Praise for *This Unruly Witness*

"For June, the struggle ultimately was about and in the service of love, and the ways this book allows both to coexist is impressive."
—**Cornelius Eady**, author of *Brutal Imagination*

"In her letters to June Jordan, contributing poet Kathy Engel says, 'We must name ourselves.' And so *This Unruly Witness* does. With loving attention, this collection of essays and poems offers readers of Jordan's work and legacy a living portrait of a great American poet. Through poignant, funny, and searing reflections by so many who walked alongside Jordan, we are invited to be reinspired by her legacy. Within these pages we meet (again) the woman who ignited others with the courage and the wisdom of her poems; the woman who connected so many through the intensity and openness of her heart; and the woman who wrestled our broken world for justice, no matter what it cost her—even when it cost her. And we are invited to name ourselves, those of us who know the abiding love that fueled her on the page and in life, those of us who practice it as the only way forward."
—**Lena Khalaf Tuffaha**, author of *Something About Living*

"As I have said of Neruda, I say of June Jordan: If you do not know this poet, no matter how many material possessions you amass—you are impoverished. *This Unruly Witness* is evidence that statement rings true. In these pages we find essays, remembrances, and powerful poetic testaments to Jordan's fierce and fabulous self-interrogations; her moral focus; and her fluent vernaculars of courage, confrontation, and compassion. Through brilliant writing and exceptional insight, *This Unruly Witness* guides the reader through the landscape that is June Jordan—not only her poems but her person, her wisdom, her civic devotion. In both the personal and political, Jordan dares us to love in the face of danger, even though to choose to love is to choose who you will lose. During this most turbulent of times we are experiencing, when many of us too often feel so far from the love and sustenance of community, *This Unruly Witness* is a trail of intentionally placed breadcrumbs left by a woman who feeds us while guiding us home."

—**Regie Gibson**, Massachusetts poet laureate

"June Jordan was an insurgent intellectual giant of her time and ours. But she was more than that. She was a principled Black left feminist internationalist voice in solidarity with Palestine and in defense of LGBTQ justice at a time when many others were quiet. Her words were companions to her actions. Jordan's clarity, courage, and steadfastness were matched only by the eloquence of her poetry and prose. *This Unruly Witness*, with its stellar roster of editors and contributors, reminds us of Jordan's powerful influence at a time when we all need to stand boldly and staunchly in her tradition."

—**Barbara Ransby**, author, activist, and historian

This Unruly Witness

June Jordan's Legacy

Edited by

Lauren Muller

Becky Thompson

Dominique C. Hill

Durell M. Callier

Haymarket Books
Chicago, Illinois

© 2025 Lauren Muller, Becky Thompson, Dominique C. Hill, and Durell M. Callier

Published in 2025 by
Haymarket Books
P.O. Box 180165
Chicago, IL 60618
773-583-7884
www.haymarketbooks.org

ISBN: 979-8-88890-457-2

Distributed to the trade in the US through Consortium Book Sales and Distribution (www.cbsd.com) and internationally through Ingram Publisher Services International (www.ingramcontent.com).

This book was published with the generous support of Lannan Foundation, Wallace Action Fund, and the Marguerite Casey Foundation.

Special discounts are available for bulk purchases by organizations and institutions. Please call 773-583-7884 or email info@haymarketbooks.org for more information.

All June Jordan poetry lines are included with gracious permission from the Frances Goldin Literary Agency. Thank you to Alison Lewis and Jade Wong-Baxter for spiriting this through.

Cover photo by Chester Higgins.
Cover design by Rachel Cohen.

Printed in Canada by union labor.

Library of Congress Cataloging-in-Publication data is available.
Library of Congress Control Number: 2025943397

For June Jordan and Lauren Muller

Activism is not issue-specific
It's a moral posture that, steady state,
    propels you forward, from one hard
hour to the next.
Believing that you can do something
    to make things better, you do
something, rather than nothing.
You assume responsibility for the
    privilege of your abilities.
You do whatever you can.
You reach beyond yourself in your
    imagination, and in your wish for
understanding, and for change.
You admit the limitations of individual
    perspectives.
You trust somebody else.
You do not turn away.

—June Jordan, from "Breast Cancer: Still Here"

Contents

Alexis Pauline Gumbs
    Foreword: A Definition of Love   1

Part 1: Poet on the World Stage

Naomi Shihab Nye
    In Response to "The Bombing of Baghdad" by June Jordan   7

Elizabeth Alexander
    Black Alive and Looking Straight at You: The Legacy of June Jordan   9

Adrienne B. Torf
    It Began as a Romance: The Collaboration of June Jordan and Adrienne B. Torf   15

Alexis De Veaux
    How She Sang the Blues   22

Zack Rogow
    June Jordan and the Renaissance of Poetry as a Performing Art   27
    Urban Ghazal   35

Margo Okazawa-Rey
    "A Report from the Bahamas": And What of Identity Politics?   37

Marilyn Hacker
    Elegy for a Soldier   46

Kathy Engel
    Letters to My Friend, for June Jordan   51

María Poblet
    ¡Puño en Alto! ¡Libro Abierto! / Fists Up! Books Open!: On Anti-Intellectualism, Literacy Brigades, and Revolutionary Consciousness   60

Mahogany L. Browne
    The Setup   66

Becky Thompson
    The Waters Are Wide: We Can Cross Over   71

Gwendolen Hardwick
    Call and Response   80

Part 2: We Are Lucky She Dared

E. Ethelbert Miller
    "Some of Us Did Not Die": Remembering June Jordan   85
    After All Is Said and Done   98

Dima Hilal
    Bit by Bit   99
    america   102

Rajasvini Bhansali
    Elphinstone, Bombay, 1993   104

Shanti Bright Brien
    "The Bombing of Baghdad": Building Connections
        in a Time of War   110

Xochiquetzal Candelaria
    Maestra   116

Ruth Forman
    Dear June   122

Ariel Luckey
    a practice of freedom   125
    not past   127

Sheila Menezes
    A Blueprint for June's Love   131

Kate Holbrook
    Choosing a Praxis of Liberation   137

Jessica Wei Huang
    On the Spirit of June Jordan: The Ultimate Capacities of a
        School's Lifeforce   144
    Standing at the Gates   149

Reid Gómez
    Stay All the Way with Reggie and Ranya   153

Dani Gabriel
    "I choose / anything / anyone / I may lose": June Jordan, Faith,
        and Holy Risk   167

Sriram Shamasunder
    Between the Knuckles of My Own Two Hands: Learning
        from June Jordan   171

Part 3: The Awesome, Difficult Work of Love

Angela Y. Davis, Pratibha Parmar, and Leigh Raiford
    A Place of Rage: A Conversation   179

adrienne maree brown
    In Response to "Apologies to All the People in Lebanon"   196

Jehan Bseiso
    After June Jordan, a Poem About Police Violence   198

Donna Masini
    For the Sake of a People's Poetry: June Jordan and Walt Whitman   200

Elizabeth Riva Meyer
    Truth-Telling as an Emancipatory Act: What June Jordan Taught
        Me About Liberation   206

Zeina Azzam
    Finding "Living Room" with My Drone   217

Will Horter
    Love Like a Mango, Obvious   221

Wesley Brown
    June Jordan: When All Things Are Dear That Disappear   231

Kelly Elaine Navies
    "Something Like a Sonnet": Reading June Jordan, Finding My Voice, and Becoming an Oral Historian   235
    Wild Grapevines   242

Ruth Nicole Brown
    Choosing My Mind Between the Mosquitos and the Moon   244

Dominique C. Hill
    A Note on Praxis and Black Girls   251

Afaa M. Weaver 尉雅風
    Become a Menace   256

Imani Perry
    Afterword: June Jordan; An Eternal Summer   257

ACKNOWLEDGMENTS   259
NOTES   261
SELECTED BIBLIOGRAPHY   273
INDEX   287

Foreword

A Definition of Love

> Love is lifeforce.
> I believe that the creative spirit is nothing less than love made manifest.
> ... And it seems to me that love, that a serious and tender concern to respect the nature and the spontaneous purpose of other things, other people, will make manifest a peaceable order among us such that fear, conflict, competition, waste, and environmental sacrifice will have no place.
>
> —June Jordan, "The Creative Spirit," 1977

This is not a book. It's a reunion, made of all the things that we do in the light of June Jordan's loving life of work. Things we must do from the dark of missing her embodied presence. Welcome. In these pages you will meet or reunite with June Jordan through her impact. Her friends, her students, and many of the thinkers, educators, and activists who work in her legacy are here, offering you what June Jordan gave us: an opportunity to love ourselves and each other more honestly. An imperative to "make love powerful."[1]

In the essays and poems that follow, you will learn how June Jordan taught us to love our communities with our words and actions, to love across generations, to love romantically within and beyond the boundaries of marriage, to love ourselves enough to tell the truth of who we are, to love ourselves when we feel like failures, to love each other when we are very angry, to love life itself where and when it is threatened, to love across species and oceans, to love across grief, to love the process when we don't know what we are doing, to love revising poems, to love our students, to love our memories, to change our institutions by loving them, to love our communities by leaving institutions behind, to love our laughter, to love our questions, to love our music, to love who we used to be and who we are becoming and who we are right now in the midst.

And there are openings for love we haven't even imagined yet.

I first read Jordan's essay "The Creative Spirit" in a quiet room sifting through archival boxes. And there it was: her typed and retyped draft of a talk for a conference about children's literature. And there it was, that sentence: "Love is lifeforce." During my visits to June Jordan's papers at the Schlesinger Library, as I open folder after folder I continue to ask myself, "What can this letter/manuscript/syllabus/etc. teach me about love?"

The material artifacts of June Jordan's life, and the miraculous gift of knowing some of her students, colleagues, and loved ones, teaches me about love in a way that never remains merely theoretical. Her theory of love permeates my life. It offers my personal and political relationships back to me to attentively wonder about and revise as if this whole planet were a Poetry for the People classroom, where how I love will be reflected back to me again and again, inviting more bravery, more truth, wiser action. Because I study June Jordan, I am becoming a more available friend, a more generous sister, a more passionate partner, a freer teacher, a more committed daughter to my given and chosen mothers.

This book, this place, this reunion, though gratefully compiled in memory of June Jordan, is not a backward-facing ceremony. It is a futuristic resource toward the possibility of more love flowing through you in all directions. And so my offering, my humble assignment to you as a belated student-teacher of the June Jordan approach, is to ask yourself as you read each essay, poem, or reflection in this book: "What can this teach me about love?" What can the experience of reading each passage, stanza, and paragraph here teach you about the love growing in your life right now?

I am so grateful to be here with you, in this printed place of infinite possibility. In this sacred shaking possible place, where love is lifeforce and therefore

June Jordan Lives!

Love always,

Alexis Pauline Gumbs

Alexis Pauline Gumbs was the first researcher to visit the June Jordan Papers at the Schlesinger Library. She gratefully calls several of June Jordan's friends, loved ones, students, and legacy bearers her mothers, mentors, community, and family. Alexis created the June Jordan Saturday Survival School and the Juneteenth Freedom Academy in Durham, North Carolina, where she co-creates a living library of Black LGBTQ Feminist Brilliance called the Mobile Homecoming Trust with her partner Sangodare. Alexis won the Whiting Award in Nonfiction for *Undrowned: Black Feminist Lessons from Marine Mammals* (AK Press, 2020) and was a National Humanities Center Fellow and National Endowment for the Arts Creative Writing Fellow. She is the author of *Survival Is a Promise: The Eternal Life of Audre Lorde* (Farrar, Straus, and Giroux, 2024).

PART ONE

Poet on the World Stage

In Response to "The Bombing of Baghdad" by June Jordan

Naomi Shihab Nye

To stand up for
  one's own self
and selves like you
  is one kind of light
    shining

but to stand up for
  other selves
    linked
by sheer humanity
  another light
    entirely

doubled
  tripled light
radiance beyond measure
  or explanation

and not for
  any personal gain
my vote
  a grand ovation
only because
  it is the right thing to do
in the garden of time

  oh June Jordan
this was you.

Palestinian American poet, editor, and writer for children **Naomi Shihab Nye** received the Wallace Stevens Award from the Academy of American poets in 2024. The same year, she was also named Texas Writer of the Year by the Texas Book Festival. Her most recent book is *Grace Notes: Poems About Families* (HarperCollins, 2024).

Black Alive and Looking Straight at You[1]

The Legacy of June Jordan

Elizabeth Alexander

I have been thinking for a long time about poetry and politics through the instructive examples of June Jordan, the woman and her work. What is the "job" or the work of a poem, and what are its limitations? Why would a writer speak in the morning in the poems, in the afternoon through their body while teaching or doing other activist work, and in the evening in prose essays? What can each form do that the other cannot? Most specifically, what do we want to protect in poetry if we believe, as I do and as Jordan did, that poetry *is* sacred speech that marks the sacred in our lives?

There are poetry people who think that politics, per se, has no place in poetry. This is silly, and it is amazing how strong a hold this idea has had when it is so empty. For time immemorial, across geographies and peoples, poetry has taken as its subject politics, that is, the affairs of the polis, the community and its people. Some people think of themselves as gatekeepers, defenders of a culture, as though culture is something that can be owned by anyone. Culture is like ambient gas; once it is released, there is no collecting it and bringing it back home. This is a great and magical thing: Culture belongs to the world that occasions it. But we could usefully think about the rich and edifying aspects of form that mark discourses in a particular genre. How should a poem attend to the business of its chosen form, the care and style with which the box is made rather than what is put inside the box? Poets do have responsibility to make images that compel, to distill language, to write with model precision and specificity; that is what poetry has to offer to other genres. It makes something happen with language that takes the breath away or shifts the mind. For the poem, which is after all not the newspaper, must move beyond the information it contains while simultaneously imparting the information it contains. Jordan's commitment to poetry was constant, and it is in those words that we find her simultaneous devotion to the largest possible picture—her keen analyses of the world situation—and to the smallest detail—her tending of language.

Jordan outlines many of these ideas in her book *Poetry for the People*, which chronicles that movement at UC Berkeley, where she taught for many years, and offers a try-this-at-home handbook for bringing together people across boundaries through the power of poetry—in order, quite simply, to make the world a better place through reading, writing, and performing poetry. To be brave and then be braver. To do the work of learning and knowing so that when you speak to the issues of the world, you know of what you speak. To travel, either literally or by learning another language and reading what people who think and speak in that language have seen of the world. To come together under the umbrella of poetry, knowing not only what we fight against but also where the love is that can unite us. "As I think about anyone or any thing," she wrote,

> whether history or literature or my father or political organizations or a poem or a film—as I seek to evaluate the potentiality, the life-supportive commitment/possibilities of anyone or anything, the decisive question is, always, *where is the love?* The energies that flow from hatred, from negative and hateful habits and attitudes and dogma, do not promise something good, something I could choose to cherish, to honor with my own life. It is always the love, whether we look to the spirit of Fannie Lou Hamer, or to the spirit of Agostinho Neto, it is always the love that will carry action into positive new places, that will carry your own nights and days beyond demoralization and away from suicide.[2]

June Jordan lived from 1936 to 2002 and was a poet, activist, essayist, and teacher. She published more critical prose than any other African American woman writer in the twentieth century, as well as plays, anthologies, children's books, and the tough-minded memoir *Soldier*. She was a proud African American Brooklynite of Jamaican parentage, but she was not mired in racial, national, cultural, or ideological groupthink. She wrote, for example, that after she was raped by a black man "it became clear to me that I had a whole lot of profound and overdue thinking to begin on the subject of what it means to be female regardless of color."[3]

Jordan tirelessly advocated for the rights of others both locally and internationally, and her essays articulated far-reaching, integrated points of view on culture and politics. She is perhaps best known as a prolific poet whose lyrical voiced linked political struggle with an ethic of love. Anyone who ever met her knew she was a fierce, brilliant, tireless, brave, direct, luminous woman who exemplified life force even as—especially as—she fought for many years against cancer.

I first read her poems as a child in the beautiful collection *Who Look at Me* that introduced African American art to young people. "I am black alive and looking back at you," she wrote, which always seemed to me to be a credo for moving through this life and its challenges. Her work, then, has always been with me, as has her example of a committed, productive artist, who was sometimes afraid but was always courageous, who saw herself as a citizen of the world, who traveled to Nicaragua and Lebanon and concluded, "The whole world will become a home to all of us, or none of us can hope to live on it, peacefully."[4] She was simultaneously a pacifist and a fighter who knew that "all war leads to death and all love leads you away from death."[5] She wrote, in her unsparing memoir *Soldier*, of the Jamaican immigrant father, Granville Ivanhoe Jordan, who brutalized her, his only child, and yet made her a fighter. That fighter is everywhere in her work: the fighter who, as a student at the University of Chicago, knew that the teacher who told her she couldn't write, who wondered if English was even her first language, was wrong, and would prove him wrong; the fighter who, as a teacher years later, told her students, "this is not my class, this is our class. I do not want to hear what I think. I need to know what you think."[6]

I saw her read several times over the years and was too shy to go up and speak to her. I read every flinty word she wrote—on Chilean poetry, the Palestinian situation, bisexuality, any number of issues of justice—and she became an example to me of someone who made a righteous and beautiful life by poems, essays, and deeds and who did not shy away from what was difficult. A few years ago, when I was about to give a reading in her home of Berkeley, California, I wrote to her, introduced myself, and asked if I could visit her. She responded by giving me a long and magical evening that I will never forget, and an email friendship ensued until she died, just a short year after. There are some deaths where you feel the earth open up and leave a physically palpable void, and June Jordan's death hit me and many others who knew her well and not at all. Her vitality, in word and in person, was extraordinary. Clichés such as "larger than life" and "force of nature" applied. She was utterly beautiful to behold, exquisite and exact and light filled, with an enormous, knowing laugh. She felt like life itself.

In her essay collection *Civil Wars* she wrote of her year teaching at Yale University in 1974–75, where I now teach: her love for students; the particular challenges of teaching "black studies" in the 1970s to "the descendants of slaves as well as the descendants of the slave owners"; and of challenging what she saw as hegemonic worship of Richard Wright in African American studies to the exclusion of necessary voices like Hurston's. She decried an "either/or" approach to African American canon formation and political thinking. "It is tragic and ridiculous to choose between Malcolm and Dr. King," she wrote. "Each of them hurled himself against a quite different aspect of our predicament, and both of them, literally, gave their lives to our ongoing struggle."[7]

At whichever institution employed her, she pressed at the boundaries of the place and challenged the status quo. While at Yale she protested an impending campus visit by pseudoscientific racist William Shockley, and along with students, she organized the Yale Attica Defense. At the anti-Shockley rally, she spoke questions that still echo for us as a community at Yale:

> What freedom does this institution care about? Is it the freedom to maintain traditions based on hundreds of years of genocide, theft, rape, humiliation and hypocrisy? Is it the freedom to protect

respectability for the forces of conservatism: social, political, academic conservatism: the conservation of bloody, terrifying, life-denying, arrogant traditions of a self-appointed elite of the world? . . . Show me the freedom that this University upholds: show it to me in its admissions policies. Show it to me in its financial aid programs. Show it to me in its curriculum, in its required readings, in the color, the sex, the viewpoints of its faculty. Show me this freedom that this institution holds dear.[8]

She offered an example for learning, living, and questioning in larger institutional contexts.

And she always wrote about love, be it in a whole book of love poems, *Haruko*, or her constantly asking, Where is the love? Do you know what you are fighting for as well as what you are fighting against? She wrote: "I am saying that the ultimate connection cannot be the enemy. The ultimate connection must be the need that we find between us. It is not only who you are, in other words, but what we can do for each other that will determine the connection."[9] It was love, in her unsentimental vision, that could blaze a path through a world in which multiple-scale violence is the rule.

Jordan wrote: "We need everybody and all that we are. We need to know and make known the complete, constantly unfolding, complicated heritage that is our black experience. We should absolutely resist the superstar, one at a time mentality that threatens the varied and resilient, flexible wealth of our Black future."[10] That "we" is the site of Jordan's poetry, over and over again, real we's of the individuals and communities she has worked with, and imaged we's of the difficult but optimistic future that calls for our clear-eyed love and bravery.

A celebrated poet, scholar, and cultural advocate, **Elizabeth Alexander** is a nationally recognized thought leader on race, justice, and the arts and is currently president of the Mellon Foundation. An author or coauthor of fifteen books, Dr. Alexander was twice a finalist for the Pulitzer Prize: for poetry with *American Sublime* (Graywolf Press, 2005) and for biography with her memoir, the *New York Times* bestseller *The Light of the World* (Grand Central Publishing, 2015). She held distinguished professorships at Smith College, Yale University—where she taught for over fifteen years and rebuilt and chaired the African American Studies Department—and Columbia University.

It Began as a Romance

The Collaboration of June Jordan and Adrienne B. Torf

Adrienne B. Torf

It began, of course, as a romance. So much of June's life was, a romance—as a child, the romance with language / the romance of and with a young white man in a yellow Oxford-cloth shirt leafletting, jacketless, on a cold autumn day / the passionate romances with women and with men / the romance of Buck, her beloved Airedale, trotting along a beach in winter ("all things are dear that disappear")[1] / the romance from a distance and the romance up close / the romance of Chet Baker, of Meshell Ndegeocello, of Jennie Portnof's cow painting holding tight to the dining room wall / the romance with students occupying the sidewalk next to CNN or on Sproul Plaza or Junichi Semitsu boldly delivering his poem at a UC Regents annual meeting / the romance of a clean white shirt, of a tennis court, of a Volkswagen GTI speeding toward home on a dark winter evening / of someone new, of someone gone / the romance of all life is possible / the romance that all love is possible, as well.

It began, of course, as a romance one snowy April night in a theater in Minneapolis. June led off the program reading poems, I played piano for a singer, and June asked to meet me. In the green room she explained, through dark glasses and the smoke of a slim brown Sherman MCD / she explained, in her impeccably tailored mocha-colored wool suit, pearl-gray silk blouse, matching hose and heels way too tall for walking in snow / she explained that others had set her poems to music

(Leonard Bernstein, Roy Brown, Sweet Honey in the Rock), but this time, she said, she wanted the poem and the music to grow together / to be conceived and created in tandem / a real collaboration, she said through the smoke and the shades and the echoes of poetry and music from the hall.

I said yes. Of course. Wouldn't you?

Yet there was nothing of course about it, this meeting, or a collaboration between so powerfully gifted and controversial a Black poet and so naïvely gifted a white piano player and composer. Nineteen years and a continent's breadth between us, we began.

At first, June sent me drafts of poems through the mail; she would read them to me over the phone and I would mail back to her a cassette of the music I'd written for those drafts. From the beginning, the music was there, embedded and alive in June's poetry, in the language, the rhythms, the imagery, the so-often lyrical lines. I found it impossible not to hear the music:

> What about moonlight
> What about moonlight[2]

> so hot so hot so hot so what
> so hot so what so hot so hot
> They made a mistake[3]

> Every night Winnie Mandela
> Every night the waters of the world
> turn to the softly burning
> light of the moon[4]

> Break the clothesline
> Topple down the clotheslinepole
> O My Lives Among The Wounded Buildings
> should be dressed in trees and grass[5]

Or I'd fly to New York, where we worked late at night in a rehearsal studio in the Public Theater, taking breaks to fly balsa-wood airplanes in the empty canyons of summer streets or to have a drink at a bar on Lafayette.

Joseph Papp and Leonard Bernstein asked to hear what we were writing, curious about this collaboration. Upon hearing our works in progress, they each, separately, made the same suggestion: "Build a story around it. It belongs on the stage."

It began, of course, as a romance.

In 1984 I moved to Brooklyn where we could collaborate in full / intertwining our lives first there, then in Berkeley, for the next eighteen years.

Two shells hinged together pretty tough at the joint, she described us. There was nothing in the artistic, cultural, or political institutions of 1980s America that suggested our collaboration in any obvious way. We were of different races, different generations, different backgrounds. Yet the collaboration flourished, rooted in our shared passions as artists and our shared responses to political events in the United States and other places around the world. Each of us classically trained, we shunned ivory-tower insulation: the sounds and rhythms of the city were our lifeblood. We wrote from the myriad voices of the people with whom we shared the streets, the subways, classrooms, theatrical and political stages. We wrote to reflect the political and musical milestones of our contemporary consciousness. We loved, and from that love we summoned ourselves and those who listened into the creative dialectics of violence and art, inhumanity and love.

By the fall, we had written the working version of what became *Bang Bang über Alles*, our full-length stage musical about a confrontation between young performing artists and the Ku Klux Klan. On the opening night of *Bang Bang*'s run at 7 Stages Theatre in Atlanta in 1986, men of the Ku Klux Klan in hoods and robes and men of the Aryan Nation in camouflage came to burn down the theater, to shut us down, to terrorize us, to shut us up. The cast and band met them in the parking lot and sang "Death to the Klan" to their faces.[6] The FBI protected the theater for the rest of the run.

That, too, was a romance: poetry and music facing off with those who opposed our love and our insistence on love, with poetry and music winning.

As we prepared to record *Collaboration: Selected Works 1983–2000*, June wrote to a friend about

> the complexity and conflict in which Adrienne and I have elected to collaborate—as artists and comrades and family—despite our own actual and apparent differences. Our collaboration, itself, testifies to possibilities of original and creative response to big events that tend, more often than not, to smother singular and creative affirmations.... And our collaboration chronicles milestone conflagrations and injuries and deaths and victories of spirit and substance, both. ... Adrienne and I aggressively insist upon our artistic capacities to encounter and engage—each other and all of the above alluded to milestones of 20th century historic explosion ... huge, difficult intersections that our art has transformed into coherent opportunities for affirmation and resistance.... [This recording] redefines "collaboration" and makes it mean something as powerful as it is engaged, as aggressive as it is beautiful, and tender.

How to keep alive "coherent opportunities for affirmation and resistance" in this century, as replete as the last with "conflagrations and injuries and deaths and victories of spirit and substance"? I turn often to *Who Look at Me*, June's first published book, the title a subjunctive, rather than a question—a possibility, a desire, an expression of uncertainty. Is that not the definition of romance? To look at another, to see in them, to have them see in us, possibilities for love?

> New energies of darkness we
> disturbed a continent
> like seeds
>
> and life grows slowly
> so we grew
>
> We became a burly womb
> an evening harvest kept by prayers
> a hallelujah little room
>
> We grew despite the crazy killing scorn
> that broke the brightness to be born

In part we grew
by looking back at you

that white terrain
impossible for black America to thrive
that hostile soil to mazelike toil
backbreaking people into pain

we grew by waiting
to be seen
black face black body and black mind
beyond obliterating
homicide of daily insult daily death
the pistol slur the throbbing redneck war

with breath[7]

And I turn to this:

Most people search all
of their lives
for someplace to belong to
as you said
but I look instead
into the eyes of anyone
who talks to me

I search for a face
to believe and belong to
a loosening mask
with a voice
ears
and a consciousness
breathing through
a nose
I can see

> Day to day
> it's the only way
> I like to travel
> noticing the colors of a cheek
> the curvature of brow
> and the public declarations
> of two lips[8]

And always, always, I turn to this:

> We need, each of us, to begin the awesome, difficult work of love: loving ourselves so that we become able to love others without fear, so that we can become powerful enough to enlarge the circle of our trust and our common striving for a safe, sunny afternoon near to flowering trees and under a very blue sky.[9]

It begins as a romance.

June Jordan (left), Adrienne B. Torf (right) in 1984. Photo by June Jordan.

Adrienne B. Torf and June Jordan were artistic collaborators and life partners for nineteen years, until Jordan's passing in 2002. Together they produced their full-length documentary opera *Bang Bang über Alles* and numerous works for performance by themselves and by ensembles, recorded on *Collaboration: Selected Works, 1983–2000* (ABongo Music, 2000). Adrienne's original compositions for piano and synthesizer are captured on three solo albums, *Brooklyn from the Roof* (ABongo Music, 1986), *Two Hands Open* (ABongo Music, 2003), and *Here I Am* (ABongo Music, 2025). Her other theater works include *Poetry for the People: The June Jordan Experience*, winner of the 2023 Theater Washington Helen Hayes Award, and *The Awesome Difficult Work of Love*. Adrienne's keyboard work appears on more than a dozen commercially released albums by Holly Near, Cris Williamson, Meg Christian, Ferron, Kay Gardner, and others. (See more at adriennetorf.com).

How She Sang the Blues

Alexis De Veaux

When I interviewed June Jordan for a feature piece published in *Essence* magazine in April 1981, I'd only recently met her. Searching through the pockets and corners of Liberation Bookstore in Harlem some years back, I'd pulled a copy of her first book, *Who Look at Me*, off the shelf as a gift for my younger sister. Flipped through it. Saw words: jubilant, shoulders-back / stomach-in words, full of hallelujah, stride across pages. A mighty march of words so black. So loud.

I bought the book. Because it talked poetry for young readers. And the title talked familiar black English. And the next month I bought a copy of *Who Look at Me*, published in 1969, for myself. I memorized the lyric rhyming. Memorized the blues sonata of the narrative. The dark sweetness of the poem. Looked for her name on flyers and announcements for poetry readings around town. Scoured bookshelves of friends and lovers for more of her work. The more of it I found, the more I discovered: June's poems can nourish the eye, the back, the feet, the soul.

But years later, I discovered an arc: At one end was that first book, *Who Look at Me*. At the other was her last in life, *Soldier: A Poet's Childhood*, published in 2000; thirty-one years later. Between them were some twenty-five or more books. These two, however, choreographed the arc and the archive of a bruise. That can come early in black life. In childhood.

To be the child June Jordan. That had been the bruise.

She was sent away to prep school for the entire academic year. And then to a camp for the summer; where the schedule was rigid and camp life totally structured. By a father who thought "a disciplined life was good for the character."[1]

For while her father wanted her far from the Brooklyn streets of her childhood (he thought she was becoming thug-like), she wanted relief from the terror at home. "I felt saved," she told me, "not from the streets but from the family. My particular family situation was so violent. I mean, I am talking about corporeal violence being inflicted upon me by my father. It was a relentlessly frightening situation at home."[2]

The writing was the antidote. To the bruise.

Written as a long and elegant paean to the blues, dedicated to her son Christopher, and shaped, primarily, by the voice of a child, the text of *Who Look at Me* traveled through an illustrated narrative of twenty-seven paintings of everyday black persistence.

In it, June announced the bruise as abuse, as a historical reality.

The voice was multigendered and multivalent: of the historian, of the ancestor, the artist. Of the child. It was June's first, comprehensive look at the whole of what black people have endured/endure in the so-called "new world." At the heart of *Who Look at Me* was the poet's understanding that black people created of life an art form, and that "all art is mysterious to some degree because it participates in magic."[3] As other though, we are beyond invisible: we are simply not recognized as human. Not mirrored in public policies. Not seen. As Jordan pronounces, we not only come from an "otherwise," we are unreadable, a sleight of hand, mysterious in this where.

Who Look at Me invited us to time-travel blackness. It was a statement by a poet about black life. Imagine not slavery but the child who comes to life enslaved. How it was: to be five or six or four years old and belong to / be property. To be put to work sun come till sun go. To be dressed in rags. To have bad teeth, from lack. Be sickly from overwork. To be terrified day and night. Imagine: to have to *obey* a master. This, as your people taught you to read the stars. The plants. A stolen book. This, as you learned to survive that evil. And learned love. And grew to require freedom.

Imagine black children surviving a daily violence.

June Jordan did.

The stain of the bruise is the racism. The rupture of (the) underlying blood vessels. *Who Look at Me* chronicled the stain and the rupture of the bruise.

It was a history book that was poetry in 1969.

Unlike other black poets and writers who found a home in the Black Arts Movement of the 1960s, June did not. She was outside the orthodoxy of black nationalism that framed much of black artistic discourse at the time. And writing, as a poet, genre-bending history, biography, and fiction for young readers when most others were not.

Who Look at Me was a project inspired by Milton Meltzer, an American historian well known for his work on Jewish, African American, and American history. Jordan's text was in conversation with reproductions of paintings by established artists, assembled by Meltzer. In concert with the text, the images acted as a counternarrative, a counterspeech, to popular constructions of black realities. The book marked her as an early advocate of literature for young black readers: *The Voice of the Children* (1970), *His Own Where* (1971), *Dry Victories* (1972), *Fannie Lou Hamer* (1972), *New Life, New Room* (1975), *Kimako's Story* (1981).

Who Look at Me told an American story. Of an American crime. The crime being the stain. The stain being racism. The rupture being the site of the bruise.

We don't just sing it. We wear the blues. It is skin. Made black and blue from racist, hegemonic, genderphobic injury. How we survive. That discoloration of the skin. The daily bleeding underneath, those microaggressions. Typically caused by intentional aggression. The rupture of one's well-being and security.

Bruising.

What the body's mind will do to the bruise. Though the wound of the bruise is forever in the body, the cells in the superficial, upper layers of skin, the epidermis, shed that black and blue. But the deeper layers of the skin, the dermis, where there is the bleeding underneath the underneath, do not do this shedding thing. Because the wound of the bruise is a tattoo. So it remains imprinted. Because the inky particles of the discoloration, that is the bruise (we see), cannot be ingested by the white blood cells that patrol the body. No matter how we construct it, the body does not heal. We are forever wounded by a bruise.

But the bruise is a place where injury can shape-shift. Where the violence of the injury to the child, the violence of bruising, can be reborn as strength, as fierceness, as the activist armed. It is the place where the father is simultaneously the adoring and terrified child's "hero and tyrant."[4] And there it was, the making of the fearless poet. The warrior.

And there it was at the other end of the arc: *Soldier: A Poet's Childhood* (2000). Published two years before she left this life. A memoir aching with clarity. Dedicated to her father, her "hero and tyrant." An account of her first twelve years as the daughter who was the only child of Jamaican parents. Of a Jamaican father who groomed her to be a soldier. Written in terse, controlled language. Sharp as it was brutal. Inflicted on the reader like the beatings she received at her father's hand. When she was "his helper, his sidekick: His son."[5] Growing up in an intense, religious household. Where there was attention to beauty. Where having a good time meant quoting scriptures from the Bible or reciting the dialect poetry of Paul Laurence Dunbar.[6] And listening to her uncle Teddy, "a master of Black English" who lived upstairs in the family's brownstone and fascinated her with stories told in a marvelous language he called Black English.[7]

And her mother the nurse. Who broke fevers and made soup for neighbors. How her mother did not intervene, did not rescue her from her father.[8] How she yearned for parental love.

The book jacket's photograph is of a young girl and a dog: "June and Spottie First Day at School." The photo credit: Granville Ivanhoe Jordan. Father of the poet soldier.

I wondered when I first read it, I wonder still: How do yearning and brutality concoct beauty and poetry in a child's spirit? Does the spirit come to life in the child always and already formed by beauty and poetry that cannot be brutalized by gender and more beauty and race and poetry?

Soldier was June's coming to terms with the bruise, the ecchymosis, of family. It was a forgiving blues. Archived in pain. It paid homage to the wonderful and the terrible. It was, as an arc, her most vulnerable, piercingly beautiful, heartbreaking work. When I interviewed her for a piece on it for *Essence* magazine, June said to me, "I think this book could win a National Book Award." It did not. Unlike *His Own Where*, it was not even nominated. Like James Baldwin, June Jordan was the recipient of several literary awards, but none consistent with her singular, prolific achievement.* Throughout her life she stood as a warrior, often alone, or ahead of the crowd, when it came to global issues. She could be easily, fiercely enraged by any slight—to herself or to another black person. If you were a friend to her, her enemies could not be your friends. She was a consummate writer. Across multiple genres. She was always writing; some of that writing was topical, of the moment; some of it is timeless. She was underrecognized. And she knew it.

The writing was a balm.

Alexis De Veaux is a Harlem-born and -raised author, poet, artist, and activist recognized for her lifelong contributions to a number of women's and literary organizations. Her work, influenced by black feminist and LGBT movements, gives voice to the racial and sexual experiences of black women while disrupting formal boundaries. She has won many awards for her genre-defying works, including the Hurston/Wright Legacy Award, the Gustavus Meyers Outstanding Book Award, and the Lambda Literary Award for her biography of Audre Lorde, *Warrior Poet* (W. W. Norton, 2004).

---

* June published twenty-eight books before her death in 2002. In the United States, she remains the foremost productive Afro-Caribbean writer of the twentieth century.

June Jordan and the Renaissance of Poetry as a Performing Art

Zack Rogow

The Experience of Hearing June Jordan Read

Goosebumps. Fireworks of laughter. Trying so hard to hold back the tears. And then wiping them away. That was listening to June Jordan read her poems in person. It was a physical experience, unlike any other I've encountered in a lifetime as a writer and a fan of poetry.

You could not remain indifferent when hearing June Jordan read her poems. You had to shake your head to express your dismay at the particular state of the world that she was illuminating. Or, you had to resist inwardly at those moments when you wondered if you completely agreed with her.

"The live reading situation for me is the final criterion for my poetry," June Jordan said in a 1981 interview.[1] "It's part of the process of creation, an indispensable part of it for me. I assume that in everything I write, whether it's poetry or an essay, I assume an audience. I assume that interaction. It's not a personal event, it's an effort at conversation. At least." For June, delivering her poems to a public audience was an enactment of the democratic impulse at the heart of her poetry. That impulse to communicate with an audience shaped the *subjects* she wrote about, and it influenced *the way* she chose to write about those subjects, and it also informed how she *presented* her poems.

June Jordan's Rebellion Against the Mainstream US Reading Style

In 1969, when June Jordan published her first poetry collection, *Who Look at Me*, there was an unwritten rule among many established poets in the United States that to perform one's poems was in bad taste. Poetry was supposed to be read with a deadpan delivery, as if in a private conversation. It was a time when a specific idea about authenticity was playing an important role in US literature. The confession of one's actual, individual experience required for some poets a restrained reading style that indicated a stamp of unaltered, undoctored, personal perspective. Look up Robert Lowell reading his classic "Skunk Hour" on YouTube,[2] for example, and you'll hear an example of this aesthetic. Robert Lowell is reading about a personal moment, not addressing a mass audience, and speaking almost to himself.

Not only that, the experimental poetry that was emerging at this time in the United States required an even more abstract reading style that emphasized a tone of detached scientific inquiry. Think of John Ashbery reading "Self-Portrait in a Convex Mirror."[3] Even poets who admired him greatly jokingly compared John's public appearances to a recitation of the Manhattan phonebook, his delivery was so dry and unemotional.

June Jordan sought to create an aesthetic that was almost 180 degrees opposite for poetry readings. By doing this, June was actually much closer to literary tradition. Bards chanted Homer's epics while strumming a lyre. The griots of West Africa recited their poems to the accompaniment of doundoun and balafon. The medieval Provençal troubadours were lyricists who invariably performed their poems with instruments ranging from woodwinds to strings. In China, poets of the Tang and Song Dynasties wrote in the *ci* style, composing lines to the meters of popular songs. Poetry and performance have been tightly braided for most of human history.

The Development of June Jordan's Poetry Reading Style

June Jordan created a dynamic style for her public readings influenced partly by the poets of the Harlem Renaissance and their predecessors, and partly by the jazz musicians of the 1960s and '70s. An accomplished musician herself (June Jordan studied classical piano at The Juilliard School in New York City), she had an ear acutely sensitive to the lilts and pacing of words. As jazz became more free-form during the bebop era and the period of *Birth of the Cool*, the unit of expression for saxophone and trumpet soloists became less the metered line of a ballad, and more the musician's breath. June absorbed this influence through certain brass soloists whose work she admired. "June *loved* Chet Baker, and Gato Barbieri was another of her favorites," said Adrienne Torf, June's partner and artistic collaborator beginning in 1983.[4] June had the extraordinary insight to create an effect in poetry that was similar to the solos of the great jazz brass players of the late 1960s and early '70s. She had the idea that a poet could keep reading/reciting until they ran out of breath, stringing together words in long, rapid bursts of meaning. That insight spawned whole schools of writing.

Allen Ginsberg had created a related technique using the unit of breath in his shattering poem "Howl," first published in 1956.[5] June Jordan and Allen Ginsberg definitely had a common literary ancestor—Walt Whitman and his long lines were a major influence on both of them. "Howl" is a fantastic poem, but Ginsberg's use of the extended line was more in the spirit of prayer and incantation. He used a voice in his readings that was like a holy monotone. June's recitation of the long line was more infused with the syncopations, the sharp inflections, the halting cadences, and the fluidity of the solos of Chet Baker or Gato Barbieri.

Unlike most US modernist poets, June Jordan also embraced a pronounced use of rhyme, alliteration, and assonance. Here, she was following the lead of Paul Laurence Dunbar, Langston Hughes, Gwendolyn Brooks, and other African American poets who recharged these techniques not as antiquated literary practices but as an extrapolation of the musicality of African American speech. June adapted these techniques in her own distinctive way.

Breaking the Sound Barrier: June Jordan and the Speed of Poetry

Beginning with her poem "In Memoriam: Martin Luther King, Jr." published in her first full-length collection *Some Changes* in 1971, June started to create a completely original way of reading and writing poetry that involved rapid delivery of words arranged in meaningful patterns with strong musical stresses. She also applied these techniques in her 1977 collection *Things That I Do in the Dark* in the opening of the persona poem "From *The Talking Back of Miss Valentine Jones*: Poem # One:"

> well I wanted to braid my hair
> bathe and bedeck my
> self so fine
> so fully aforethought for
> your pleasure
> see:
> I wanted to travel and read
> and runaround fantastic
> into war and peace:
> I wanted to
> surf
> dive
> fly
> climb
> conquer
> and be conquered
> THEN
> I wanted to pickup the phone
> and find you asking me
> if I might possibly be alone
> some night
> (so I could answer cool

>   as the jewels I would wear
>   on bareskin for your
>   digmedaddy delectation:)
>   "WHEN
>   you comin ova?"[6]

If you time this segment on your phone from the recording on her album *Things That I Do in the Dark and Other Poems*,[7] June takes only thirty-two seconds to read this opening sequence, which has 117 syllables. She reads so quickly, riffing the words to stress their rhythms. The speed of her reading also hammers in the urgency of the character Valentine Jones's irritation and her limited time—Valentine has demanding work as a homemaker and mother of a sick child.

Now, let's go back to Robert Lowell's "Skunk Hour." If you time his reading of that poem, by the time he gets to syllable 117 (midway through the line "was auctioned off to lobstermen"), he's been reading for a leisurely forty-seven seconds. That means that June Jordan was reciting her poem at a clip that was *almost 50 percent faster* than Robert Lowell's, which we could call the norm for US poetry at that time. Had anyone ever performed poetry as fast as June Jordan read "Valentine Jones" in the mid-1970s? Not that I ever heard.

Part of what makes June's poetry reading style so revolutionary is that she fast-timed poetry in a way no one ever had before, just as bebop sped up jazz not only to respond to the velocity of modern urban life, but also to answer the need to express pressing emotions and ideas that could not be communicated through traditional artistic restraint.

And catch this: Even though June was going at daredevil speed in "Valentine Jones," her phrasing is incredibly rich with artistry and creativity. Who else but June could come up with the phrase:

>   cool
>   as the jewels I would wear
>   on bareskin for your
>   digmedaddy delectation[8]

Check out how she rhymes "cool" and "jewels," "wear" and "bareskin"; the alliteration of "digmedaddy delectation"; and the inventiveness of that last phrase with its neologism that spell checks will never abide and its combination of street lingo and erudition. And so sexy!

Poets Influenced by June Jordan's Reading Style

Even though she was only thirty-three when her first book *Who Look at Me* was published in 1969, June (born in 1936) was in many ways the leader and senior member of an extraordinary and multitalented circle of younger poets in the 1970s and '80s. The poets in this group quickly learned from June's innovations, adapting and morphing them as they created their own styles and projects. Just two examples among many: Ntozake Shange (1948–2018) and Sekou Sundiata (1948–2007).

Ntozake Shange incorporated many of June's techniques in her now classic play *for colored girls who have considered suicide / when the rainbow is enuf*. Shange began performing sections of *for colored girls* in cafes in the San Francisco Bay Area in 1974, and the play then premiered on stage in New York City in 1975. The original published edition of the play, printed in 1974 by Shameless Hussy Press, is dedicated by Ntozake to June and four other collaborators or influences. In *for colored girls*, Ntozake adapted many of June's reading and writing techniques, including the rapid pace of poems, particularly in her "somebody almost walked off wid alla my stuff."[9] Ntozake also picked up on, and went way beyond, June's experiments with spelling words the way they're phonetically pronounced in African American speech—the poem title "somebody almost walked off wid alla my stuff," for instance. The ensemble members in *for colored girls* often danced during their performance of the poetry—another innovation that Ntozake created, calling her play a choreopoem.

Sekou Sundiata also borrowed from and extended June's techniques. He focused even more attention than June on the performance facet of his work, choosing to record his poems on a CD with a band rather than publishing them. On his 1997 poetry album *The Blue Oneness of Dreams*, Sekou doesn't limit himself to live performance, adding effects engineered in the studio, such as overdubbing and backup singers. Where Sekou borrowed most directly from June was in the speed of his delivery and his use of the dramatic monologue. He went even further than June in speaking at a pace where the words asymptotically approached pure music, as in his long persona poem "Space: A Monologue," which he included in his play *The Circle Unbroken Is a Hard Bop* (1992).

June Jordan went on to her own distinguished projects involving stage performance, songwriting, and writing as an opera and musical librettist. Her collaborators included the composers Leonard Bernstein, John Adams, Bernice Johnson Reagon, and Adrienne Torf. For June, poetry stood in relation to the other literary arts very much like the connection between mathematics and the sciences—it was a discipline that also made many related fields possible.

June Jordan's Legacy

June's writing and reading style had an enormous impact on spoken word, slam, and rap poetry. These schools flow directly from the style of performance she created. Some of June's impact on performance poetry came through her own work, and some through writers she influenced, such as Ntozake Shange and Sekou Sundiata. The breakneck speed that spoken word poets often use on stage definitely derives from June's poetry. The ability of contemporary performance poets to speak openly and impactfully about their life experiences and their politics also owes a great deal to the trails that June blazed. June has influenced almost every performance poet, whether or not they know her work or even her name, just as Petrarch has influenced almost everyone who's written a love sonnet, whether the writers are aware of their lineage through his poems or not.

Of course, June's work as a writer encompassed so, so much more than just talking fast about personal and political issues. She wrote everything from a sculpted love lyric such as "Sunflower Sonnet Number Two," to brilliant dramatic monologues like "Unemployment Monologue," to her heart-ripping tribute to black women "Getting Down to Get Over," to her dazzling manifesto in verse "On a New Year's Eve," to her stunning appraisal of the work of poet Phillis Miracle Wheatley, to a stirring defense of Black English as a medium of literature.

June Jordan's readings remain for me the most exciting poetry events that I've ever attended. When I was an undergraduate studying with June as my mentor, it was hearing her read that energized me to pursue writing and performing my poetry throughout my life.

In a generation that gave the world so many amazing poets, June Jordan stands out as the writer who expanded the possibilities of poetry wider than any other author of her time.

Urban Ghazal

Zack Rogow

for June Jordan

You know how little hope buys in the big city—
Everyone pulling at the same prize in the big city.

Women who wear their clothes like wings
Leave a trail of eyes in the big city.

The kid on the corner tries not to look
Like he's living on ketchup and fries in the big city.

Sometimes a dream boards a bus to get here,
Then turns to smoke and cries in the big city.

I love the unforeseen hats and the gymnastic words
And the tightly clad thighs in the big city.

Near to, but not at, the bottom of the pile—
That's where they rise in the big city.

It's not about Saint Francis of the A Train.
It's about whatever flies in the big city.

Zack—how can you call this nerve ending a home?
But don't stop asking the whys in the big city.

Zack Rogow is the author, editor, or translator of twenty books and plays. His most recent book of poems, *Irreverent Litanies*, was published in 2019 by Regal House. Rogow's other books of poetry include *Talking with the Radio:*

poems inspired by jazz and popular music (Kattywompus Press, 2015). His play *Colette Uncensored* (coauthored with Lorri Holt) had its first public reading at the Millennium Stage of the Kennedy Center in Washington, DC, and was subsequently performed at The Marsh in San Francisco / Berkeley and the Canal Café Theatre in London. Rogow is the editor of *The Face of Poetry* (University of California Press, 2005). He serves as a contributing editor of *Catamaran Literary Reader.*

"A Report from the Bahamas"

And What of Identity Politics?

Margo Okazawa-Rey

> I am reaching for the words to describe the difference between a common identity that has been imposed and the individual identity any one of us will choose, once she gains that chance. That difference is the one that keeps us stupid in the face of new, specific information about somebody else with whom we are supposed to have a connection because a third party, hostile to both of us, has worked it so that the two of us, like it or not, share a common enemy.
>
> —*June Jordan, "A Report from the Bahamas"*

I am reaching for the words to name with whom I want ultimately to be connected: What needs would we find? What can I do for them? What can they do for me? What could we do collectively? And for whom and for what purposes?

I seek in this essay to locate myself in relation to the questions of identity politics and the politics of identity. I begin with my most recent experiences in Palestine.

"There"

Sitting in the kitchen in the house of ninety-three-year-old Um Hani, as she is known by her culturally traditional name of Mother of (the Eldest Son); Wadi Joz East Jerusalem; Occupied Territory; Palestine. Mrs. Wedad Abu Dayyeh, the beautiful and amazing mother, grandmother, great-grandmother, who adopted me as one of her family, is the mother who outlived the third child of the four children she bore. Her beloved daughter, my sister-friend/comrade Maha Abu Dayyeh, may she rest in peace and power, introduced and invited me into this country, the women's human rights center she cofounded nearly thirty years ago, and into her life in 2004. When I first met Um Hani, her body was sturdy and her mind sharp.

Today, Um Hani is frail, although her powerful mind and will keep her mobile however slowly and gingerly, keeping going, doing many things for herself, going to work in the finance office of the business she cofounded with her late husband before "'48." Her frailty brought me to share her home, as nominal backup, while her eldest daughter Freda is on holiday "outside." A powerful coincidence of me being "inside" the country and Um Hani needing someone inside the house through the night brought us together in this way. She, for many years, has proclaimed me one of the family—"I really appreciate and never forget everything you did for Maha"—but this is the first sharing of space and meals over days. And one of the ways I could reciprocate for her kindness over the years.

Although sparse, our conversations consist of the Israeli Occupation and changes she has observed and experienced, from before the Nakba catastrophe of 1948 and since. The undeniable role of the US state in enabling, facilitating, sanctioning, financing, and justifying the Occupation and the cowardice of the international community. Um Hani also shares family gossip, drama, and sources of pride.

Um Hani, most other friends, families who claim me as "blood" relative, and colleagues at the Women's Centre for Legal Aid and Counselling actually rarely mention my gender, race, class; occasionally "American" comes up, usually in the context of the actions of whomever resides in the White House and his minions or some popular-culture phenomenon. We are not directly bound by external forces, "a hostile third party." We are heart-connected. That's how we need, and have needed, one another, in various ways during my fifteen-year relationship to the place and people.

I learned, later in the day, that Israeli officials demolished houses and buildings in the Sur Bahir neighborhood of East Jerusalem that morning—as Um Hani and I were sitting together eating breakfast the day of writing this essay. In this context, given my citizenship and Um Hani's social location, what do we need from one another?

How did I get here, in this geographic and political space of Palestine? In this historical moment, considering I am not even supposed to exist?

Origins

And I would not exist, or be here, if Okazawa Kazuko, my Japanese, upper-middle-class mother, and Sidney Mayfield Rey, my American, Black, and working-class father, had remained in their mandated respective social and political positions as Occupied and Occupier after World War II. But they did not; thus, I have a complex story to tell.

That story begins with the question of home. As many marginalized peoples have, I too ask, where and what is home? Where and what is my original home? Where do I belong? Who recognizes me in ways that they then can and will claim me as one of their own? Where do I feel belonging and know that I am claimed?

From all the family lore I carry with me, I know, and imagine even more vividly, that War-time and post-War Japan were difficult. Although the Okazawa family fared well given my お爺ちゃん's (grandfather's) class background and position in a major shipping company, Kobe was in shambles thanks to operations of war.

But Kobe was different from most other Japanese cities long before World War II, up to now—characterized by cosmopolitanism and internationalism:

> Kobe was opened as a treaty port for the outside world in 1868 and rapidly developed into an international port that thrived on trade and transport.... Yokohama was another international port, similar to Kobe, but Kobe was closer to Hong Kong and Shanghai where Britain had already established trade centres in the Far East. Kobe also benefited from the two wars Japan fought and won against China and Russia as those wars stimulated industries and trade. World War I provided further opportunities for expansion. The Great

Kanto Earthquake in 1923 brought more business to Kobe, as many trading firms shifted their offices and operations from Yokohama. In the 1930s, the military and colonial expansion of Japan to the Asian continent also stimulated business in Kobe because a large volume of goods went through the port.[1]

Kobe and its citizens, not to mention Japan, benefited from industrialization, wars, and colonization from as early as 1868, five years after President Abraham Lincoln formally issued the Emancipation Proclamation, freeing the enslaved people of African descent. As its origin suggests, Kobe was intended to be an international city. Its reputation today is just that, with all the signifiers such as French bakeries, German sausages, and Chinese, Mexican, and Indian restaurants, for example. People of Kobe are reputed to be "high tone" precisely because of their assumed cosmopolitanism.

However, post–World War II Kobe was an Occupied Kobe (1945–1952). Citizens were under the formal power of the US. "Home," even for citizens, was always conditional. For a child like me, it was even more so. I was stateless until 1953, when the US military gave my father permission to marry my mother. At the time, Japanese citizenship was patrilineal only.

My first physical home was in Rokkō Mountain, where my お母さん (mother), an unwed woman bearing a mixed-race child, was allowed to live in the Okazawa family summer 別荘 (villa). Stories go that a whole cadre of friends and family (especially her sister, my aunty Yoko) collectively raised me those first years of my life. Among them were the US military people who knew my father, an Italian American GI and African American military couple who wanted to adopt me, and the Japanese women friends of the two sisters. My home then, as with the rest of Kobe, was international and, in a sense, transnational, as my entire existence now is. I am unable to recall how I felt, but I am certain those early years of both deeply Japanese and international child-rearing and language-learning laid the foundation for whom I have become and for my transnational and feminist perspectives that drew me eventually to Palestine. (I began learning formal English in the first grade at St. Michael's International School in Kobe, founded in 1946 by Miss Leonora Lea, a British Anglican missionary, and Japanese Anglican Bishop Michael Yashiro).

In 1952–3, my father returned to Japan to reunite with his family after discharge from the US Army and serve as a civil servant with the US Air Force. That prompted our family move to Kunitachi (国立市), a village then, now part of Metropolitan Tokyo, near the old Tachikawa (立川) Air Force Base. My home there was, by Japanese standards of the day, large and modern, on land that my お爺ちゃん bought for the daughter he had disowned several years before.

We were the only Japanese, Black, American, Western family then, but my mother's class position, demonstrated by landownership, mitigated what I imagine would have been severe discrimination otherwise. It was a place where I felt I belonged with friends and neighbors, and even students at the nearby music university who used to invite me to play with them. The story goes that I would bicycle there regularly to meet them, that I became a kind of "mascot" in the kindest of ways because I "すごく可愛かった" (was so cute).

This was home. Even though I traveled school days to the base dependents' primary school as a second grader, my heart was 国立市. The American students and teachers (all white) were strange, foreign, and spoke and acted in ways different from what I knew and understood. Early on, having been required to recite the alphabet (it was silly in the first place in the second grade), I diligently complied—except at the end, "zed" came out because of my British English education at St. Michael's, instead of American "zee." The entire class, including the teacher, faced me and laughed. I clearly did not belong in the school, and in that moment the whole class let me know, so I believed.

Transpacific Journey and Beyond

Our family made our way to the US in winter 1960 due to my father's job transfer—to Utah, a place I knew only as "America." Others in the US, even the non-Mormons around us in Utah, thought the place strange with their atypical religious customs—no alcohol, tobacco, caffeine, for example—and their requirement for young people to complete their stint as a Mormon missionary in various places outside the US. I and my family as a whole were "strangers in a strange land," to be sure, but I could not have predicted what was to come in the decades ahead.

Now, back in the US in 2019, social and political relationships are too often bound by externally imposed categories. This, of course, is directly related to the interlinked histories of oppressions including legal segregation based on categories, which predated formation of the US and was created to establish and buttress the settler-colony that is called "America," especially where race was concerned. The numerous and varied movements organized to resist, to create change, and to free ourselves all began with identities and the histories of colonization, slavery, and racism institutionalized in both.

From experiences and lessons learned in Utah, across several states in the country, and finally in California, I became socialized—though with great fear, trepidation, and discomfort more often than I can count—to become an "American," African American, woman. During the course of six decades after first landing in the US, I have wended my way to knowing myself and to being known by others as a radical, African American and Japanese, transnational feminist, community worker, and academic. Throughout these decades, I have noticed that folks, including me, are compelled to ask others of whom they cannot confirm easy, presumed-correct identities, Where are you from? That is, are you really one of us? Can we claim you? Do you claim us? As a Black, mixed-race Japanese and African American woman of color, I know these questions shaped my relationships to people and social movements, and I have been both included and excluded for the same answers.

The politics and dynamics of identity-based, interpersonal, individual interactions operate within and across contemporary social movements in the US, as they have in the past and do even more so today. Now, the Right and white-supremacist movements again rely on assumed connections among their people. Indeed, they are emboldened to rally "white people" to "make America great again" and white.

Folks in progressive movements, despite our intellectual understanding—"they're socially constructed"—too often treat as real the existing sociopolitical classifications and categories, particularly race and gender in the US, and lay them into the foundation of mobilization and galvanization.

The progressive-movement organizing principle of centering the voices of the most-affected people and of focusing the work primarily around *experiences of oppression, impacts on affected people*, I argue, have placed parts of the progressive movement into a roundabout, a rotary, around which we move in circles, despite appearances to the contrary. An aerial view of how we conceptualize both the problems and the responses might enable us to see ourselves, still relying on "identities" based on classifications not of our making. Indeed, these classifications serve to keep tying us to the oppressors and dominant frameworks, which do not serve us obviously, and reinforce a reactive politics that reinforces the seeming inextricable connection between oppressor and oppressed: the powerful set the agenda, in a sense, of our struggle. As June Jordan says; "The ultimate connection cannot be the enemy. The ultimate connection must be the need we find between us. It is not only who you are, in other words, but what we can do for each other that will determine the connection."[2]

Turning the Decade, Experiencing the "Need Between Us"

I embrace my seventieth year wholeheartedly, knowing the preciousness of every day we live, not to mention seven decades! In Palestine, I feel more deeply that preciousness, for obvious reasons of the Occupation. However grueling the grind of daily living, Palestinian folks live with beauty, joy, love, and commitments to relationships, alongside the other emotions. This "interior" is what I observe, what I hear, what I smell and taste, what I experience when I am "home." It is there I need and am needed.

The interior of Birthday Week in Palestine was beyond my imagination. Everyone to whom I am connected created a spectacular, deeply connective, and love- and joy-filled birthday week. During the first family conversation on the eve of my birthday, the children Ali, Yasmin, Zaina, and Tala, and parent Samar (who also spoke for me), shared what we meant to one another over the years—what each person liked about me and the activity they most enjoyed doing with me, and I shared the same with each in turn. During her turn, Tala, the youngest, confessed something she had been nervous to mention before: "I didn't go swimming with you early in the morning because summer holiday is when I can sleep late." Um Hani decided we should go to Beit Sahour, near Bethlehem, for lunch. The significance is that these days, she rarely ventures past her office and home because of physical challenges. (At ninety-three years old, her mind is sharper than yours and mine combined!) We paid tribute to Maha at the Abu Dayyehs' section of the Beit Jala cemetery, had a small adventure getting lost, and laughed a lot! She agreed my feminist driving is good enough to become part of the NET Tours driver team after I retire from university teaching. Um Hani wanted to celebrate me, no doubt, and must have sensed I needed her company and energy and to remember and honor Maha this birthday week. I brought her silver-gray hair coloring that can only be bought in the US.

Two parties marked the cultural practices of life in Palestine. The family party was attended by all members, women, men, children.

And, on the last evening of Birthday Week, Nadeen, Salwa, Samar, and I, the moon-gazers' "Moon Ladies" group we created last summer (mostly over WhatsApp), sat together over tea, mixed nuts, and sweets. We read Angel Cards, as has been our practice, and shared "inside stories." I needed the conversation, as I believe the other women did too.

In the vignettes shared here, the stories taken together, our needs are both mundane and profound. "Birthday Week" activities, and others like them, will not result in uppercase Revolution or Decolonization, but they signify life-affirming connections that help to rehumanize and to remind: our connections must be based on generative values and principles and on authenticity, coming and going to one another, simply and fully as we are. Connections based on categories not of our making will never hold.

Ahead of Us

I argue that the penultimate connection is to a *vision* of a life-giving and life-affirming world. It is our collective connections to our dreams of justice, genuine security, peace, joy, creativity. More fundamentally, our connection is rooted in our collective and interpersonal experiences of the mundane and the profound, of our daily encounters with life dilemmas, and in the contradictions between our social locations and our deeply held commitments to one another.

It occurs to me that much organizational grief could be avoided if people understood that partnership in misery does not necessarily provide for partnership for change: *When we get the monsters off our backs all of us may want to run in very different directions.*[3]

And not only that: even though both "Olive" and "I" (Olive, Bahamian Black woman maid in tourist hotel; June Jordan, African American woman, professor SUNY Stony Brook) live inside a conflict neither one of us created, and even though both of us therefore hurt inside that conflict, I may be one of the monsters she needs to eliminate from her universe and, in a sense, she may be one of the monsters in mine.

Let us unite, therefore, based on our shared dreams of liberation and freedom where creativity, joy, and love guide our decisions, undergird how we decide who we can become, "what we can do for each other," and our deeply held belief and faith that another world is truly possible.

Margo Okazawa-Rey is an activist-educator who has been working on issues of militarism for nearly thirty years. She has long-standing activist commitments in South Korea and Palestine, with Du Re Bang and Women's Centre for Legal Aid and Counselling, respectively. She is also a founding member of the Combahee River Collective and International Women's Network Against Militarism, and was the most recent board president of AWID.

Elegy for a Soldier [1]

Marilyn Hacker

for June Jordan, 1936–2002

I.
The city where I knew you was swift.
A lover cabbed to Brooklyn
(broke, but so what) after the night shift
in a Second Avenue
diner. The lover was a Quaker,
a poet, an anti-war
activist. Was blonde, was twenty-four.
Wet snow fell on the access
road to the Manhattan Bridge. I was
neither lover, slept uptown.
But the arteries, streetlights, headlines,
phonelines, feminine plural
links ran silver through the night city
as dawn and the yellow cab
passed on the frost-blurred bridge, headed for
that day's last or first coffee.

The city where I knew you was rich
in bookshops, potlucks, ad hoc
debates, demos, parades, and picnics.
There were walks I liked to take.
I was on good terms with two rivers.
You turned, burned, flame-wheel of words
lighting the page, good neighbor on your
homely street in Park Slope, whose
Russian zaydes, Jamaican grocers,
dyke vegetarians, young

gifted everyone, claimed some changes
—at least a new food co-op.
In the laundromat, ordinary
women talked revolution.
We knew we wouldn't live forever
but it seemed as if we could.

The city where I knew you was yours
and mine by birthright: Harlem,
the Bronx. Separately we left it
and came separately back.
There's no afterlife for dialogue,
divergences we never
teased apart to weave back together.
Death slams down in the midst of
all your unfinished conversations.
Whom do I address when I
address you, larger than life as you
always were, not alive now?
Words are not you, poems are not you,
ashes on the Pacific
tide, you least of all. I talk to myself to keep the line open.

The city where I knew you is gone.
Pink icing roses spelled out
PASSION on a book-shaped chocolate cake.
The bookshop's a sushi bar
now, and PASSION is long out of print.
Would you know the changed street that
cab swerved down toward you through cold white mist?
We have a Republican
mayor. Threats keep citizens in line:
anthrax; suicide attacks.
A scar festers where towers once were;

dissent festers unexpressed.
You are dead of a woman's disease.
Who gets to choose what battle
takes her down? Down to the ocean, friends
mourn you, with no time to mourn.

II.
You, who stood alone in the tall bay window
of a Brooklyn brownstone, conjuring morning
with free-flying words, knew the power, terror
in words, in flying;

knew the high of solitude while the early
light prowled Seventh Avenue, lupine, hungry
like you, your spoils raisins and almonds, ballpoint
pen, yellow foolscap.

You, who stood alone in your courage, never
hesitant to underline the connections
(between rape, exclusion and occupation . . .)
and separations

were alone and were not alone when morning
blotted the last spark of you out, around you
voices you no longer had voice to answer,
eyes you were blind to.

All your loves were singular: you scorned labels.
Claimed *black*; *woman*, and for the rest eluded
limits, quicksilver (Caribbean), staked out
self-definition

Now your death, as if it were "yours": your house, your
dog, your friends, your son, your serial lovers.

Death's not "yours," what's yours are a thousand poems
alive on paper.

You, at once an optimist, a Cassandra,
Lilith in the wilderness of her lyric,
were a black American, born in Harlem,
citizen soldier

If you had to die—and I don't admit it—
who dared "*What if, each time they kill a black man/
we kill a cop?*" couldn't you take down with you
a few prime villains

in the capitol, who are also mortal?
June, you should be living, the states are bleeding.
Leaden words like "Homeland" translate abandoned
dissident discourse.

Twenty years ago, you denounced the war crimes
still in progress now, as Jenin, Ramallah
dominate, then disappear from the headlines.
Palestine: your war.

"To each nation, its Jews," wrote Primo Levi.
"Palestinians are Jews to Israelis."
Afterwards, he died in despair, or so we
infer, despairing.

To each nation its Jews, its blacks, its Arabs,
Palestinians, immigrants, its women.
From each nation, its poets: Mahmoud Darwish,
Kavanagh, Sháhid

(who, beloved witness for silenced Kashmir,
cautioned, shift the accent, and he was "martyr"),

Audre Lorde, Neruda, Amichai, Senghor,
and you, June Jordan.

Marilyn Hacker is a translator and the author of fourteen poetry collections, including *Blazons* (Carcanet, 2019) and a book of essays, *Unauthorized Voices* (University of Michigan Press, 2010). She received the 2009 American PEN Award for poetry in translation. She lives in Paris.

Letters to My Friend, for June Jordan

Kathy Engel

> Your Danny is dead.
> And how can we honor his heroic wish: "to change the world"?
> I have no simple answers.
> But perhaps our willingness to listen and to say all that we know, and feel—all that we dare—perhaps that will help us to build something better than we can even, now, imagine.
>
> —*June Jordan, "Letter to My Friend"*

Dear June:

I begin writing this sequence of letters on your birthday, July 9, 2019. Attempting some kind of lucidity, articulation to submit to a collection honoring and engaging with your legacy.

I've wondered if you felt underacknowledged when you were here breathing so fiercely on this planet, this sphere, living so very fully, with your mighty daring generous brilliance. I'm glad we at MADRE honored you for our sixth anniversary—was it 1989? I remember asking you how other honorings had been and being shocked when you replied that it was the first one.

How can we learn to honor each other better while we're still here, together? Isn't it critical to do so as part of building *beloved community*, the phrase we sometimes speak as easily as a sip of coffee? I might say it is one of the most challenging, painstaking, and essential acts in creating the possible. To truly honor while living. You did that in multiple ways.

You invited me to read at Stony Brook when others in the field didn't recognize me as a real poet.

You did those things, nurturing young poet/activists, always taking the time. Those stretches and affirmations in real ways. Not merely nods but leaning all of your being into the support of another, one whose life you would change with your loving presence, response, and readiness.

When students in one of my classes first read "Letter to My Friend" and I saw the impact, I asked them to write their own versions. I suggested writing to someone important to them about something hard to discuss. I revised the syllabus, and the semester's work evolved from that project. The most powerful, honest, vulnerable writing emerged. Some in the class worked with junior high school students in the Bronx with the same prompt. At the end of the semester, we hosted a sharing of the work at NYU, inviting the junior high students and their teacher to join. This was a beautiful, transformative process.

Ever since, my students have engaged in different ways with the letter-as-essay and specifically "Letter to My Friend," the invitation to write intimately and into the world in the same breath. You exquisitely and in some sense delicately embodied that practice and risk. As you write, "My life seems to be an increasing revelation of the intimate face of universal struggle."[1]

Happy birthday, June. I love you. I miss you. I float your words constantly. I never studied with you in an institution, but you were/are one of my greatest teachers. Even the lessons of how to understand sudden disruptions and misunderstanding in intense friendship and comradery. Those bruises and healings. That time we didn't speak for a while. I didn't understand then your readiness to fist with words in a friendship. The suddenness. I came to understand more deeply, even after we had reconciled, when I read *Soldier*. I didn't know then that it was just a moment, a misunderstanding, that love and shared passion were stronger. That my hurt didn't have to turn into pride or become a wall. Becoming sensitive to what provokes strong reaction and discomfort, or readiness to attack in another, even a good friend, is a lifetime practice. As intimate as anything. As political as anything.

Slowly, carefully, we returned. In Washington, DC, at the inauguration of the MADRE group there, with Bernice Johnson Reagon, Jacqueline Jackson, Congressman Ronald V. Dellums's top aides, and the book of letters and signatures from Nicaraguan women requesting that the US president and congress stop killing their children. The book the women entrusted to you. The book that constituted the artifact that asked for the formation of MADRE. I will never forget the head of the Nicaraguan Women's Association running up to us in the airport in Managua, breathless, handing you the book, saying: *We didn't know what to do with it, but you will. Please tell your president to stop killing our children.* (I think how many uncountable mothers have asked the same of "sisters" regarding the killing of their children by a US president and congress). You held the pages on your lap as if they might shatter when the small plane lifted from the Sandino Airport; your smooth, articulated hands, caretakers of ink, blood, the memories and prayers of a country of mothers. 1983. Then in June, 1984, we were there, on the local news in DC, and the book was entered into the Congressional Record. Our promise. Archive of friendship across borders.

Then there was a performance, your opera, a reading. One gesture, one message, one presence. When I saw you, June, 1987, at Leslie Cagan's birthday celebration at Ruth Messenger's Upper West Side apartment, Ella was a tiny baby we carried in a laundry basket! You asked what we needed or wanted for the baby, loving that we named her after Ella Baker, this little pink girl! I said a poem, without pausing. Within weeks a handwritten "Lullabye for Ella" arrived in the mail. It's on her wall in her home now.

Meaning, we found our way back. Remember our conversation after the decision about O. J. Simpson? Your essay about not choosing between being a woman and being black, rejected by *The New York Times* op-ed page, published in *The Progressive*? The constant struggle to find the spaces to share the words.

Your handwritten notes and letters. I can hear your giggle through your handwriting! And your love. And sometimes your rage.

So I keep writing a Letter to My Friend. Hoping to be that letter. That friend. That giggle. Be that home of fear and daring love. How we work to hold all our loves and strains, each devastating misunderstanding, write through them, into some light. How we did somehow. How Split This Rock honored you. How Melissa Tuckey, poet and editor of the first eco-justice poetry anthology *Ghost Fishing*, explains you were inspiration for the book, that your poems helped her see what eco-justice poetry is and what it has been and you made that.

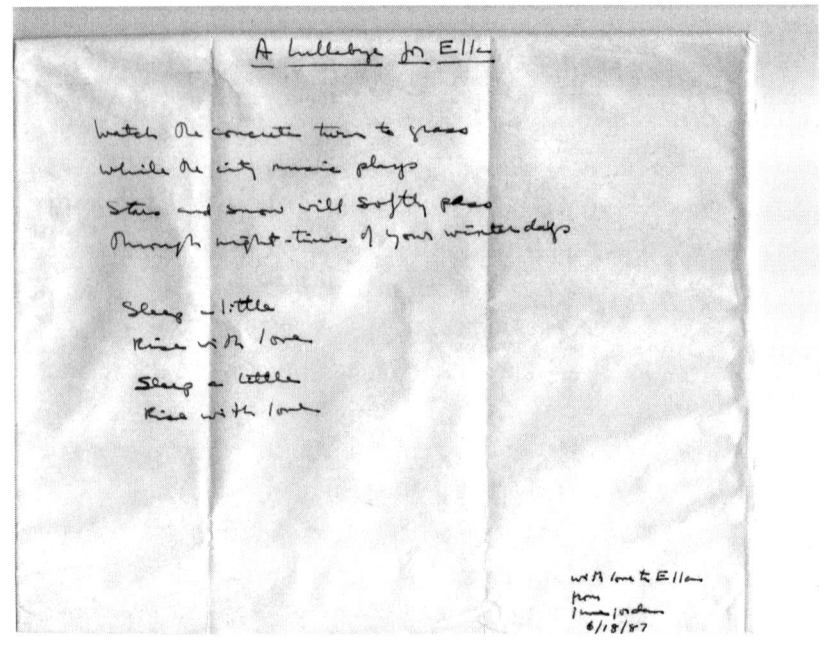

"A Lullabye for Ella." Photo by Kathy Engel.

Every day in some way. Because that's it. *We're on*, as you wrote at the end of the foreword to *Civil Wars*:

> And then if you're lucky, and I have been lucky, everything comes back to you. And then you know why one of the freedom fighters in the sixties, a young Black woman interviewed shortly after she was beaten up for riding near the front of the interstate bus—you know why she said, "We are all so very happy." It's because it's on. All of us and me by myself: we're on.[2]

On. And through the letters, our words, our lyrical testimony, we continue, often stumbling in the dark, and still, the words, the pull . . .

Love, Kath

July 2019

Dear June:

Kamal Boullata has died. I'm thinking about our summer, 1982. Vivian and I visited you and Sara in Bearsville. We talked about *Sisterfire*. Dreamed up *Moving Towards Home* with Kamal. CNN every hour. We couldn't shake the dissonance, how at the great peace march and rally, June 12, 1982, there was no official mention of Palestine.

I watched Kamal emerge every day at Blue Mountain Center late June, 1982, from the wooden phone booth, tears streaming down his face, having spoken with family in Beirut. I listened to Holly Near's "No More Genocide in My Name" again and again like an adolescent soaking in a love song. It is a love song.

Darwish wasn't allowed into the US for *Moving Towards Home*; Kamal read his poem. The Israeli poet attacked you after the reading. A week or so later, PEN voted to disassociate from our event. Your letter to PEN, resigning from the board, has been recovered recently by poet/scholar Anjuli Fatima Raza Kolb while researching Edward Said's archives at Columbia.

Etel Adnan told us she'd never before shared a stage with an Israeli. I still have the CBS news clip from that November night in NYC at the Ethical Culture Society; show it to students. Etel was, at ninety-four, still making art and language. Your essay "Life After Lebanon" tells it. I regularly read aloud your poems: "Moving Towards Home," "Apologies to All the People in Lebanon," "To Sing a Song of Palestine," and more. Poems that broke silence, shattered the censor, pierced the muzzle, passionately, oh so stunningly. Still do.

Then all those years later, after you had left us in your bodily pain, Kamal and I made *We Begin Here: Poems for Palestine and Lebanon*, dedicated to you and Eqbal Ahmad. That's how I met one of the editors of this collection I'm writing for, Becky Thompson, through the making of that anthology. Through Ethelbert. I mention all the names of those with whom we are threaded because this is how we move together. Nothing just happens. We must name ourselves, each other, when we're able, when it won't potentially annihilate any of us. Because when we don't name, we contribute to erasure, brutal amnesia. Remember, in Nicaragua during that initial postrevolution period of elation, there was a saying: *Whenever you say your name aloud it means victory.* We weave our words, intentions, and passions, our impatience and patience, our ways of being related. Learn through misunderstanding, listening, wounding, and trying again.

And over the years I kept losing Kamal through distance and time zones. But never really.

June, Toni Morrison passed the day before Kamal. A planetary shift. A gulf opened. In addition to the waters and mountains of her words, her mind, I keep remembering how you went to bat for her, started a campaign, appeared on talk shows and wrote letters to people in important places, when she was passed over for the National Book Award. You did what others might consider. Or not. Those were things you did.

I'm not sure how to make sense of much my dear departed still-here friend, but I remember you, me, Jon, Sara trembling in the hills of Teotecacinte after two international journalists had been killed, a mortar attack. And dancing in the hot night on Corn Island. I remember you were a rock star in your ironed skirt and blouse in a dusty arena in Bluefields, during war and revolutionary exhilaration. I remember you never stopped and always made time to have fun.

We said *I love you* in your last days. You wrote me a wobbly note after Safiya passed, honoring the friend I was to her. And I made a class in a university studying your work. Not a week goes by when I don't repeat something I learned from you to my students. And tell them, in the story of things, how you introduced me to Alexis De Veaux and Sekou Sundiata. Alexis Pauline Gumbs, who's written volumes about your work, who was born into this world on the day of the march, June 12, 1982, made art from your image, gifted to me by Alexis De Veaux for my sixtieth birthday, framed on a wall facing all who come into my university office. Unavoidable, your singular gaze and reach. We are all (some quilt of a *we*) together in some sense in these different iterations and ways of making.

In the eighties, we took a long walk in Virginia countryside after the reading *American Poets on Lebanon* hosted by Congressman John

Conyers in the Rayburn House Office Building, following *Moving Towards Home*. You asked if the walk constituted a hike? We care about what we call things. We laughed—who knew when a walk became a hike, but it was so much fun, wasn't it?

Love, Kath

August 2019

Dear June:

Last October my friend, Sandra Garcia-Betancourt, was organizing an event with Voices of a People Speak, which she was directing at the time, to build momentum for midterm elections, at the Nuyorican Poets Café. I was asked to read a piece by Naomi Klein and one by Susan B. Anthony. I said I wasn't comfortable reading Susan B. Anthony unless I could offer a context, given what we've learned about her racism. Sandra then offered me a piece by you to read. When I mentioned your name a colleague leaned forward, her eyes opening wide and almost touching mine, and said something like: *I probably wouldn't be here doing what I do if it weren't for June Jordan.* Immediately I felt an intense connection with her that had little to do with our jobs at a university. She told me that when she was in graduate school and trying to find her way, perhaps lacking self-confidence, you approached her and asked if she would read a manuscript of essays, tell you what she thought. The faith you, a literary and political shero, showed, your respect for this graduate student, became a turning point for her. That story gave me permission to ask a beloved recent alumna, René, if she would read this piece for me, made me feel it wouldn't be crossing a line but hopefully offering us both a gift.

Thank you.

Love, Kath

August 2019

Dear June:

I met a friend I hadn't seen in a long time. She told me about travels she planned, spiritual journeys to ancestral lands overseas. One she anticipated was to Jerusalem. She explained to me that she supports Palestine but has always wanted to make this journey and it's not political. There was that split second where I tried to decide whether to say anything or not. I said: *When it comes to Israel there's no way for it not to be political.* She said: *I can. I can make it not political.*

We let it drop and said how wonderful that she's going to Egypt and that I once was part of a project MADRE organized with the brilliant Egyptian feminist/scholar Dr. Nawal El Saadawi.

There was that space in the air. Our visit ended lovingly. I don't know if it was right or wrong to say what I said, but I felt I had to. Part of the letter. A week later she wrote to me that she'd learned about the boycott and was reconsidering.

Somehow writing this letter in conversation with your Letter is opening up a letter that doesn't want to end, that doesn't know where the beginning or end of this conversation might be. That may be the way we're immortal. That may be the way spirit speaks. That may be how we conjure *our willingness to listen and to say all that we know, and feel—all that we dare—*

Yes, *perhaps that will help us to build something better than we can even, now, imagine.*

Where's the rage? Where's the love? Right here, my friend, living together across heartbeats still pulsing and those in another world—as you signed your books and letters—*with faith.*

Love, Kath

Kathy Engel is a cultural worker, poet, essayist, organizer, and founder and cofounder of projects including MADRE, East End Women in Black, Poets for Ayiti, Riptide Communications, Lyrical Democracies, and East End for

Peace. She is associate arts professor for the Department of Art and Public Policy at Tisch School of the Arts, NYU. Her most recent book is *Dear Inheritors* (Get Fresh Books, 2024). Learn more at www.kathyengelpoet.com.

¡Puño en Alto! ¡Libro Abierto! / Fists Up! Books Open!

On Anti-Intellectualism, Literacy Brigades, and Revolutionary Consciousness

María Poblet

I'm pretty sure the first time I heard the word "Anti-Intellectualism," I said, "that word is so elitist!" Luckily, I was in the company of one of my greatest teachers, June Jordan. After giggling uncontrollably (her giggle-fests were legendary), she asked me what I thought the word meant. Little did I know we were beginning a dialogue that would last more than a decade and shape my view of the world.

I explained my logic to her: "If I label something as inaccessible because of its advanced vocabulary, then I'm defending the working class, right? I mean, even if I know what the word means, that's just because I had the privilege of education. And we're all responsible for building a movement culture that doesn't exclude people!"

June did not giggle. She peered over her glasses, ashing the Nat Sherman she was smoking, and cocked her head, as she did when things got interesting. "Really? Have you ever asked a working-class teenager if she would rather be fed easier words or get an education that allows her to read any word she wants?"

It was such a powerful example of the problem with anti-intellectualism (hostility toward intellectuals or intellectual work), that I still remember it, fifteen years later. Well . . . that and the fact that she was calling out my paternalistic view in no uncertain terms. Here I was, getting good grades at a fancy university, claiming the real problem in society was big words. I worked three jobs and accumulated a huge debt to attend the school where she taught. If education was that important to me, why would it be less important to anyone else? Lucky for me, she was patient with my contradictions, and her passion was contagious.

"Come over here." She continued, "Did I ever tell you about the Sandinistas?" June started to tell me of her experiences in Nicaragua in the 1980s. The Frente Sandinista de Liberación Nacional (Sandinista Front for National Liberation, known by its Spanish acronym FSLN), a left-wing political organization, led the 1979 overthrow of dictator Anastasio Somoza, ending his family's right-wing political dynasty in the country and ushering in an era of profoundly progressive social and economic change. June was proud to have been the first Black journalist to travel to Nicaragua and document the success of that movement. Following Sandinistas around with a steno notebook from a meeting in Managua to a school in Estelí changed her life forever. "The feeling," she said, "was like falling in love." She described the wave of enthusiasm; the desire to give your best self to this joyful, complicated, collective process. The feeling that everyone you met was a cousin who had just arrived at some kind of revolutionary family reunion.

She wrote a stark portrait of dignity and poverty, which was also a portrait of the work of the literacy brigades.

Third Poem from Nicaragua Libre: Photograph of Managua

The man is not cute.
The man is not ugly.
The man is teaching himself
to read.
He sits in a kitchen chair
under a banana tree.
He holds the newspaper.
He tracks each word with a finger
and opens his mouth to the sound.
Next to the chair the old V-Z rifle
leans at the ready.
His wife chases a baby pig with a homemade

broom and then she chases her daughter running
behind the baby pig.
His neighbor washes up with water from the barrel
after work.
The dirt floor of his house has been swept.
The dirt around the chair where he sits
has been swept.
He has swept the dirt twice.
The dirt is clean.
The dirt is his dirt.
The man is not cute.
The man is not ugly.
The man is teaching himself
to read.[1]

She had arrived shortly after the FSLN began implementing Carlos Fonseca Amador's vision of a strong relationship between literacy and militancy. Fonseca Amador was a librarian, teacher, and founder of the FSLN. Years after his death, his ideas lived on and took the shape of literacy brigades. This visionary project sent one hundred thousand volunteers into peasant communities to end illiteracy. Drawing from the example set by the Cuban Literacy Campaign, which literally eliminated illiteracy in that country, they adapted the concept to their own unique conditions. Jesuit priest Fernando Cardenal, who coordinated the effort, described it this way:

> Not only would we teach people letters and what those letters mean, we would also make it possible for peasant farmers and urban workers to learn about their own situation and the economic, social, and political context in which they lived. We were going to teach them to answer questions like, why am I poor? We wanted them to learn to distinguish between a tragedy like a drought or an earthquake and a tragedy like poverty. We wanted them to learn that nature provokes hurricanes while human beings create poverty. Making this distinction is what *concientización* is all about.[2]

Their consciousness-raising was deeply influenced by the methods and theory of Brazilian educator and militant Paulo Freire. Freire's theory

(*Pedagogy of the Oppressed*) and methods (*Popular Education*) had the goal of *concientização*. Originally coined in Brazilian Portuguese, and common in Spanish (*concientización*), the term refers to the process of developing critical consciousness. Which is to say, learning to read the contradictions in social, political, and economic life, and learning to take action against the oppressive aspects of reality.

Illiteracy, the brigades said, was not an individual problem. It was a social problem that everyone had responsibility for, and it required a community-based solution. And this community-based solution would not only eradicate illiteracy; it would also raise consciousness. Volunteer *brigadistas* learned as much as they taught. They returned from their work with peasant communities humbled and inspired by the resilience of the families they lived and worked with, and ready to support the struggle for economic justice that the peasant organizations were leading inside a broader progressive front.

Rural communities learned too. Not only how to write a number or read directions, but also about the relationship between their often-isolated experiences of struggle, and the political system the society was only just starting to cast off after an electoral victory by the FSLN. Education was flowing in all directions. And, as the poetic Sandinistas tended to do, they gave their project a beautiful slogan: "Turn our country into a school!"

In the United States, the right wing has been so successful in tying working-class identity to anti-intellectualism that we can hardly tell the two apart. And that confusion shows up inside our movement as well. We often critique intellectual work as if it has a class nature in itself, instead of recognizing that, like artistic, scientific, or therapeutic work, it can be put to the service of any class. If intellectual work is associated with the capitalist class and with class privilege, it's simply because the capitalist class has control over it.

And it's a power shift when intellectual tools are in the hands of oppressed people who know they are oppressed and are seeking a path toward liberation. June knew that when she started Poetry for the People, which supported young people in finding their voice, and required that students teach in the community, giving classes at Glide Memorial

Church, FCI Dublin women's prison, Berkeley High School, and Mission Cultural Center. I served as artistic director of the program and found that what I was learning from this collaboration with her was much more than poetry. Working with June taught me the function of critical consciousness in society and taught me to understand writing as a form to explore and convey that.

Literary critics often praised June Jordan for being "a voice for the voiceless," but she rejected that characterization. As I began my transition into community organizing and movement-building work, we discussed this question often. "Who has no voice?" she asked me. I described the communities I was organizing with: Salvadoran grandmothers hanging on to rent-controlled apartments in SF's mission district, African American teenagers treated as criminals in West Oakland, queer couples unable to hold hands on the street. "Do they have no voice?" she probed, cocking her head. It finally clicked. There are no voiceless people, only people who are not being heard.

This epiphany led me from poetry to community organizing. I came to understand community organizing as the process of building a giant megaphone, so that oppressed and exploited people could be heard. It turned out that the core of organizing wasn't that different from teaching poetry. People needed a space to make sense of their experiences, longed to deeply see and connect with each other, and wanted to be able to imagine something beautiful. After Poetry for the People, I worked alongside many dear comrades in the community to build Causa Justa / Just Cause in the SF Bay Area, bringing African American / Black and Latin American / Latinx folks together for social, racial, economic, and gender justice. While some traditions of organizing avoided ideology and stuck to a focus on concrete winnable policy reforms, we took a more radical route. We engaged deeply in the world of ideas, read and wrote voraciously, and worked hard not to shrink our imagination down to the scale of what we could do with our current amount of political power. Amid campaigns for rent control and immigrant rights, we built cross-racial unity by putting our disparate experiences into a shared political context, and understanding why things were the way they were, particularly for Black and Latinx working-class people.

Even in a country steeped in anti-intellectualism and individualism, we found that people in our working-class communities were eager to come together and make meaning. Causa Justa / Just Cause became both a power-building project, and a process of development of critical consciousness. These days, I get to work with groups like this across the country, building strategic frameworks for transformative movements at the Grassroots Power Project.

As we face the crises of today, I draw on June Jordan's wisdom and her passion for deeply human critical consciousness. Community organizing, direct action, and mobilization are powerful tactics. But without critical engagement in the world of ideas, they are not enough to win the scale of change we need in our communities and in our world. Our whole social movement is struggling to reclaim the power of intellectual work, and to put it in deeper relationship with grassroots power-building. Instead of letting anti-intellectualism narrow our view, let's turn our movement into a school! As the Sandinistas said, "Fists up! Books open!"

María Poblet has a couple decades of community-organizing experience, a smart mouth, and an optimism of the will. She is Chicana and Argentine. María serves as executive director of the Grassroots Power Project, facilitating strategic breakthroughs in social movements. She cofounded the grassroots racial and economic justice powerhouse Causa Justa / Just Cause, the US chapter of the World March of Women, the Feminist Organizing School, and Left Roots.

The Setup

Mahogany L. Browne

it's like he forgot
how his own mother
cowered beneath the shadow
of a small sad man
his own voice booming louder
to drown out his failed dreams

it's like he can't remember the outline of a woman's body
alone in the house that raised him and his siblings

the way they called him bastard instead of latch key
the way his kicks were snuffed and his head a marble
pinned up against the lockers after school
or against a blacktop on the weekends
or beneath their fists initiating him into a house of bricks
or like the time he swung on his first girlfriend
or his second girlfriend
or the girl at the bus stop that refused to give him her name
because her ego towered over him
because her smile was louder than his
because her talents were too shiny
because he got a backbone with a fractured memory
because ain't nothing in history tell him
"we will not forgive you for how you mistreat our sisters"

it's like the time he read books and wrote a dissertation
about the corrupt system he never witnessed firsthand
still similac stoic behind his mother's sadness
still almost man penning penal confessions
of the brave bruised boys he aspired to become
still burgeoning boy burrowing into this hollow
idea of Black masculinity

it's like he ain't know this was a setup
he ain't know this was a setup
to fight women that look like your mother
to wed women because they don't look like your mother

it's like he ain't never worn cotton before

it's like he ain't never wiped the syrup of mango
from an extended elbow

it's like he a machine gun jammed and pointed
at the rest of us women
too Black and brash and here
we remain
left to pick up the pieces
and forgive r. kelly
still we stand
stone wall women pretending
chris brown and miles davis
ain't like the blood on our lips more than the breath in our body
and the beat goes on
because they don't want us to remember america
done weaponized Black men to destroy
what whiteness can't

whiteness so fragile in its excess to exist
look how it release the bullet
without a guilty verdict
without an arrest warrant
holding their great-grandchildren's name
without stocks and bonds crashing
to the same symphonic melody as black wall street
without the fear of the help
coming back into the big house
with shotguns and spiked sticks

it's like he don't remember the noose
he don't remember the noose
how the song of wind picked away at scabs of our feet

and I ain't got time to talk about kings,
not today
I want to talk about the privilege of forgetting
how I live to fight in a country that
needs us to think only one kind of woman
is worth believing
how I birthed a Black daughter in a country
that needs us to believe in respectability
and silence and shame and shame and shame

so, yea I got time for the sundown towns
the Black boys they want us to forget
the Black men that swing into the sweet dark
and woman flesh with the same intensity
I said I got time   I got time   I got time

they want us to leave our Black men in the prisons they built
like condominiums in Brooklyn
they want us to focus on gentrification and bail bonds and school
  debt

like we ain't from a lineage of buoyancy
like we ain't seen these film credits before
like we can't differentiate charred wood from charred flesh
still the smoke goin' rise
like any good fire
like the sweat from a forked tongue

I will speak up against the man
who pulled his piece out in a car ride

I will speak up against the man
who pulled his piece out during an interview

I will speak up against the man
who pushed me against a crumbling scaffold

I will speak until the dawn breaks its beak wide
and we will sweep a circle until there is enough room
for those ready to undo the ragged rope
for those ready to unhinge the desire to flee

we will keep wake for the soft-eyed
slew-footed and unyielding brothers
together we will hold space and standards
for the short-tempered & ill-mannered man handlers

we will not buy his books / we will not
attend his concerts / we will not
bop our heads to the beat / justify
how he beat / women to the tune of genius

we will vow to end his days in the light
we will vow to end his days in the light
if he should ever reach for another's woman throat

we will become a nuisance   a nuisance?   yes!
we will become a nuisance to the carnage collectors

and the bones of our enemies
will line neatly
on our dinner plate
like any good meal

Mahogany L. Browne, a Kennedy Center Next 50 fellow and MacDowell Arts Advocacy awardee, is a writer, playwright, and educator. A recipient of numerous fellowships, her acclaimed works include *Vinyl Moon* (Crown, 2020), *Chlorine Sky* (Crown, 2021; optioned by Steppenwolf Theater), *Black Girl Magic* (Roaring Brook Press, 2018), and banned books *Woke* (Roaring Brook Press, 2020) and *Woke Baby* (Roaring Brook Press, 2018). Founder of the Woke Baby Book Fair, she tours *Chrome Valley* (Liveright Publishing, 2023), celebrated by *Publishers Weekly* and *The New York Times*, and is the 2024 Paterson Poetry Prize winner and Lincoln Center's inaugural poet-in-residence.

The Waters Are Wide: We Can Cross Over

Becky Thompson

It is marvelous to be part of the growing community of people influenced by Jordan's work, the myriad ways she is a mirror for us now, reflected among change agents globally. What we have in common is admiring how Jordan refused to get or stay in little boxes. She lived her life as if it were a rushing river, with inlets for rest, and rapids where she insisted that she and all those she was around hold on for dear life. While I have revisited much of Jordan's writing, my most beloved essay is "Many Rivers to Cross" which traces her early years as a mother, artist, and daughter. The essay begins with "When my mother killed herself I was looking for a job."[1] You read that first line, and all you can say is "help!" How can you start there—quintessential Jordan—an economy of words, keep emotions at the center, keep it real. She had me right there, as someone whom I love very much tried to kill herself twice before I was born. And then Jordan had me for the rest of the essay, as we learn that she was looking for a job so she could support her son after she and her husband split.

We learn that her father couldn't tell whether his wife, her mother, was dead or alive. We learn that Jordan's mother might have killed herself so her daughter would get her life insurance policy. We learn that when June did make the terrible announcement that her mother was dead, she committed to do what she could to ensure that people would know definitely whether she was alive or dead.

Such a commitment meant knowing that there would be "many rivers to cross," one of many examples of Jordan's exquisite use of metaphor—in this case, as water runs through much of her work. Both of

Jordan's parents were born in Jamaica, a country that works, lives, and rests with the sea. Jordan was born on July 9, 1936. Her sign is Cancer, the water of all water signs. Most of Jordan's life was lived by the ocean—in New York and then Berkeley. So many places that Jordan wrote about were sea-loving places: "Nicaragua: Why I Had to Go There," a country sheltered by the Pacific Ocean and Caribbean Sea. "Report from the Bahamas" opens with a description of the Caribbean salt water—used to attract tourists, kept from the people who live there. In "Life After Lebanon," water embroiders the city of Beirut— one of the most alive cities in the world, where shellings from previous wars are woven into the sidewalks, the architecture, and the scents of being alive.

It makes sense that water runs through Jordan's writing. Hers is a quintessential example of embodied work. Our bodies are 80 percent water. The earth's surface is 80 percent water. In her poem "Of Nightsong and Flight" Jordan writes, "There are things lovely and dangerous still // the rain / when the heat of an evening / sweetens the darkness with mist."[2] In Jordan's writing, water is a source of energy, a site of sweetness, company in the dark, as "These words / they are stones in the water / running away."[3] Water, and its many attendants—the sun, moon, tides, and clouds. Clouds hold the water until the rain of change takes place.

Jordan was a willing witness for change on so many issues, particularly when unequal access to power was involved. I am thinking, for example, of how she responded to "post-structuralist" and "deconstructionist" language that invaded academic writing through the last decade and first of this century. Jordan explains that the imposition of these "values on the human activity of writing and reading should be seen as nothing more than that: a cloud passing over a big, big sky that will outlast every one of us who loves the world and lives inside it."[4]

Jordan also draws upon water for her love poems, her many love poems. For example, in "Alla Tha's All Right, but," she writes, "Somebody come and carry me into a seven-day kiss . . . I need an absolutely one to one a seven-day kiss."[5] Where would kisses be without water, without moisture, without the softness that moisture makes? The moisture of kisses, the moisture of food, as she writes in "Free Flight": "Nothing fills me up at night / I fall asleep for one or two hours then . . . I must arise / and wandering into the refrigerator / think about evaporated milk homemade vanilla ice cream / cherry pie hot from the oven with Something Like Vermont / Cheddar Cheese disintegrating luscious / on top while . . ."[6] Jordan insists on the beauty of language, the fragility and strength of the world, strawberry shortcake, the big sky, the way that writing can emerge as prose or poetry or a combination of both, indeed as a way to cross rivers . . .

> perhaps starting with the Combahee River
> 750 slaves and Tubman
> the intimate treacherous losses
> can't be calculated
> only out of the rapids
> onto dry land to the next crossing
> to the river Jordan
> close to the Tigris and Euphrates
> Jordan was not afraid
> to make love in the dark
> so many lovers with initials and named
> willing to weave passion
> into the Intifada
> # 1 and # 2
> and still another
> at Standing Rock
>
> Jordan would be there by the Missouri River
> the heart and the beat
> of the Lakota Sioux
> inheritance, a rush
> Madonna Thunder Hawk still standing
> at seventy-nine, raising money
> for grandmothers' vans
> to pick up children and bring them to schools
> they call them survival
> as in schools, protectors

their relatives
more than 100 activists now
hijacked by courts
the Missouri a river worth
standing
living for

Jordan a river
beyond agent orange
by the rivers of Babylon
where we sat down
and got up
again.

In "Many Rivers to Cross," Jordan's wish is that her mother had been able to get up again. Jordan summons us to lift up the people who have been taken as well as the freedom fighters who are still alive, keeping others alive. Water, what we drink. Water, what we treasure, Water, that keeps us alive.

Tricky Crossings

In these past years, Jordan's water work, her word work, her work as a teacher have been a guide for me, particularly as I have accompanied people in transit from the Middle East and North Africa. In 2015 I found myself at the epicenter of a crisis in Lesvos, Greece, when hundreds, and then thousands, and then by the end of the year a million people passed through this tiny island on their way to other countries in Europe.

As I became part of a grassroots movement of people greeting rafts of people coming from Syria, Afghanistan, Palestine, and many other countries, I had Jordan's work as a model. Her first lesson: Start by listening. Whatever the mainstream media began to say, turn that on its head. What they began to call the "refugee crisis" was an outrageous example of "undemocratic language" since it put the onus on refugees, rather than on the geopolitical conditions that force people to leave their homes. "Refugee crisis" is an example of a phrase that is missing the agent of the sentence—which governments are forcing people to risk their lives to try to save their lives. This is not unlike the utterly common phrase, "I was raped," that Jordan uses as a powerful example of passive voice in "Problems of Language in a Democratic State."[7] Actually, what we have been witnessing is the biggest multilingual, intergenerational, multinational peace march since World War II.

From Jordan I learned, if there are many rivers to cross—or in the case of Lesvos, first a perilous sea and then many mountains to cross—get a bicycle and loop people's backpacks on the handlebars. When the NGO leaders are asleep, find the key to the warehouse and liberate the shoes and diapers and warm pants and Band-Aids that said NGO is saving for an emergency. Lay all of the supplies out on the beach in rows so children can come by and pick out just the sneakers they want, so no one has to stand in line for clothes that were intended for them to begin with.

From Jordan I learned, when the time comes for people to write their stories about their journeys, certainly don't ask them to write them in English. The cadence, rhymes, emotions, and reasons in their stories are in their own languages. There will be time to translate the writing later. First get it onto the page. Poetry for the people starts with phrases about how people make a "way out of no way." It includes funny stories because even in tragedy there is humor. Yes, the stories include love and tenderness and fighting and hurting and despair and community and connection and audacious, behind-the-scenes and in-front-of-the-police acts of resistance.

From Jordan I learned that coediting a volume of poetry by and for refugees needed to include poems by people currently in transit. Yes, the book could include revered poets in exile, poets from refugee families who have established a poetry of protest in response to forced migration. But the first feminist collection of refugee poems would not be complete without the voices of those who are still walking, still in detention, still living in containers. This meant offering poetry in refugee centers in Thessaloniki and Athens and Mytilini, which has meant falling on my face a lot. Like the time I arrived to teach a class only to learn that several people could not read or write in any language. That I needed to start with the oral tradition. Teaching poetry has much to do with voice as we can always hear in Jordan: say something real to someone real ("Nobody Mean More to Me").[8] And by the way, there were five children that parents brought who wanted to draw, paint, and sing while the class continued. Like the time I showed up with a packet of poems translated into Arabic and Farsi only to learn, after I was in class, that the formatting hadn't transferred the Farsi correctly; that those poems were actually confused scribbles on the page. Like the time I agreed to offer a series of poetry-writing classes at a refugee center to be translated by a refugee from Afghanistan who, it turns out, was also a professor in his country—which meant we needed to coteach the class, he being the one, actually, who knew how to teach the class in multiple languages. And so we did. Jordan modeled that shared leadership for me.

Jordan taught me that poetry for the people includes children and the elders. That "many rivers to cross" includes seas. Staying in a country where barrel bombs and sarin gas are served by the government for breakfast may be a form of suicide that people will take extraordinary measures to avoid. Jordan committed herself to do all she could to ensure that her loved ones, which to her meant the world, would not see suicide as an option. Jordan taught me that getting the word out to the press, to communities of resistance who are physically far from a crisis, starts with stories of heroes/sheroes. Individual eighty-year-old grandmothers dressed in elegant abayas whose families pulled their wheelchairs on inner tubes behind the rafts. An individual Syrian woman who had the audacity to divorce her three-timing husband and commandeer a raft without the use of any smugglers across the Aegean. Almost impossible. But she and her adolescent sons did it. And along the way she took an Afghan mother and three young children with her. Just for the record, as the mainstream media consistently focus on interethnic conflict, not the stories of interethnic solidarity, the point is love, the point is tenderness, the point is saving each other's lives.

Liquid Batons

With her voluptuous life, her willingness to go to "danger" zones and report back intense critiques about the people responsible for the danger, her multiracial gaggle of friends and lovers, Jordan also modeled for me what to do with my body, my particular queer, white, mixed-class, US-born, English-speaking body. All those identities shape what resources I have access to, but none of them can fully explain next steps. For that, I have learned I need to size up the situation and then act.

At several points in finding myself in complicated sea-border-crossing situations, I have consulted Jordan's work, asking, what would she say? Where shall I put my body, ethically, spiritually, politically in these fierce times? Over the years, I come back to Jordan's words: "I am saying that the ultimate connection cannot be the enemy. The ultimate connection must be the need we find between us. It is not only who you are, in other words, but what we can do for each other that will determine the connection."[9] From what I have understood: If June Jordan believed she needed to be Nicaraguan to speak up against US military intervention in revolutionary change made possible by the Sandinistas, she never would have written "Nicaragua: Why I Had to Go There." Or her book of poems *Living Room*. Jordan didn't need to be Lebanese to protest consistently against Israeli bombing of Lebanon and the open-air imprisonment of Palestinians. In fact, she eventually made a truly bold swerve when she announced, "I am become a Palestinian."[10] Perhaps that is what looking cruelty in the face clearly for decades will do for you, teach you that no border, no identity, no checkpoint can stop us from building a politics of solidarity. We take identity politics into account and then move, with passion. Five years before reaching a half century in her rich life, Jordan wrote, "My life seems to be an increasing revelation of the intimate face of universal struggle."[11] May we all aspire to that awareness.

When June Jordan passed on to another realm, she threw out a thousand batons. In the twenty years since her passing, we have been witnessing people carrying them. When I think of June Jordan's batons, I hear Dominique Christina, in particular her poem "Karma" and how much it resonates with Jordan's "Poem About My Rights."[12] I think of the cadence and texture of twenty-year-old spoken-word artist

Sara Abou Rashed's poem "Welcome to America."[13] I think too of Palestinian poet Jehan Bseiso's "No Search, No Rescue," dedicated "to the families and lovers at the bottom of the sea, trying to reach Europe."[14] The baton-tossing makes me think of Alexis Pauline Gumbs, who opens her coedited volume *Revolutionary Mothering* with June Jordan. The book illuminates mothering as leadership—most often revealed by biological and chosen mothers known within their own families and communities. The book chronicles the outrageous, everyday acts of conscience that mothers teach, preach, and imprint on our consciousness. This is how Jordan taught, loved, activated, and moved us forward. The first quite unexpected sign that I'd caught a baton appeared when I started to write a statement for her memorial service in Boston. Instead of prose, a poem popped out—the first in twenty years. That poem catapulted me to study with many political poets, to expand my teaching of Jordan's work, to incorporate her Poetry for the People pedagogy into my own teaching in the US, China, Thailand, and Greece.

One of the many problems, of course, with getting a baton from someone who has passed into the next realm is that it is not immediately clear how to check with them about how we are doing. How are we faring with our interpretations of your words? Our responses to Agent Orange? To the continuing open-air prison in Palestine? The devolution of democratic rights to land and education in South Africa? The delicious range of people whose daring continues to be shared by Jordan suggests that the batons she passed on still have energy, twenty years later. It might be reasonable to say that the statute of limitations is up by now, but seriously, in a moment when I have really not known what to do, something in June Jordan's language, something in her rivers, something in the water has delivered me to another shore. Jordan has taught me that what connects us as people may be less about solid identities and more about liquid, the moisture that we share. And maybe that goes for our connection with ancestors as well—through the sea, a wet sky, remembered kisses. I know for me, when I have consulted Jordan the most has been when I am crying, an ancient form of moisture the body makes, and then gives away. The batons, silvery, glistening, star-like, liquid packets to keep us going.

As someone indebted to June Jordan, not in the money kind of way, but in the learn from my elders and treasure their courage, their stamina way, I hear her asking, what kind of water work can each of us do in these red times?

Becky Thompson, poet, scholar, activist, and yogi, is the author of several books, including the recent *To Speak in Salt* (Ex Ophidia Press, 2022), *Teaching with Tenderness: Toward an Embodied Practice* (University of Illinois Press, 2017), and *Making Mirrors: Righting/Writing by and for Refugees* (coedited with Jehan Bseiso; Interlink, 2019). Her years of teaching and activism in Thailand, Greece, the US, and China have all been touched by June Jordan's life and legacy.

Call and Response

Gwendolen Hardwick

CALL

I.

It could be
a late afternoon
sometimes
dinner is barely on the plate
or
we be snuggling watching TV
maybe
in the wee hour of the morning bodies entwined clinging to sleep
and each other
the phone rings
my lover answers the phone, "it's June," she says

WE GOTTA GO!

II.
be prepared

III.
grab revolutionary necessities:
    sneakers- check
    loose clothing- check
    bandana- check
    small 1st aid pack- check
make signs/practice chants . . . "a people united will never be defeated"

"no justice no peace" . . . . . "what do we want . . . when do we want it . . ."

RESPONSE

reject
refute
resist

        tendencies to be
        silent
        passive
        tentative
        victimized

fight back
fight against
fight to end

        mass incarceration/ mass murders
        children in cages
        hunger/ food insecurity
        homelessness/ joblessness
        water/ air/ land pollution

take the law into your hands
        into the streets
        into the courts

form . . . . a SQUAD

Gwendolen Hardwick is an educator, playwright, director, and educational theatre specialist. She is a trainer in applied theatre practices for social justice/ change and community activism as well as conflict-resolution techniques.

She has been a consultant nationally designing issue-based drama for theater companies and/or community-based organizations, educators, teaching artists, and arts institutions. Internationally, she has designed and facilitated projects in South Africa, Zimbabwe, Norway, Nigeria, Jamaica, and Ireland.

PART TWO

We Are Lucky She Dared

"Some of Us Did Not Die"

Remembering June Jordan

E. Ethelbert Miller

There are times when a gentle rain falls, and I think of my friend, June Jordan.

There are times when I watch or read the news, and I think of this woman who was fierce and fabulous. Yes, our world is a dangerous place to live, but somehow we survive. Many days of my life have been made more beautiful because of the words written by this woman. I wish every month were June, and she were still here.

When I was writing my memoir, *Fathering Words: The Making of an African American Writer*, one of the first sections I wrote was about meeting June Jordan. I wanted to write about her first, because she had a significant influence on my development as a writer. She wrote the introduction to *Season of Hunger / Cry of Rain*, one of my early collections of poems. Jordan was my model of the activist and writer. Her politics are tightly woven into a sensual compassion for human life. Her work retains a lyrical quality enhanced by her understanding of black speech. We met in 1974. I was twenty-four years old, and she was thirty-eight. Here is an excerpt from my memoir:

> It was Toni Morrison, who told us (Ahmos Zu-Bolton and [me]) to fix the chairs, since we were early at the Random House affair. We were insulted, but we did as we were told. The evening was young, and there was no reason for someone to give us a black eye and spoil our trip. The stars would come out, and Ahmos and I would watch them enter the room: Melvin Van Peebles, Angela Davis, Nikki Giovanni; and then there she was, the woman poet I had heard

about, the woman whose work Stephen Henderson said was "heavy" language and saturated with blackness. She came into the room, and Sun Ra was behind her. It was how he always opened a performance. The Sun Goddesses, beautiful women walking the stage showing the audience the way to Egypt and the next stop being Jupiter. Sun Ra coming behind, his genius a light for those who had ears.[1]

Looking back many years later, this first meeting seems almost mystical.

At a New York book party celebrating the work of Henry Dumas, I would meet this outspoken poet. By this time, June Jordan was already a woman with a strong moral vision. She was willing to comment and offer clarity on a variety of issues: from the Middle East to Nicaragua; from Black English to bisexuality. During her lifetime, Jordan was not just a poet; she was the author of five children's books, a novel, three plays, books of essays, and a memoir.

When it comes to the importance of love and passion in her thought, her body of work can be separated into nine categories, with some overlapping:

(1) The Middle East

(2) Black studies and Black English

(3) The fight against cancer

(4) Prison and police violence

(5) International affairs

(6) Bisexuality

(7) New York (Harlem and Brooklyn)

(8) Love poems

(9) Humor

In 2006, Valerie Kinloch published the biography *June Jordan: Her Life and Letters*. Kinloch's book provides background information about June's West Indian heritage, her childhood, and her relationship with her mother and father. Even though June had a complex—if not complicated—relationship with her parents, when she accepted the 1998 Lifetime Achievement Award from the National Conference of Black

Writers, presented at the Fourteenth Annual Celebration of Black Writing in Philadelphia, she began by saying:

> This award is an incredible capstone to my personal history. And on this occasion, I wish to thank my mother and father by accepting it on their behalf. Two more faithful human beings have seldom walked this earth. And I would like to acknowledge, with loving gratitude, the decades of support and counsel I have received from the black poet, E. Ethelbert Miller.[2]

In the poem "Ah, Momma," Jordan described an intimate relationship with her mother, Mildred Jordan.[3] She is a witness to her mother's secrets. There is also a desire to fulfill her mother's dreams and to make her proud.

The reach of Jordan's love is personal but extends into the political. As a single mother, her love for her son, Christopher—whom she had with Michael Meyer—would be a motivating factor in her career decisions. In her collection of poems *Living Room*, we see her dedicating the book to the children of Atlanta and to the children of Lebanon. In the essay "Love is Not the Problem," published in *On Call*, Jordan writes about her interracial marriage to Meyer, a marriage that ended in divorce in 1965 after ten years. Considering that in many states interracial marriages were illegal during the 1950s, this marriage was radical, and Jordan understood this, writing: "And I know that in America, one out of two marriages fails nowadays: the institution itself is not well, evidently. And I know that I do not regret my marriage. Nor do I regret my divorce."[4]

In her foreword to Jordan's *Haruko / Love Poems*, published in 1994, Adrienne Rich asks, "What is this thing called love, in the poems of June Jordan, artist, teacher, social critic, visionary of human solidarity?"[5]

Rich provides the answer to her own question:

> First of all, it's a motive; the power Che Guevara was trying to invoke in his much-quoted assertion: "At the risk of appearing ridiculous . . . the true revolutionary is moved by great feelings of love."

... But the motive is "directed by desire" in Jordan's poetry, and desire is personal, concrete, particular and sensual.[6]

Yet, in her own words, June Jordan says:

I am a stranger
learning to worship the strangers
around me

whoever you are
whoever I may become.[7]

In 1982, the Arab American Cultural Foundation released *And Not Surrender: American Poets on Lebanon*, edited by Kamal Boullata. This anthology of nineteen poets (including me) was compiled in response to the Israeli bombing of Lebanon, during the months of June and September 1982. Jordan contributed four poems to the book. One was "Moving Towards Home," a long poem that ended with the lines:

I need to talk about living room
where I can sit without grief without wailing aloud
for my loved ones
where I must not ask where is Abu Fadi
because he will be there beside me
I need to talk about living room
because I need to talk about home

I was born a Black woman
and now
I am become a Palestinian
against the relentless laughter of evil
there is less and less living room
and where are my loved ones?

It is time to make our way home.[8]

Palestinian poet Suheir Hammad used Jordan's words for the title of her first book, *Born Palestinian, Born Black*. In her author's note, Hammad wrote: "The last stanza in June Jordan's 'Moving Towards Home' changed my life. I remember feeling validated by her statement. She dared speak of transformation, or re-birth, of a deep understanding of humanity. The essence of being Spirit, something no labels can touch."[9]

June Jordan was also outspoken when it came to sexual matters. In her July 1991 *Progressive* magazine column "Just Inside the Door," Jordan presented the essay "A New Politics of Sexuality." She made three statements:

> I believe the Politics of Sexuality is the most ancient and probably the most profound arena for human conflict.
>
> . . . I can voice my ideas without hesitation or fear because I am speaking, finally, about myself. I am black and I am female and I am a mother and I am bisexual and I am a nationalist and I am an antinationalist. And I mean to be fully and freely all that I am!
>
> . . . Bisexuality means I am free and I am as likely to want and to love a woman as I am likely to want and to love a man, and what about that? Isn't that what freedom implies?[10]

In 1994, while editing my anthology *In Search of Color Everywhere*, I wanted to include poems I felt were essential for understanding everything from black history to black love and black achievement. I wanted authors to be represented by work that would be instructional to a mother or father reading to his or her child in the evening hours. I wanted the book to provide poems that might simply remind the reader of the complexity of black identity. I examined Jordan's poetry looking for work that would be timeless or at least survive many winters in America.

I selected four poems: "Poem About My Rights"; "Poem Against the State (of Things): 1975"; "Grand Army Plaza"; and "The Test of Atlanta 1979–".[11]

"Poem About My Rights"

June Jordan described this poem as one of her breakthrough poems. Writing it was an act of courage. The poem was written after she was raped in her home on Long Island in 1970s. It was first read at one of the National Black Writers Conferences held at Howard University. I was in the auditorium and recall the emotional shock of the audience when Jordan described what had happened to her. Her poem makes one immediately aware of what a woman faces every single moment, no matter her age, race, or where she might be living.

The first twenty-two lines are a sweeping indictment of the conditions women face. What follows is a legal definition of rape and where the poem begins to take an international perspective. When she wrote this poem, a number of African nations were in the headlines:

> I was wrong I was
> wrong again to be me being me where I was/wrong
> to be who I am
> which is exactly like South Africa
> penetrating into Namibia penetrating into
> Angola and does that mean I mean how do you know if
> Pretoria ejaculates what will the evidence look like[12]

Jordan's poem takes issue with blaming the victim of rape. Her assertion is that she is not the problem. She shouldn't be blamed; she is not wrong. Within the poem, not only do we see Jordan making connections between the personal and the political, but she also shows how gender, class, and race can also victimize us. In the poem she refers to her father walking across her college campus, believing he was in the wrong place. Being in the wrong place places one at risk. By the middle of the poem, Jordan summarizes and connects the dots and presents a powerful defining line—*I am the history of rape.*

Here the scope and vision of June's work is as embracing as anything Walt Whitman might have written. In "Poem About My Rights," Jordan speaks for the multitudes. Her poem is militant and concludes as a proclamation of defiance and resistance.

In an interview with Jill Nelson, published in the *Quarterly Black Review of Books* in the summer of 1994, Jordan explained: "I happen to think rape is one of the most heinous things that can happen to anyone. But there's a victimization of people that is systematic, that we as black folks have to survive some kind of way."

In a 1981 Karla Hammond interview, Jordan made the following comment:

> I sent Ethelbert a copy of the "Poem About My Rights," and he said, "you should take your mother out of that." And I said, "Why?" And he said, "Because, until you get to your mother, everything you're talking about; who has done something to you—whether it's South Africa or the guys in France—is male. It's a man in some form violating you." And I said, "Listen, I don't give a damn who it is that violates me. Violation is violation. When my mother asked me to have braces on my teeth, plastic surgery on my nose, and straightened my hair, she violated me and that was the first woman I ever knew. She stays in that poem."[13]

"Poem Against the State (of Things)"

Ahmos Zu-Bolton and I first published this poem in *Hoo-Doo* magazine #4. We heard June read it on the campus of Howard University on April 21, 1975. June was the second guest poet to appear on my Ascension Poetry Reading series, which I started in April 1974. June does not include "Poem Against the State (of Things)" in her collection *Naming Our Destiny: New and Selected Poems*, which was published in 1989. Why did she not select it? The poem in *Hoo-Doo* has a different title: it's "Poem Against the State (of Things): Dedicated to the Memory of Brother LD Barkley." Barkley, whose full name was Elliott James "LD" Barkley, was one of the leaders among inmates at Attica prison. He was killed during the September 13, 1971, retaking of the institution. During the retaking of the prison, forty-three people were killed, including twenty-nine inmates and ten hostages. Whereas authorities would say Barkley was killed by ricocheting bullets, others said he was targeted and shot in the back at close range.

The removal of Barkley's name from the original title is interesting. In *Things I Do in the Dark*, Jordan replaces Barkley's name with the year 1975. This change airbrushes Barkley out of a poem that is very descriptive of the Attica prison riot.

Jordan's poem is not just about a prison riot, uprising, or disturbance, however—it is a poem about human rights versus the power of the state. The reference to Salvador Allende, the socialist leader elected in Chile and then overthrown with US help, shows once again Jordan's decision to make international connections with things happening in America. Her vision is always large and all-encompassing. She is a master of the metaphor, as well as a writer of witness. The fourth section of her poem is like a coda to the first three sections:

> *wherever I go (these*
> *days)*
> *the tide seems low*
> *(oh) wherever I go (these*
> *days)*
> *the time seems very*
> *very low*
>
> *God's love has turned away*
> *from this Almighty place*
> *But*
> *I will pray*
> *one prayer while He yet grants me*
> *time and space:*
>
> NO MORE AND NEVER AGAIN!
> NO MORE AND NEVER AGAIN!
>
> A-men.
> A-men.[14]

"God's love has turned away from this Almighty place." I think about this many years after Attica. I think about it as I read about the endless documentation of police brutality. Where is God's love?

Jordan refuses to accept defeat:

But
I will pray
one prayer while He yet grants me
time and space:[15]

"Grand Army Plaza"

June Jordan's love poem "Grand Army Plaza" was published in her book *Passion*. It's one of several poems she wrote in response to something I had written to her. My own poem, also titled "Grand Army Plaza," was published in *SOL*, a small newsletter published in October 1980. In both poems we find the words "civil war." Jordan used the phrase as the title for a 1981 book of essays. How do we learn to disagree yet still create movements that embrace us all? Friendships and love should not end in tragedy.

Jordan begins her poem with a question and realization:

Why would anybody build a monument to civil war?

The tall man and myself tonight
we will not sleep together
we may not
either one of us
sleep
in any case
the differential between friend and lover
is a problem
definitions curse
as *nowadays we're friends*
or
we were lovers once[16]

My poem "Grand Army Plaza," which I wrote after leaving June's Brooklyn apartment in 1980, was about the geography of relationships; the distance and difference that often defines the confusion between love and friendship. There is a reference at the end to the Draft Riots of 1863 that took place in New York City. When I wrote my poem, I was thinking of young men afraid of going south to fight in the Civil War. I was also aware of a relationship ending. I began the poem with the image of someone standing outside a subway and the underground, which I felt was symbolic of death at the time. June's poem in response to mine is important for its ending. Native American poet Joy Harjo placed it at the beginning of her own book, *In Mad Love and War*, published in 1990:

> We are not survivors of a civil war
>
> We survive our love
> because we go on
>
> loving[17]

These last lines are important. June Jordan and I would have a major disagreement around Nicaragua and US foreign policy. We would even find ourselves in an elevator at a major writers' conference and not even acknowledge each other's presence. It was an example of how politics can often destroy relationships, and it was also an indication of how passionate June was about what she believed in. In her essay "Nicaragua: Why I Had to Go There" in *On Call*, she wrote: "All my life I've been studying revolution. I've been looking for it, pushing at the possibilities and waiting for that moment when there's no more room for rhetoric, for research or for reason: when there's only my life or my death to act upon."[18]

In the Givens Collection, housed at the University of Minnesota, are the letters June Jordan wrote to me from 1975 to 1999. There are no letters for 1984. I visited Nicaragua in 1983 and had mixed feelings about what was going on in that country. By coincidence, I bumped into June in the Miami airport, as she was heading to Nicaragua, and I was returning to the United States. Little did I suspect a considerable amount of time would pass before we talked and laughed together again.

"The Test of Atlanta 1979—"

This poem is similar to Jordan's "Poem Against the State (of Things)." Here, we find her once again being a writer of witness. The subject is the mysterious murders of twenty-eight black children that haunted the city of Atlanta for two years between 1979 and 1981. It begins with a haunting opening line: "What kind of a person would kill Black children?"

What follows are lines asking the same question over and over:

> What kind of a person could kill a Black child
> and then kill another Black child and then
> kill another Black child and then kill another
> Black child and then kill another
> Black child and then kill another Black
> child
> and stay above suspicion?
> What about the police?
> What about somebody Black?[19]

Note the reference to the police as suspect. A number of June Jordan's poems question police violence. It is one of the reasons why her work continues to be important and timely. "Poem About Police Violence," for example, sounds like something written by the hip-hop group N.W.A.:

> Tell me something
> what you think would happen if
> everytime they kill a black boy
> then we kill a cop
> everytime they kill a black man
> then we kill a cop
>
> you think the accident rate would lower
> subsequently?[20]

Her use of repetition reflects a blues element. The repetition is not just for sound but also to underscore and emphasize a political point of view and message. Jordan's work is not just an indictment of the status quo; it offers hope and optimism. Jordan must be viewed as a woman who saw her work being defined as the poetry of the New World. Her essay

"For the Sake of People's Poetry: Walt Whitman and the Rest of Us" outlines the nature and content of the type of work each new generation of writers should be challenged to produce.

If nothing else, June Jordan wanted to redeem our language for the purpose of telling the truth. Her vision was a global one. Jordan wanted to know what was going on in Africa, the Middle East, as well as the boardrooms of our major corporations. As an American writer living in one of the most powerful nations in the world, she vowed to become as serious as her enemies.

Two hundred of June's letters are housed in the Givens Collection. Thanks to Adrienne Cassel, whom I met at the Bennington Writing Seminars in 2003, the letters have been transcribed, edited, and bound. Cassel compiled the letters under the title *Survival Letters: Correspondence from June Jordan to E. Ethelbert Miller 1975–1999*. On April 21, 2005, I presented a lecture on the campus of the University of Minnesota. The title was "When Love Turns into Letters."

On January 21, 1997, June Jordan gave a speech at Emory University celebrating the life of Dr. Martin Luther King Jr., in which the future of hope was never in doubt:

> Is there reason for hope? Is there anywhere a trace, a phoenix of revolutionary spirit consistent with Dr. King's preaching and true to the democratic, coexistent values of Beloved Community?
> I know there is.
> It may be small. It may be dim. But there is a fire transfiguring the muted, the daunted spirit of people everywhere.[21]

At the end of my memoir *Fathering Words*, I included a letter June wrote after reading about how I described our first encounter. I wanted to know if I had gotten it right. She responded with these words:

> Dearest Ethelbert:
>
> Tonight it's the first rain of the New Year, the last year of millennium.
> And it is tonight that I sat at the table, reading your autobiographical excerpt.
> Well, I am still breathing, and thank God for that!

You do bless my life.

To go on loving means not to forget and you remember you testify and no one could doubt your love. And I do not forget your love, or mine—my love for you. I remember.

And the rain seems beautiful now. Clean and soft and everywhere just gentle and not to be denied.

Thank you. Adambert.

Thank you for what you have chosen to remember, and why.

You the Tallman, always.

The Tallman and The Loving Poet of my life.

June[22]

When I read June's words, I am moved by how she connects human love to nature. The rain is falling, cleansing the space in which we live. There is something eternal about the rainfall. Maybe it's because at times we wait for it to rain, and our lives are thirsty for meaning and goodness. June's words are a reminder of the importance of memory. We struggle not to forget. Our failure only makes us human. Our attempt to remember restores our faith in the unseen. It's why I do not forget June's name. It's why I whisper it in the dark and it gives me light to continue living.

E. Ethelbert Miller is a literary activist and author of two memoirs and several poetry collections. He was given a 2020 congressional award from Congressman Jamie Raskin in recognition of his literary activism, awarded the 2022 Howard Zinn Lifetime Achievement Award by the Peace and Justice Studies Association, and named a 2023 Grammy nominee finalist for Best Spoken Word Poetry Album. In 2024, Miller was awarded the Furious Flower Lifetime Achievement Award.

After All Is Said and Done

E. Ethelbert Miller

(for June)

Some nights I remember
the poems a lover once
wrote to me.

Words like
flowers still bring the scent
of memory as if it was
picked by moonlight.

How do we harvest
this unspoken passion
for the living things that
struggle to survive?

What things must we
continue to do in the dark?

Oh, lift me to the light
so that I might call you
star.

Why do others
call you love?

Bit by Bit

Dima Hilal

In the spring of 1996 my dearest friend, my closest companion, my grandmother, passed away after heart bypass surgery. This devastating, maddening experience was followed that summer by reports of an Israeli plane flying over Qana, bombing a UN refugee camp in its wake. I read reports, my blood chilling at tales of blood-soaked shoes, sobbing mothers, and heartbroken UN workers who stared at photographers, eyes glazed in shock. Having left Beirut in the height of the civil war and immediately after the Israeli invasion that ravished the city, I felt like my universe was imploding. I read every story and watched every television segment until, too quickly, the headlines disappeared, not even an outline of the story remaining behind.

That summer I picked up an article written for *The Progressive* by June Jordan, called "Eyewitness in Lebanon." Her words, eloquent, haunting, described the crisis back home. I was rapt at this woman's courage, at her humanity, and most of all at the power of her witnessing. "*But I went there, to Lebanon. And I'm back. And I'm real. And Lebanon is real.*"[1] I cut out the article, folded it in half, and saved it. To finally be seen, heard, and believed felt nothing short of miraculous. And when I needed it most, a spark of hope ignited. At the bottom of the article, in the fine print of bylines, her name and title stood: Professor June Jordan, UC Berkeley.

One autumn day I trailed a friend to Poetry for the People, a class held in the bowels of Barrows Hall. I sat in the corner of the room trying to take up as little space as possible. Twelve students surrounded a conference-style table and sat shuffling papers.

June entered the room, sunglasses on. Although much smaller than I had pictured her, she was still immensely imposing. She slid her backpack off her shoulder and set her books and notepad on the desk. She sat down, slowly removed her sunglasses, and folded them neatly in front of her. For the next hour and a half, she skimmed through heavily marked passages of a green leather-bound Quran, exploring Islam and its followers with unmatched intensity and challenging her students to think outside of their cultural bounds. The class read Haas Mroue's poetry out loud, the first words of this Lebanese American poet I had ever heard, covering me with goosebumps and making me blink back sudden tears.

Elated, I approached the professor at the end of the class as she jotted in her notepad. My friend gave me a nudge and gently murmured, "June, this is a friend of mine from my poetry workshop." June said something like, "Uhn." She didn't look up.

"I am so amazed and moved by this class," I gushed. "As a Lebanese and a Muslim, I just want to thank you for this, for—"

In the midst of my raving and my genuine gratitude, June lifted her head and stared straight into my eyes. She grabbed my left arm unexpectedly, and with more than a little force, and asked, "Do you want to be in this class?"

I stammered, "Uh, yeah . . . I mean, yes! I would be honored."

And I was.

I managed to write "Bedouin Eyes," an emotionally charged poem that aimed to dispel the prevalent view of the Arab as the enemy, a faceless, nameless terrorist. I wrote in a fury, trying madly to convey to the world that those video-game blips on the screen were really resounding blasts, shattered windows, and shaking children.

The next day I brought the poem to class. I shyly read it, and after a productive workshop, June motioned me over. She smiled and said, "I'm doing a commentary called 'Flashpoints' on Pacifica radio. Would you allow me to read this poem?"

Before I could even utter "of course," or "duh," or "hell yeah," June had paused, reflected, and continued, "Actually, why don't *you* come read it yourself?"

I can still hear the pride and strength in her voice: "And I give you nineteen-year-old Arab American poet . . . offering you her words, her heart, and her hurt." I read nervously, mechanically, and it still sounded amazing nestled between her intro and conclusion. I am convinced that I easily could have recited the "Pledge of Allegiance" or my car manual and, with her by my side, it would have come across as music.

And so, I did just that—I wrote from the heart about my family, the old country, Palestine, issues that flowed through my veins.

Dima Hilal holds a bachelor of arts from the University of California at Berkeley, where she was mentored by June Jordan. Hilal's work has appeared in the *San Francisco Chronicle, Aramco, The Poetry of Arab Women: A Contemporary Anthology* (Interlink, 2000), and elsewhere. Hilal currently resides in Dana Point, California, with her husband and two sons.

america[1]

Dima Hilal

we cross from Andalusia to these Pacific shores
carry memories in a single suitcase
abandon brothers, skyscrapers and tight alleyways
villages framed with grape leaves and fig trees
the land of Jesus and Abraham

we flee fighter jets and darkening skies
escape shrapnel scenes,
for the American dream
we brush off dust from the old country
unearth the clay from beneath our nails

we fade into the fabric of these united states
pay our taxes, pledge our allegiance
lose ourselves in its thick folds
success finds us and we find success
intoxicating

until a plane carves a path through steel and glass
smoke billowing from two wounded skyscrapers,
the aftermath all too familiar
just the epicenter shifting
we know the endless sorrow
of life snatched without warning or reason,
we seek solace in our neighbors
see our own blanched faces
reflected back at us

until the sudden sidelong glance,
the step back
wait, isn't that where you're from?
let's bomb them back to the stone age
those arabs
never should have let them into our country
those arabs
never should have let them in

we'll show them
those arabs
we'll teach those turban-wearing, towel-headed,
dirty, camel-loving terrorists
a lesson they'll never forget
fractured skull, baseball bat,
crushed bones, clenched fists
battered bodies, a switchblade, crowbar
gunshot blast

it's us versus them
are you with us
are you with us
are you with us
or against us?

we cross from Andalusia to these Pacific shores
carry memories in a single suitcase
we flee fighter jets and darkening skies
escape shrapnel scenes,
for the American dream
for the American dream
the American dream

Elphinstone, Bombay, 1993

Rajasvini Bhansali

> How easily we killed them—without shedding a tear, without establishing a commission of inquiry, without filling the streets with protest demonstrations. . . . We killed them because it was not important for us not to kill them.
>
> —*Ari Shavit, "How Easily We Killed Them"*

squalid Elphinstone Street
leaves betel nut stains on my salwar
pinches my butt in a crowded bus
my city of thirteen million catcalls and whistles
then laughs at the sour twists of bare midriffs
in polyester sarees

this January morning
imminent unrest crackles Elphinstone Street
hindus destroy a muslim shrine
level the mosque built allegedly on top of a temple
remove a last sacred place of a minority
trivial
in this mass of overworked commuters slumdwellers artists
industrial workers bureaucrats businessmen teachers
and us students
"bunking" classes for vada pao
outside St. Xavier's college
a train and a bus away from home
in breakfast company of school friends

white sarees drape the body of a boy
who cleaned cars
in the parking lot of the highrise apartment building

I call home
the boy who this morning smiled shyly when I passed him on the
way to school
and now, at dusk, I watch him fall
was he hindu
was he muslim
shot in the back as he walked
out on the street
probably to his second job

some boys shoot bullets
the way they play with cricket balls
polyester catches fire first
I see my neighbor's window shatter and fall
glass pours into our balcony
like unseasonal monsoon rain
moments before giant licks of fire
smolder the buildings nearby
slums burn while I live in tenth floor protection
in Elphinstone's middle class neighborhood

150000 flee
100000 in refugee camps
about 1500 dead
about 5000 injured
the only numbers I can find
about
on an average
approximate
around

by the year 2000
Bombay will have 20 million people
from village homes to city streets
and I will never know where the 150000 fled

I will never know why Rizwan was burnt alive in his family's 8 square foot hovel
I will never know why a group of boys threw bricks at Vanessa on her way to church
late for sunday morning mass
not hindu
not muslim

I say let's clean this street
still strewn with shards of broken windows and hopes
a brittle collage
of incomplete memories
abandoned inquiries into the riots, the deaths
the sudden skyscrapers
on refugee land

they have used amnesia as an excuse and called it beauty
it's ugly, they say, to inquire into undesirable things
let's move on, once again we are told, we have bigger fish to fry
buildings to build
markets to occupy

I still savor the bitterness
every stubborn betel nut stain
takes me home to Elphinstone Street
as I vow
never ever to forget again
that even
about
on an average
approximate
around
100000 is a large number
to be out
and then gone

In Islam, ghaflah is considered the sin of forgetting one's divine origins. In June Jordan's class for student-teacher poets in 1995, I wrote a poem related to the concept of ghaflah as my heart and mind traveled home to Bombay, where my activism first ignited, where I learned to make sense of unfairness and injustice, and where I first began to place myself inside the dynamics of power, privilege, violence, and displacement all around me. As a new UC Berkeley undergraduate student enamored by the activism of the moment, I was beginning to forget a critical moment that had shaped me. I had witnessed firsthand the discrepancy between the political narrative of communal hatred and the brutal reality of real estate developers leading the charge of killing and displacing scores of working-class and poor people, expelling them from urban land. As the 1990s wore on, many of us progressive Indians fell prey to neoliberalism-induced collective amnesia, forgetting the calculated project of mass displacement as a strategy for power-grabbing by the elites. Now in India we are witnessing an even more vicious time. Elites scapegoat Muslims to advance an agenda of profiteering from human suffering. I wrote this poem to remember; to undo the sin of forgetting of my own divine origin; to remember reality when I knew the future would be manufactured and history revised to suit those hoarding political and financial power. In response to this invitation to participate in this historic project to memorialize June Jordan and her immense contributions to the world, I recovered this old poem with a faltering heart, to contend with the fact that India is once again in the throes of a similar crisis of disappearance, displacement, and deaths of dissenting peoples.

A new citizenship law called the Citizenship Amendment Act and an accompanying National Register of Citizens were enacted into law on December 12, 2019. While benefiting persecuted religious groups from three neighboring countries, especially Hindi, Sikh, Jain, Parsi, and Christian refugees, the amendment specifically and deliberately leaves out Muslims from Afghanistan, Pakistan, and Bangladesh. India is in the midst of an uprising—daily protests all over the nation coordinated and led by civil-society organizations and student groups to protest this heinous law. Millions of Indians from housewives and grandmothers to political writers and intellectuals have risen up in protest. The government and its police force respond with increasing violence. Protestors remain steadfast and continue to increase in numbers all throughout India in defense of dignity, pluralism, secularism, and equality.

From protest art to chants that spring forth like poetry, ordinary people in India have finally said enough to state-sanctioned Islamophobia. Iconic antiauthoritarian, antifundamentalist poems and poems of witness and resistance by revolutionary poets Faiz Ahmad Faiz, Mahmoud Darwish, Bismil Azimabadi, and many more have been revived by students all across India to motivate, inspire, and energize this movement further. We confront once again a chance to remember and be reignited in solidarity with the many on the streets today. My poet's heart is bursting with inspiration like 1996, when I first penned this poem under June's guidance and with her feedback on craft and truth-telling. My spirit is moved to act. The divine ancestry of the poetry of Faiz, as well as that of Jordan, is moving us to imagine and commit nonviolent acts of remembering, resistance, and solidarity that are necessary in these times.

June wrote, in her brilliant essay "Nicaragua: Why I Had to Go There":

> All my life I've been studying revolution. I've been looking for it, pushing at the possibilities and waiting for that moment when there's no more room for rhetoric, for research and for reason: when there's only my life or my death left to act upon . . . I had to go there [Nicaragua] . . . I wanted to see for myself what was happening. I wanted to face the violence reported by the newspapers and supported by my taxes: to make my witness to this First World dream before it buckled into yet another nightmare colony, another "vacation paradise," another "vital" outpost of the big guys. I wanted to get real: to put my life, as well as my words, on the line. I had to go to Nicaragua.[1]

In this essay, she documents her firsthand witnessing of the struggle for daily life in Nicaragua, but also a revolution very much in progress with signs of wins—free literacy programs, free health care for all, equal pay for equal work for men and women, a society reclaiming its own freedoms, a culture filled with warmth and generosity in spite of its own struggles. June left Nicaragua inspired and deeply accountable to what she had been given, the opportunity to bear witness in the struggle of Sandinistas. She understood the profound way in which the changes being brought about in Nicaraguan society were there to stay: "They have given to me and to all of us an amazing example of self-love. With their bodies and their blood they have shown us the bravery that self-love requires. They persist. The new laws and the new programs integral to their new life persist."[2]

June's witnessing of not only the material conditions of Nicaraguans but also the poetry of their self-love inspires each of us to see the world through such a lens that appreciates a deep noticing of each other in struggle and solidarity.

So, I offer this poem because memory is a weapon against coercive revisionist history. I offer this poem today in deep reverence to the protestors all across India as tribute to their courage, to their resilience, and to their immense self-love, the kind of love that transforms repression into freedom. For those of us in the diaspora, this moment is a reminder that we must align all our privileges in the United States with democratic uprisings in our beloved motherlands. May we fight back against each and every fundamentalist, sectarian, imperialistic, xenophobic, regressive force that stands to destroy our humanity, to make us forget our own lived experience, to sacrifice the lives of some of us for just the benefit of a few of us. May we invent and/or find the possibilities and then act upon them with our power, and "seize the world around us with our freedom."[3]

Rajasvini Bhansali is executive director of the Solidaire Network. She advocates for participatory grassroots-led social change and is a community organizer, researcher, planner, and policy analyst. Born and raised in India, Vini earned a master of arts in public affairs from the University of Texas at Austin and a bachelor of science from the University of California, Berkeley, where she had the honor of working with June Jordan's Poetry for the People and initiating the writing program at FCI Dublin women's prison.

"The Bombing of Baghdad"

Building Connections in a Time of War

Shanti Bright Brien

A sense of relentlessness and irrationality pervaded the University of California, Berkeley campus and the country during the Persian Gulf War. I remember watching news coverage of the bombings. Every day for forty-two days the pictures looked the same: bright-orange explosions against the black sky of Iraq. It seemed to never stop. I felt overwhelmed and helpless and scared. I was eighteen years old, a freshman at UC Berkeley and a student in June Jordan's class, Poetry for the People.

June Jordan's poem "The Bombing of Baghdad" is about the Persian Gulf War. It also addresses the genocide of Native Americans, colonialism and systematic violence, violence against women, shame and responsibility, and the use of poetry to address all of these. Barely an adult, this was my first war. I had just begun to know my father, a Native American man and graduate student at UC Berkeley. I had never really read or understood poetry. To hear June speak with such specificity and power about these new critical aspects of my life kind of blew my head open. This truth—that my daily life, national events and politics, and even intentional violence were all connected, that I played my own role in them, and that writing and speaking out can challenge those systems of violence—shaped my young adulthood and who I would become as a lawyer, mother, and writer.

"The Bombing of Baghdad" opens with an explosion of irrational violence. The bombings

began and did not terminate for 42 days
and 42 nights relentless minute after minute
more than 110,000 times
we bombed Iraq we bombed Baghdad
we bombed Basra/we bombed military
installations we bombed the National Museum
we bombed schools we bombed air raid
shelters we bombed water[1]

Jordan repeats "bomb" and "bombing" thirty-one times in the first section, creating a feeling of relentlessness. And then the poem contrasts that dehumanization and destruction with a short section, starkly intimate and soft, about "my body and the breath / of my beloved."[2]

Then the poem steps back again, in scope and in history, to General Custer and Crazy Horse. The poem connects the white westward expansion and the attacks and murders of Native Americans with the Persian Gulf War. "I hear Crazy Horse singing as he dies / I dedicate myself to learn that song / I hear that music in the moaning of the Arab world."[3]

After the poet "cheer[s] for the arrows / and the braves," "The Bombing of Baghdad" circles back to the war, recognizing it as "terrorist activity" and "against the peoples of the Middle East." At this point, she takes responsibility for her role in the violence. She lives "inside [Crazy Horse's] grave" and she recognizes that those who bombed Baghdad "traveled from my house / to blast your homeland / into pieces of children / and pieces of sand."[4]

With this gruesome image, the poet asks her readers to confront the horrors "perpetrated in [our] name."[5] We see the connections between violence over time and geography, but also see how our lives touch those threads, intersect those stories, and even benefit from that violence.

I began to make those connections around the time of the Persian Gulf War as a student in June Jordan's class.

My father, Hal, a member of the Muscogee (Creek) tribe, was also in the Poetry for the People program, as a student-teacher poet. He had left me and my mother when I was about two years old, and I remember seeing him just once before middle school. When I arrived in Berkeley, Hal was a graduate student there and heavy into being Native American. He read me poems about the four directions and "Mother Earth." So as we learned and wrote poetry together and began to be father and daughter together, we explored what it meant to be Native together.

Getting to know my father meant "learning that song" that "The Bombing of Baghdad" names, because being Native means living with generations of violence and sadness. Sadness, especially, overwhelmed my father; it was as relentless and exhausting to watch as the bombings.

Yet as a woman, being Native meant something slightly different for me. "The Bombing of Baghdad" addresses the colonizers' abuse of Native women and use of them as objects of conquest: "He pushed westward / to annihilate the savages / ("Attack at dawn!") / and seize their territories / seize their women / seize their natural wealth."[6] I seemed to live this history out in high school and early college with a series of white men who treated me like an object and then ignored me. I wrote poems about being part Native and part white, about identity, and about my father and grandmother.

I used June Jordan's lessons ("Let me be / very / very / very / very / very / specific") and her "Guidelines for Critiquing a Poem" (especially "avoiding the verb to be")[7]—but just as valuable were June's introductions to a world of diverse poets, most notably for me, Joy Harjo.

In 1993, Joy Harjo came to Berkeley as a guest poet and teacher of Poetry for the People. Joy Harjo is a Muscogee woman, poet, musician, writer, and survivor of domestic violence. I read and reread her poems until the pages wore thin. Especially one.

> She had horses with long pointed breasts.
> She had horses with full, brown thighs.
> She had horses who laughed too much.
> She had horses who threw rocks at glass houses.
> She had horses who licked razor blades . . .
>
> She had horses who waltzed nightly on the moon.

She had horses who were much too shy and kept quiet in stalls of their own making[8]

Eventually, we find out, "These were the same horses."[9]

And to me, this is the same idea as "The Bombing of Baghdad": The war in Iraq, white colonialism, oppression and violence, the Holocaust, these are the same horses. And we each have our role and inherit our part in these histories. We live in Joy Harjo's "stalls of our own making." Sometimes we inherit from both the colonizer and the colonized. And as Jordan reminds us, sometimes "the enemy travel[s] from my house."[10]

The enemy still travels from "our house," and so "The Bombing of Baghdad"—its connections and call for responsibility—could not be more relevant today. The wars in Iraq, Afghanistan, and Syria continued for over twenty-five years and only recently ended. As a US citizen, a voter, a taxpayer, and a consumer, I reap benefits from these wars, and I must face my responsibility for them. Since 9/11, the wars we waged in the Middle East resulted in approximately 500,000 human deaths, about half of those civilians.[11] This fact fills me with shame.

I recently visited my family in Oklahoma and the small town in "Indian Country" where my grandparents grew up. I saw the trailer that hosts City Hall sagging under the weight of poverty and hopelessness. I learned my cousin relapsed again. The Muscogee tribe built an impressive new district court and legislative building, and the steel and mirrors of the casino soar high above the river. Still, Native America in general faces the highest rates of poverty and addiction in the country. Men inflict violence, disappearance, and murder upon Native women at unfathomable rates.

And yet the white part of me protects me from all of this. It's been relatively recently that I've understood that I, like the poet in "The Bombing of Baghdad," "live inside [Crazy Horse's] grave."[12] Quite literally I have a home in the East Bay, land that the Ohlone people stewarded for thousands of years before it was stolen from them. But I also have innumerable privileges from my whiteness, my education, my marriage to a white man, and my American citizenship. And thus I return to the poem's question: "how shall I negotiate the implications / of my shame?"[13]

I have answered this, as June Jordan taught, with poetry and writing, advocating and speaking out. In my last year at Berkeley, I cowrote a book about the Poetry for the People experience so that other schools could replicate the model. I later went to law school intending to help people say what they needed to say to those in power. I hoped to end sexual harassment or race discrimination in corporate America. I ended up writing appeals for those convicted of crimes and held in prison. In legal briefs I connected issues like race and justice, violence and redemption. I explore this more in my book, *Almost Innocent: From Searching to Saved in America's Criminal Justice System* (2021). It is about the criminal justice system and the tragedies, the human stories, the contradictions, and the resiliency found there.

I also write essays—published in national publications, local newspapers, and essay collections—about the themes of "The Bombing of Baghdad" played out today. Being a modern Native American living with a legacy of sadness. The Me Too movement and women reclaiming power through our own voices. Speaking out for others while recognizing my own part in oppressive systems like white supremacy, the criminal justice system, and American wars abroad.

As cofounder of Fogbreak Justice, an education company for criminal justice professionals and civic leaders, I teach people how to reduce bias, increase empathy, and build community trust. Vital to our curriculum and the workshops I lead is the idea of connection. The racism and inequity we see in the criminal justice system connect back to the history of racial violence in our country. Many of us have inherited benefits from these and other systems of control and violence. I am quick to speak about my own biases and admit the privileges I have gained through my whiteness, my education, and my status as a lawyer and an American. This connects me to those I teach because we are all in this together, learning from each other, having difficult conversations, taking responsibility.

For almost thirty years I have continued to learn and relearn June Jordan's and Joy Harjo's teaching: *dedicate yourself to learn that song*, see what is *perpetrated in our name*, recognize *the stalls of our own making*. It's important—it's survival, really—to learn that song and speak those connections.

This is the message of "The Bombing of Baghdad" too. That in poetry we forge on, we connect with humanity, we live despite the violence:

> And this is for Crazy Horse singing as he dies
> And here is my song of the living
> who must sing against the dying
> sing to join the living
> with the dead.[14]

Shanti Bright Brien is an author, educator, criminal defense attorney, and cofounder of Fogbreak Justice. Her memoir, *Almost Innocent: From Searching to Saved in America's Criminal Justice System* (Amplify, 2021), was named one of 2021's "Best Indie Books" by Kirkus Reviews. Shanti teaches others how to write their stories through workshops and writing circles. She is an enrolled member of the Muscogee (Creek) tribe and a mother of three.

Maestra

Xochiquetzal Candelaria

Fuchsias bloom for the most part in June. They require both sun and shade in equal parts. They grow in clusters like a series of hearts. When I go running these days, I do it only long enough to hear my heart beating hard against my chest, and I talk to June at these moments; I can still see her eyes looking up and away, gathering all the words that seem just overhead.

Fuchsias seem to have mouths that open when forefinger and thumb apply delicate pressure, making a popping sound. For me, they have always been flowers capable of speaking. I learned the word "fuchsia" when writing a poem in June Jordan's poetry seminar in the spring of 1994. I had known the flowers as a small child, but I encountered them alone and so never knew what to call them. I didn't know June had just survived cancer. I didn't know much of anything about her as she walked into the room wearing reflective sunglasses and a neck brace. All I could really read was her smile.

Many of us say that we delighted in June's laugh, how unforgettable it was. Yet, I don't think that is why we remember it. It was the laugh paired with that way her eyes would meet our own, then look up into the air above our heads, where she seemed to find words; their music she'd release to our hearts' inner lining, producing simultaneously the wonderment of the big and the small:

> Next to the roasted mushrooms/onion/shrimp and chunks
>   of ripe red pepper
> Next to the wine and the cooler and the candle and
>   the flashlights
> Next to the gigantic redwood tree

> Next to the mountains receding but never
>   shadowy or lost
> Next to the very spot where Venus
>   blinked delirious as I felt close
>   enough to feel the Milky Way
>   collapse into the aerial Big
>   Dipper poised above our bodies
>   close enough to feel
>   our bodies close
>   together.[1]

Her words did not sacrifice the particular, did not ignore the immense. They called us out in an orchestral language, so that our souls could celebrate our sacred struggle to exist.

I intimately knew fuchsias from early childhood, as they hung overhead and seemingly watched over me as I walked the skinny sidewalk beside my grandmother's rickety, pale-yellow house. I'd look up at them and they'd look down at me and slowly I'd work my little five-year-old hand behind one of their observing heads and a sound of surprise would fall into the air. *So many red, delicate mouths,* I would say to myself. I was outside and observing:

> Before you knew my name
> I knew
> nobody treads the earth
> as close
> as light
> as you[2]

Inside of the house, I was afraid that my grandmother would be arguing with my mother. Anger, it seemed sometimes, was the only means of power accessible to the women of my family, a kind of caffeine that allowed them, for centuries, to get through the day and keep the children protected. My great-grandmother was married off at twelve years old; she eventually escaped, crossing the Sonoran Desert with her four children. She had previously evaded being enslaved and sent to a silver mine in Sinaloa by resisting, like many others, the regime of Porfirio Díaz.

So anger I knew as a tool growing up. Not a very refined tool, but a tool nonetheless. So it seemed natural that I study rhetoric, the science of argument, when I attended college. Shortly before the first time I met June, I had finished a course covering Friedrich Nietzsche's *The Birth of Tragedy*, and my heart, like the fuchsia, seemed to have popped. I felt alone with ideas that I believed if put into practice could change the world for the better, could chart a course beyond anger into communal grace.

But the way we studied in the Rhetoric Department made it seem like everyone was alone, lonely, and without actionable concerns. I wanted to be in touch with the primal unity, the collective power that Nietzsche claimed existed beneath the appearance of things. He said that poetry was one of the only ways to reach the primal unity, and that there, at the heart of existence, things were complex, powerful, and true.

I was lonely and my heart hurt, so I looked in the UC Berkeley course catalogue and found a poetry seminar in the African American Studies Department taught by a Professor Jordan. What I remember most about those first few days in class was the energy that seemed to surround June. It was an energy with the power I associate with flowers, water, and blood.

In *Translating Neruda*, a book June gave me, Cesar Vallejo is quoted as saying that poems reach out to us "in the cardiac rhythm of life."

I learned later that I didn't qualify to be in June's class because I hadn't taken a much larger introductory course. Still, June made a place for me. I wrote tiny, terrible poems most of the term, and I was completely happy to do so. I felt comfortable being the worst poet who was trying her best. I felt fed by June's delicate and inspiring lectures that would often end in her laughter or slow, measured, expanded cadence.

She described writing poetry as "wrestling with an angel," letting us know that we were going to lose, but that the experience was blessed and transformative. In some greedy corner of my heart, I wanted June to myself, but my heart as a whole knew that what we all shared was greater than anything we could achieve on our own.

I believe the magic of June's work and teachings is that she did not compromise when it came to the singular and its connection to the architecture of our physical, spiritual, and political lives. June Jordan knew how to inspire young writers to find the words to match the images and actions already animating their lives and the lives of those they loved. She called on us to be emissaries, heart warriors. Our lives with all their particular details mattered because they were, in the act of being named, a portal to tenderness, truth, and political dignity:

> The dirt floor of his house has been swept.
> The dirt floor around the chair where he sits
> has been swept.
> He has swept the dirt twice.
> The dirt is clean.
> The dirt is his dirt.
> The man is not cute.
>
> The man is not ugly.
> The man is teaching himself
> to read.[3]

In "Nobody Mean More to Me Than You and the Future Life of Willie Jordan," June describes how the students in her class could not enjoy the Black English found in *The Color Purple* because they hadn't seen their own speech patterns written down before. I remember distinctly, just before I met June, feeling uncomfortable writing in English, though it was my native language. I felt somehow that what I wanted to say was often crushed by the form. June writes, "None of the students had ever learned how to read and write their own verbal system of communication: Black English."[4] The idea that I was entitled to my own verbal system of communication broke my heart wide open. I was in love. I was in love with Black English to begin with, and then I was in love with my use of Spanglish, and lastly, I came to delight in standard English.

She taught students at Stony Brook University to formalize their understanding and appreciation for Black English, and she did so in the face of heartbreaking police brutality. She galvanized the students to take the murder of their fellow classmate—Willie Jordan's brother, Reggie Jordan—as a call to action. In fact, in the face of trauma and disdain for the lives of people of color when many of us would have collapsed, June led, listened, and loved with her whole self.

In her house on Carlotta Avenue in Berkeley, June had a piano, a modest upright with keys that caught the light coming in through breaks in the lavender growing around her entrance. One day, for only a couple of minutes, she played something for me. She most likely was writing the libretto *I Was Looking at the Ceiling and Then I Saw the Sky* at the time. The way her hands moved like water across the keys, the way the notes seemed to arch in every direction, rearranged the atoms of my body, and kissed everything in the room. I was inside and all the fuchsias I could ever want were dangling and bobbing above me. It was so beautiful that it hurt.

It was as if her talents were infinite in those moments when my ears absorbed the "the catapulting music of surprise that makes me / hideaway my face."[5] It hurt because all the love embodied in her musical talent is the heartbeat behind the breast beating out a primordial account and organizing principle: love, love, love.

Somehow June was never unaware of her gifts or pretentious. She didn't choose a false dichotomy for understanding one's place in the world. She writes: "What I can envision is the possibility that enough people will come to understand that because I have power equal to your power doesn't mean you have less power. . . . The current idea is that if other people (not like me) have as much freedom and power as I have, then what I have is less meaningful, less valuable or just plain less. This is a hideous, fatal, long-standing error of conceptualization."[6]

Once when she invited someone to join our poetry collective, someone who I considered to have genius abilities, she asked us to help him learn the ropes of our poetry community. He was exceptional and in need of training; the two were not mutually exclusive.

I'm not trying to claim that June was perfect or beyond critique, but her herculean synthesizing abilities I believe only future generations will fully comprehend. She was constantly composing a collective bloom, rainstorm, heart song.

I have a copy of *The Complete Poems of Keats and Shelley* that June gave me. On the inside, she wrote, "Someone gave this book to me and so I pass it on, hoping you will someday be as blessed as I am by yourself and find your own Xoch—to pass it on." June, through her work and teaching, was always giving us back to ourselves and inspiring us to pass ourselves on to others. Ahh, Momma, *mi querida maestra*; I'm still trying.

Xochiquetzal Candelaria is a poet, essayist, and teacher based in San Francisco, California. She is the author of two books of poetry, *Empire* (University of Arizona Press, 2011) and *Show Me the Bells* (Tia Chucha Press, 2024). Her work has appeared in *The Nation*, *Tin House*, *Colorado Review*, and other magazines. Her honors include fellowships from the LEF Foundation and the Barbara Deming Memorial Fund and an individual grant from the National Endowment for the Arts. Her writing has been anthologized, most recently, in *Other Musics: New Latina Poetry and the Poetry of Capital*. She teaches creative writing at City College of San Francisco.

Dear June

Ruth Forman

September 13, 2019

Dear June,

    I will never be as courageous as you, but your courage steps with me. You live in my heart, even when I forget to say a prayer for you. Your pen my pen's teacher, your voice my inspiration and challenge, your laughter tinkling like bells in my ears. How can one be such a powerful warrior with such beautiful and delicate laughter? Bells cannot match it, though they do come close. Your laughter somewhere between light bells and wind chimes, I can still hear it. You challenged us to lift and defend the human spirit. Even from my first poetry days and collection (*We Are the Young Magicians*), I try.

    I wonder if you could survive these days. With all that fight, the cancer came and stole you from us. What would these days do to you? Would you even sleep? You would be writing and speaking, protesting and traveling. June. Oh June. Warrior spirit. I miss you. I miss you. How would you fight in these days?

    Your spirit carries forward in my instruction. I use your "Guidelines for Critiquing a Poem" every time I teach a creative writing class. At VONA (Voices of Our Nations Arts Foundation, a multigenre workshop for writers of color) with writers, Bread Loaf (an intensive summer master's program) with teachers, creative writing workshops—I try to build in the community and justice, celebration and solace. I carry those guidelines from the *Revolutionary Blueprint* into every class. We reflect on them as guidelines—not as hard rules—but things to seriously consider. Punctuation always a rich axis for conversation. But we challenge ourselves, try them on, test them, work with them until we know them, as we discuss our own and each other's work. Call them out:

2b. Poetry: The achievement of maximum impact with a minimal number of words.

2c. Poetry: Utmost precision in the use of language, hence, density and intensity of expression.

3. What is its purpose?

7b. Singularity and vividness of diction.

7d. Avoidance of abstractions and generalities.[1]

Experienced writer or novice, each student has a common place to speak from as they help each other clarify their words. To work from as they consider their own poems. And the work becomes so clear, so powerful. So many times, our class is knocked back by what students are able to express. Afterward, writers often bring your guidelines to their own fiction or memoir; middle school and high school English teachers often bring your guidelines to their own classes.

June, you gifted us a way to bring forth the clarity and power in our words. I try to pass this talisman on for others' voices spilling out onto the page when it all is too much. Minimal words for maximum impact. Descriptive verbs. Specificity, precision, horizontal and vertical rhythm. June, you sing in every classroom through their words.

So I guess that's what you would do in this time. Sing through your students' words and their students' words and their students' students' words as they speak about what matters to them. As they speak about what they see, their lives and their rights and the rights of human beings on this planet. As they name. As they witness. You hover in their words. You live in our words. You thrive in our words. You dance in our words. You laugh and smile and sob in our words.

And our words, in the midst of this crushing world, they are beautiful.

Thank you.

Love,

Ruth

Ruth Forman is an acclaimed author of poetry and children's literature. She is a founding member and former teacher-poet with June Jordan's Poetry for the People program at UC Berkeley, former teacher of creative writing with the University of Southern California, and a longtime faculty member with the VONA writing program. She is currently a professor at the Middlebury Bread Loaf School of English. Ruth's most recent children's books are *Like So* (Simon & Schuster, 2024), *Light* (Simon & Schuster, 2024), and *One* (Simon & Schuster, 2023). You can find out more at ruthforman.com.

a practice of freedom

Ariel Luckey

1999. Berkeley, California. I gathered in the streets in front of KPFA Radio Station with hundreds of people, strips of white cloth bound across our mouths to symbolize a gag order. The community was rallying to defend the station, long known as a champion of free speech, from a hostile takeover. At the center of the mass civil disobedience was a small stage and a microphone. Between the chants and speeches, a slight African American woman with close-cropped hair and a sparkle in her eye read a poem, her lyrical voice at once playful and deadly serious. I didn't know who she was, but I was deeply moved by the honesty and urgency and artistry in her words. The woman passed the mic to a handful of young poets, who I later learned were her students. Each read a short but powerful piece of their own, simultaneously an embodiment and advocacy of speech as a practice of freedom. This was my introduction to poet and professor June Jordan. The following semester I enrolled in Poetry for the People at University of California, Berkeley to study the poets and the peoples of the world in a small class with June, her insatiable intellect and fiery spirit leading us in a rigorous pursuit of humanity.

In class we read, wrote, discussed, critiqued, and revised poetry constantly, often using June's "Guidelines for Critiquing a Poem" as a framework. One of them, that poetry is the art of telling the truth, became a cornerstone for me as I dedicate my life's work to the collective healing of intergenerational trauma. Digging into the layers of race, class, migration, and property ownership in my own family history has provided an entry point to question our society's relationship to the land we live on. In this light, the art of telling the truth is no small task. I have been honored to collaborate closely in this work with Sogorea Te' Land Trust, the first Indigenous women–led urban land trust in the country. Sogorea Te' facilitates the return of Indigenous land to Indigenous people in Lisjan Ohlone territory in the San Francisco Bay Area, cultivating urban gardens, building community centers, and revitalizing Indigenous culture. When Corrina Gould, a Lisjan Ohlone leader and cofounder of Sogorea Te', invited me to speak at a community prayer ceremony called Standing on This Land Together at the West Berkeley Shellmound, I read the following poem. I dedicate it to Corrina, for her fierce love and leadership, and to June, who showed me that the proper place for a poem is in the streets with the people.

not past

Ariel Luckey

I was born and raised in colonized California
in a city named for oak trees that were quickly cut down
this is the only place I've ever lived
the only place I've really known
my home
and yet my family's roots here are paper thin

in the library of living literature of this landscape
we are just the latest tweet
a popular yet passing trend
a blink of the eye
relative to Ohlone time

my children
the first in six
generations on every branch of our family tree
to grow up in the same
place as their parents
we are diaspora
we are visitors, settlers, squatters,
migrants, refugees, gentrifiers
we forget where we come from or call home to other places
but we live here

this sacred and haunted and broken and gorgeous land
Chochenyo and Lisjan
unceded and unrecognized and unrequited

how can we live here

with death beneath every step
like the bodies still under Bay Street
echoes on the edges of the wind
purple screams of Mission slavery
tattooed on the earth's skin
pulled taut like a drum
there is still tension
in the shadow of the cross

who are we to live here

we sleep in beds we didn't make
dreaming of being at home
but we are out of practice
out of balance
out of place
we are hermit crabs at Alameda Beach
eucalyptus trees in Tilden
we make our home in someone else's
living rooms cluttered with ghosts and dirty laundry
we don't even know what we don't know
I can only just gesture in the direction of the loss
it's beyond beyond

a breaking of the imagination

heart failure

and every hipster bar and restaurant
every workshare cafe and high-rise condominium
everywhere we go
sits on these tectonic plates
shaken skeletons of social decay
however visible

this blood stain
the past is not past

so how should we live here

what ethics of reconciliation
should shape our footprints
what practice of repair
could possibly come close
our humanity dangling by a thread

how can we pay rent or a mortgage or property taxes to anyone
but the Ohlone

who else can claim this land
with a story unauthored by theft
who else can show us how to live here
in accordance with the canyons and the creeks
informed by the fog and the bay
the protocols and rituals of their elders
who else

what if reverence for the redwoods
was as common as techie entitlement
what if our culture demanded we tell our children the truth
what if we stopped using plastic
what if we ripped up the concrete that suffocates these shellmounds

what if Indigenous women made a circle
and built a sacred arbor
and said
maybe
if you shut up and listen
if you tell your story when invited
if you get your hands dirty and organize your people

if you give Shuumi
and help us rematriate the land
then maybe
one day
we will welcome you
home

Ariel Luckey, born and raised in Oakland, California / Lisjan Ohlone territory, is an interdisciplinary artist and activist. He is development director at the Sogorea Te' Land Trust, the first urban Indigenous women–led land trust in the country, and cofounder of Jews on Ohlone Land. Ariel is a storyteller, strategist, and coalition builder, and was a student-teacher poet with June and an artist-in-residence at June Jordan's Poetry for the People. He lives in an urban forest with his beloved and their two sons.

A Blueprint for June's Love

Sheila Menezes

"I have evolved from an observer to a victim to an activist passionately formulating methods of resistance against tyranny of any kind," June wrote in the introduction to *Some of Us Did Not Die*, her final publication before cancer took her from us in physical form.[1] June dedicated this book to a few of her students, including me, and many of us remain close. June exists as our anchor, touchstone, guide, and our bond. We are all her methods of resistance. With every step we take toward justice and equity, we carry forward her refusal to accept the status quo.

In this essay, I write about the art and legacy of June's mentoring, guided by the principles of June's "Poetry for the People Blueprint." It isn't just a guide for writing poetry—it's a framework for activism, teaching, and creating art with integrity and purpose. Poetry and the lives we choose to live can be tools for truth, resistance, and transformation.

This is what I learned from June:

1. Read it aloud. I wrote a poem in May 2002, a month before June passed, and I read it to her that same day. I wrote it with speed, the same speed with which I attached the mattress teetering on top of my car. I was leaving the Bay and heading down to Santa Barbara for graduate school. My words were raw, ragged, and unfinished. But they were urgent, and they were for June. I sat on the edge of her bed, reading my poem as she listened with grace. She thanked me regardless of the obvious need for revisions—even as she sunk exhausted into bed, she encouraged and mentored me. I would be gone for months and feared this could be the last time I saw June. It was.

2. Is it a poem? . . . Poetry: A medium for telling the truth. As her Poetry for the People (P4P) student, a student-teacher poet, later the P4P program coordinator, and her personal assistant, I often visited June's home during her final battle with breast cancer. One day, I walked through the front door and found her standing in the kitchen as sunlight streamed through the window, danced in her hair, and illuminated her face. She tilted her head up, and with closed eyes and a profound clarity, she said, "My life has been rich." I also recall a phone call with June, where she calmly shared that she had woken up that morning blind in one eye because the cancer had spread to her brain. This was the reality she faced daily during those months—sometimes a new physical decline, other times a slight improvement. She reassured me not to worry. She eventually regained her sight. June believed her body had betrayed her. She knew she had so much more to do.

3. What is its purpose? The rest of her words from that final day lie buried in my old journals, waiting to be unearthed. Yet, those particular words matter to me less than the entirety of her words: her mentorship, friendship, love, care, and wisdom, all of which flow through my veins today. That guides me at critical decision points, when I feel like giving up, or when I can't see a way out. She inspired, encouraged, and taught me that: Even though trauma can stop me in my tracks, and I will be tenderly impacted by what happens to me, I am not what happens to me. I am what I do with what happens to me. I have a purpose: to speak up when I see harm and intentionally create spaces for marginalized voices. To tell my story. To push for more than what media and dominant culture present as possible. To remember that there are always more possibilities. To say no to any "normal" that includes oppression. To say, "Wrong is not my name." To be fierce and relentless until there is equitable change for all.

4. Is it coherent? June was serious. June unwaveringly believed that all human beings deserve equal rights, humane treatment, and dignity. She lived the belief that we are responsible for and to one another. She instilled in me that to the extent that I have more power and privilege than someone else—in whatever form—I am obligated to contribute to creating a world that does not perpetuate the current inequities. Things must get done, and we gotta do it. As June wrote, "We are the ones we have been waiting for."

5 & 6. What are the strengths of the poem? What are the weaknesses of the poem? Once, I sat with June in her dining room while her dog Bingo barked incessantly at nothing. June's face crumpled as if the bark were crashing cymbals. Mid-sentence, she excused herself, walked to the dog, and declared, "Bingo, we have to coexist." He stopped barking. June lived her beliefs. She showed me that coexistence is a strength, a fundamental principle in navigating people and creatures on this planet, no matter our differences. We are interdependent and need each other for laughter and love as much as for exposing oppressive and racist systems that cause harm—the kind of harm that steals sleep from Black, Indigenous, and Brown mothers who fear their children may be killed. June named these truths with precision, and through her unwavering clarity, she empowered me to embrace the values that had long been quietly present in my heart.

7. Is it a good poem? June's foremost impact on me was through her written word and mentoring, showing me how to find my voice with paper and pen. June modeled the infinite ways one can engage as an activist. She was a creator, and when she met barriers or roadblocks, I witnessed her figure out another way to go about something. Sometimes, the way through was a poem. She was strategic and lived the fact that taking action is as simple as speaking. She brought it into focus for me that one small move matters, and when we write words, these words become our bodies on the line. One poem can derail a trajectory of harm toward something completely different and potentially beautiful. June made it clear—writing wasn't just survival. It was resistance, transformation, and a call to action. In June's poem "Scenario Revision #1," she describes her noncompliance with breast cancer:

> I roll away
> I speak
> I laugh out loud

> Not yet
> big bird of prey
> not yet[2]

As June described, she evolved from observer to victim to activist. June taught me that through observation, we become aware of how we have been and are being harmed. This awareness is radical because, during the process of writing about our experiences, our resistance against cruelty and oppression activates. She encouraged me to let go of self-judgment, lean into my beloved community, and process my trauma by writing about it in poems and finding choice. I can shrink from the weight of harmful experiences or catalyze my power through words.

8. Is it complete? Is it a dramatic event? Does it have a beginning that builds to a compelling middle development and then an ending that "lands" the whole poem somewhere fully satisfying to the reader? June asked questions. She helped with any problem I let her know about, because June believed in taking action. Her care for my welfare, physically and emotionally, was undeniable. She coached me to care for myself and others and take action in writing by documenting individual experiences through specifics and verbs—strong, active verbs, lots of active verbs!!—to demand attention. She taught me to rewrite history for the people, to create poetry for the people, from the people, and of the people. To acknowledge the innate existence of difference by studying various cultural belief systems and poems from different cultures and celebrating them.

June required specificity because she experienced how broad strokes, labels, judgments, and generalizations erase people's lived realities. The complexity and sometimes contradiction of our human lives require our specific stories. The dismantling of tyranny requires our specific stories to describe exactly what our lives feel, look, smell, and taste like. And if we're gonna dismantle the cruel and unreasonable use of power and control, we sure as hell need specific instructions.

9. How does it fit into or change a tradition of poems? I learned from June that I could do something; I could teach young people at Berkeley

High School with Poetry for the People, and I could go into a prison and participate in a poetry slam with men incarcerated with life sentences. June's acceptance of me encouraged my acceptance of others. She reminded me of my humanity—my desire to be loved and cared for, my urgency to protect all people from harm, and my delight in humor and the spoken word. She helped me feel safer in the world by letting me know that I, in particular, just like everybody else, mattered. She helped me humanize people around me. Over twenty years ago, in that poetry slam in state prison, I let the label "prisoner" dissolve and saw instead the human being who wept as I read a poem about my grandmother. That day propelled me toward future work in transformative justice. For the past ten years, it's been no coincidence that I've spent every week facilitating groups in that same prison—teaching nonviolence, communication, emotional intelligence, and healing to help people transform reactive, harmful behaviors into intentional, compassionate responses to life's challenges and relational struggles. June directed me to the places most broken in our society and systems to find the most hope, grace, and beauty.

On the last day I saw June, I read her a poem. I invite you to write your own.

June built a community of writers and activists. We resist tyranny in hospitals, prisons, and schools. We build healthy equity and transformative justice organizations. We brew our actions with love and nonviolence and strategically plan together for travel, weddings, birthdays, concerts, and hospital stays. We share meals, watch basketball, and revel in conversation alongside our children and families. June, we are here. We still learn from your words and your love of love. You still guide us toward our deepest truths, toward our collective humanity, and you continue to inspire us to resist.

Sheila Menezes is the founder of Compassionate Return, LLC, where she supports leaders and teams through coaching and consulting. Certified through the Co-Active Training Institute, she trained in nonviolent communication, emotional intelligence, Gabor Maté's trauma-healing approach,

136 | THIS UNRULY WITNESS

and Marshall Ganz's Leadership, Organizing, and Action at Harvard. Sheila focuses on empathy and equity, transforming disconnection into connection and harm into healing. Since 2015, she has been leading weekly compassionate communication and trauma-healing groups for incarcerated individuals. Sheila believes leading with love fosters healing and change.

June Jordan and Sheila Menezes. Photo courtesy of Sheila Menezes.

Choosing a Praxis of Liberation

Kate Holbrook

Poetry for the People continues to deeply shape my ritual speech and written word, who I am as a spiritual leader, and how I support people in my role as interfaith college chaplain. It has given me a profound appreciation of June Jordan's poetry and teachings, especially the technical checklist.

To be trusted to hold space and find language for grief, compassion, the voice of the dead, and the needs of family and community is a sacred act. There is nothing abstract. I have walked families and communities through many deaths, some peaceful and many tragic. To the beloved, to the loved ones, death is always concrete. And so the dead in their silence, and the grieving in the wildness of emotion, need to have space to express their grief in a way that works for them, however that might look.

In my office, the first thing I see when I walk in the door each day is a black-framed print of June Jordan's poem "On a New Year's Eve" (with a drawing of June by former Poetry for the People student Hal BrightCloud). And each day, I am present with the free, yet precise, flow of words of June's poem. A reminder of clarity of language. The power of giving voice. I am surrounded by June's words, this poem a daily reminder of impermanence: the choice to open to life, to love and suffering. Even to the mystery in impermanence, knowing as June wrote, "I know // all things are dear / that disappear."[1] I hold this knowing close because I have always been aware that as June was transitioning toward death in the spring of 2002 and Junichi Semitsu was starting as director of the Poetry for the People program, I was joining this community that would help me find my self/voice and wrestle out my experiences. Concrete language in liminal space, which we held and wrote together that semester. Then summer and fall came, and we continued in grief and celebration of June's life, empowered, resilient—ready to resist power. And somehow, with other student-teacher poets, I began to live into her legacy one word at a time.

In the winter of 2002, I fell into Poetry for the People with dedicated passion. And for three and a half years, it was a lifeline. An embodied spiritual practice of liberation—of life-giving empowerment that taught me the collective healing power of transforming silence into language. To give voice to what I was too afraid to name and speak in my own life and what was happening in the world. I was a queer theology student seeking spiritual leadership in a tradition that at the time wasn't institutionally welcoming. The US declared war on Iraq, again. Declared war on terrorism. Then moved into Afghanistan. Hate crimes surged. Racism, Islamophobia, xenophobia continued to grow. Rhetoric of fear tried to assert control in mainstream media that encouraged silence.

And in this space, Poetry for the People cultivated a communal praxis of resistance. As a community of trust, it taught the power of claiming the truths of one's experience through a birthing process of finding clarity of speech. Every voice was important. Every word mattered.

Because to claim the realities of our lives; to claim our identities; to speak our love freely; to acknowledge our suffering, our joy; to name the injustice we witnessed, heard, experienced was critical to reclaiming our humanity, our essence, our own power, and the power of our communities. It was essential to our refusal to stay silent and instead actively call forth what was just and healing. And to do this, we needed to find and claim our language: To speak, instead of be spoken for. Poetry for the People taught us how to live a new reality rooted in a love and trust of ourselves that no one could take away.

In the introduction to *June Jordan's Poetry for the People: A Revolutionary Blueprint,* June writes that "Poetry means taking control of the language of your life."[2] And in that process, an expansiveness opened so wide inside of me that, having discovered my voice, I found name and strength that nothing external could change.

In Poetry for the People, we recognized urgency in language and poems. The world was waiting to hear your words, your poem. There wasn't time to be wasted on abstraction. Every noun. Adjective. Verb mattered. Clarity and precision in speech were critical. For others to hear us, we needed to be clear. If what we wrote was confusing, vague, abstract—though it might sound poetic, smooth, and nice—our meaning would be lost. We needed to have a purpose. Our words needed to be clear because it was essential to making language visible and breaking silence. And in the political situation of language, according to June, is something that "every one of us must move against, because our lives depend on it."[3] Because of this, June Jordan's "Guidelines for Critiquing a Poem" came into being, a means by which the abstract poem could become a concrete poem—the poet found their voice, found themselves, and was heard. Twenty years later, I remember:

(1) every poem should have purpose

(2) avoid abstractions, generalities, and the "to be" verb

(3) be specific

(4) use concrete images and active voice

(5) and make sure it is a complete dramatic event written with urgency

This technical checklist guided our lives as student-teacher poets. In fact, we lived by it, workshopping every poem. At first the guidelines were intimidating. Like others, I had been taught to use passive voice, to avoid and talk around what I wanted to say, to be vague; and I had been given messages about staying silent on certain topics. Through June's guidelines, my language and my life, my life—like that of so many others in the Poetry for the People world—changed. As June said a few times in her poem "Study #1":

Let me be
very
very

>   very
>   very
>   very
>   specific[4]

And so, I learned how to be very, very specific. I also learned the meaning of maximum impact, minimum words. In her article "Problems of Language in a Democratic State," June writes that someone who is in a position of less power tends to evade language, to "evade a further confrontation with the powerful."[5] Poetry for the People taught us that by learning to make language tell our own truth by using active voice, we claim our own power and resist dominant language and ideology that would otherwise seek to keep us alienated and silenced, collaborating unintentionally with the powerful. At its heart, June insists it's an issue of democracy and our survival. As June often asked or said in a variety of ways, "And I ask you: Well, what are we going to do about it?"[6]

At the time, as a student-teacher poet in Poetry for the People, I was so focused on the act of crafting a poem and finding voice, the urgency of speaking the truth to power now, in this moment, that I didn't see beyond the immediacy of the Poetry for the People "Guidelines for Critiquing a Poem" into the larger vision. I was fully aware of how empowering the workshopping process was; I witnessed that transformation every day for three and a half years. Yet I didn't get the fullness the guidelines embodied. I didn't fully see then how extraordinary June was/is as a poet. I also didn't see or read the subtle changes of grief between some of her earlier and later work. June continues to be an incredibly gifted poet as she speaks of/with/for the dead and in naming personal and communal injustice and suffering.

Time and life experiences, especially as I have accompanied people in grief in my current position as an interfaith college chaplain, have changed how I connect with June's work. For example, in her poem "Poem in Memory of Alan Schindler, 22 Years Old"—told from the perspective of Alan Schindler's mother, whose only son's murder was a hate crime, whose son "lived and died loving / other men."[7] Before, I focused primarily on the hate crime. I see how June's repetition of "I have buried him" later followed with "I have buried him now / beneath the earth that allows for no / distinctions among men," is an expression of grief and resistance,[8] the burial an act of reclaiming Alan's dignity/equity in a horrific death. June's use of the tattoo at the beginning of the poem—"Except for the tattoo / how could I recognize / my son"—and at the very end—"except / Thank God! / except for that tattoo"—is significant.[9] Previously I focused on the tattoo primarily in relationship to violence. Now, I read the tattoo with more complexity. In this poem, the tattoo reclaims Alan as subject, not an object as his perpetrators made him to be. The tattoo enables his mother to bury him with love and dignity, something she can do in her grief. When I read the poem now, I am always left thinking not only about Alan, but about all bodies, current and historical, who can/could not be buried because they are/were not identified due to hate crimes, violence, and other accidents.

Another example is in "For Michael Angelo Thompson," a powerful poem dedicated to a fourteen-year-old Black boy who was deliberately killed by the city after being taken off a bus and then denied access at the hospital in 1973. June is very specific that Michael was killed—he "has not 'died' / he / has not 'passed away' // the Black prince Michael Black boy // our youngest brother // He was killed / He did not die."[10] "Passed away" may comfort a family member whose loved one died peacefully, though it remains unclear. When used by others after someone is killed/murdered, "passed away" erases the violence/cause of death, frequently leading to failure to hold the perpetrator(s) accountable.

Poetry for the People taught us to explore and find language for our own and the world's pain and suffering, rather than run away or deny them. In an "Argument with the Buddha," June engages in a conversation with the Buddha about what they may agree and disagree on. This includes suffering and renunciation. She writes, "I renounce / renunciation!" intentionally choosing to immerse herself in the world; to be engaged even with pain, instead of detached.[11] She writes:

> I choose and cherish
> all that will perish
> The living deal

The balance of my bliss
with pain

excites my soul
perhaps to no enlightenment
but
. . . .
I hope to fend
off enemies
and bend with
lovers
endlessly

I choose
anything
anyone
I may lose

I renounce
renunciation

I breathe
head to head
with suffering[12]

continuing with "I know // all things are dear / that disappear," from "On a New Year's Eve."[13]

June chose to embrace what she loved. She loved and fought for life, knowing that what was dear to her might disappear. In doing so, she invited us to do so also—to embrace love more deeply, to fight for/be in solidarity with those we love and with others, even if we didn't know them—holding systems/leaders/community/ourselves accountable as we lived in the present, knowing our time with each other is precious, with all its realities.

And instead of avoiding suffering, June writes, "I breathe / head to head / with suffering."[14] To breathe into our pain. To uncover and name it, instead of avoiding our pain and living in silence. We knew that to do so was part of our healing—individual and collective. After

9/11, June wrote, "I realized that regardless of tragedy, regardless of the grief, regardless of the monstrous challenge, Some of Us Have Not Died," later going on to question, "And what shall we do, we who did not die? How shall we grieve, and cry out loud and face down despair?"[15] She allowed space to acknowledge grief, yet called and challenged us to move from any complacency and despair, because, as June put so clearly, "Some of Us Did Not Die / We're Still Here / I Guess It Was Our Destiny To Live / So Let's get on with it!"[16]

So I get on with it. As Poetry for the People has taught me to do.

Kate Holbrook is a practitioner of contemplative and embodied spiritual practices who values her capacity for helping us stay grounded. She has been an interfaith college chaplain since 2006. A teacher of Wisdom Healing Qigong, she is passionate about finding creative ways for people, especially young adults, to bring their heads and hearts together and engage meaningfully together in community and in the world. Ritual is important to her, as is working with families and individuals in crisis, including during times of death. She lives in Colorado.

On the Spirit of June Jordan

The Ultimate Capacities of a School's Lifeforce

Jessica Wei Huang

I sat in room 335C in the rear of the rectangular building as part of the circle of adult educators. I glanced at the professor and felt—for the first time in months—my body starting to relax. Even though I was the principal of this small high school named after June Jordan, the fate of the next two hours were not in my hands. I looked around the room and into every person's face. These folks all had a stake in our school's community. I knew that I was just a part of this puzzle, a puzzle that had been badly shaken and broken in places. I hoped the pieces would start to come together to form a new picture—perhaps different than the one before, but just as beautiful and complete.

I had decided to do something unconventional this year; to host a college class, Poetry for the People, as the staff professional development for the entire fall semester. Lauren Muller was to be the professor and facilitator. She was June Jordan's teaching assistant when June taught the class at UC Berkeley, and was editor of *June Jordan's Poetry for the People: A Revolutionary Blueprint*. When a trusted colleague recommended that we spend time in our professional development studying June Jordan's work, I hesitated at first. What about all the other things we needed to get done to keep the school running? When I first started my school leadership journey, I read June's memoir, *Soldier: A Poet's Childhood*. I needed June Jordan's voice again, to show me how to be a compassionate soldier.

Just two years earlier, on October 18, 2016, there had been a shooting in the school parking lot. I remember hearing the "pop, pop, pop" and wondering, "Who is playing with firecrackers in the parking lot?" On my way outside, I dodged kids running inside, diving into classrooms. School had been dismissed a mere thirty seconds prior, after the closing of an assembly about the impact of oppressive words and horizontal violence. Now the community was in real physical danger.

After the school was locked down, I stood outside with a colleague to wait for the police. I tried to remember to breathe. Many staff and parents who had been in the parking lot had seen the intruders run into the park behind the school. The person shooting was not inside the building, but that did not keep my small frame from bending over and taking a moment to hyperventilate. I was a thirty-eight-year-old Asian American woman. Was I enough to protect and defend this community against the outside forces trying to harm it? When the police finally arrived, they were in full active-shooter gear with assault rifles drawn, and they were about to enter a school building full of people of color, young and not so young. I refused to open the front gate unless they put their guns down. For this, I would experience both criticism and acclaim for years to come.

From my first years working at June Jordan School for Equity, I felt a fierce loyalty to defend and protect the community. If I were to attempt to summarize the meaning of the school for me, it would be this: a school with the mission to empower working-class youth of color. We intended to pave the way for young people to be changemakers in the world. This school was a dream of many. Then the team of students, parents, and educators who started the school had to troubleshoot it into existence. It took us many years of collaborative dialogue, fighting with one another, the larger district that it was a part of, and the community it served. I have now worked in many types of schools around the world. We were not a perfect school—but we trained warrior-scholars of a caliber I have yet to see at other schools.

The young people at June Jordan School for Equity continue to inspire me. There have been published critiques of our school, and also many celebrations of the work we have accomplished. I lament that the community that is possible at June Jordan is beautiful and diabolical at the same time. Like a kaleidoscope, move it one way, and it looks in disarray;

move it another way, and you can see perfectly formed crystals sparkling in the sun. That is the work of schools. Dynamic, always changing. Folks that write about schools are always writing about a passing moment, a thing that once was, while the real school is moving, changing, and busy existing. A school is the people in the building—the students, staff, and community who drive the mission and vision forward in an amoeba-like growth, living, moving, and changing as it lives.

I soon came to realize that what happened that day in October really broke the adults. We had worked so hard to establish a safe and liberating community, an alternative haven from the oppressive structures of the world. In Sam Chaltain's piece about June Jordan School for Equity in April of 2016, just five months before the incident, I was quoted as saying, "We have real honest conversations here about the things that matter to us. But that's taken years to build."[1] It felt like what happened in ten seconds on October 18, 2016, had torn down what we took years to build. We had a clear direction, a teacher-pedagogy training program, a strong sense of identity and self. This incident rattled the sensitive balance that kept our kaleidoscope in its crystal form. I was crushed that I could not protect the school in that instance, resulting in physical and mental harm to everyone in the school building.

In *Revolutionary Mothering: Love on the Front Lines*, Alexis Pauline Gumbs states that "those of us who nurture the lives of those children who are not supposed to exist, who are not supposed to grow up, who are revolutionary in their very beings are doing some of the most subversive work in the world."[2] My body and my mind were suffering, but my spirit kept me moving and doing, seeking to help my community heal so we could continue to be strong guides for our young people. This is where I looked to our namesake June Jordan for her words and vision.

Back in the talking circle, the professor, Lauren Muller, was introducing the purpose of the class: to use June's poetry and writings as a jumping-off point to create our own writing, and to meet and discuss June's work with her closest friends and colleagues, her former students, and twenty-first-century scholars.

Drawing upon the strength of our community and the spirit of June Jordan to have honest conversations, we found a way for our community to return to our roots. Hosting this learning experience worked to build community and to heal together. This professional development was a way to recenter the school on the bigger picture of why we were all here together. It was the catalyst to activate the "lifeforce" of our school and to reenergize our love for our work.

> When we run on love, when we move and change and build and paint and sing and write and foster the maximal fulfillment of our own lives, as well as the maximal fulfillment of other's lives that look for us for help, for protection, or for usable clues to the positive excitement of just being alive, then we make manifest the creative spirit of the universe: a spirit existing within each of us and yet persisting infinitely greater than the ultimate capacities of any one of us.[3]

This impulse for "maximal fulfillment" fuels June Jordan School for Equity. In fact, before the school's first graduating class chose to name it after June Jordan in the spring of 2003, it was called "Small School for Equity." The mission was to establish a small high school in southeastern San Francisco that fused "Community," "Independent Thinkers," and "Social Justice" as its three pillars. At the time, the city of San Francisco had no small alternative programs. All students in the San Francisco Unified School District attended large comprehensive high schools, which did little to change the status quo for working-class students and families in San Francisco. June Jordan School for Equity offers a different kind of educational space for students: one set in the foundation of strong relationships, small class sizes, and alternate assessment methods. A community of teachers, students, parents, and organizers (the San Francisco Organizing Project) worked together for a study period of two years to do research about small schools—most of them existing on the East Coast in Boston and New York—and come up with a proposal for the school. It took a year to even get a meeting with the superintendent at the time, Arlene Ackerman. After building more support and getting more people power, the school board and the district agreed to the charter for the school written by the organizing group. The school first opened its doors in the fall of 2003, one year after June Jordan's death, in the basement of Burk Hall at San Francisco

State University. It was a year of big hopes, many challenges, and the start of a revolutionary way of thinking about the purpose of education. It was love that welcomed sixty new freshmen to the school.

All of us who collaborated to start this school did it out of a love for the community and a belief that all humans deserve better. As its current leader sixteen years later, I was tasked with the duty of bringing power with love to rectify the hurt that had assaulted our community and to get back to our foundational beliefs of education. As June reminds us, we have this responsibility as educators to tap back into our own lifeforce and creative spirit in order to do the work we came here to do, which is to educate young people.

I learned a lot in the Poetry for the People class—I read a lot more of June's work than I ever had. The class took place in the fall of 2018—just after a new anthology of her work, *We're On*, was released.

The reading of June Jordan's poetry soothed us. Her words were truthful and brave and song-like. Every Wednesday afternoon after I attended Lauren's class, I felt like I had sat in meditation for two hours. To read someone who wanted to tell the truth so poetically and beautifully was healing in itself.

And so we read and we wrote our own poems. It was both liberating and frightening. Below is a poem that I wrote and read, about my experience leading our school as a woman of color. It was inspired by one of June's most famous poems, "Poem About My Rights."

Standing at the Gates

Jessica Wei Huang

> My name is my own, my own, my own
> —*June Jordan, "Poem About My Rights"*

Who is in charge here? Can't be me!
wearing jeans
and boots
walkie-talkie walking around the corner

Smiles fade
into the hot sun that bakes the fall classrooms to
90-something degrees
presumptions escalate
burn

Blood boils
I watch my tone, my anger, my insistence
in a man it's powerful
in a woman it's aggressive
bitchy

Nice nails
until they aren't
pretty to look at but hurt

alone
drowning in the words of those around me who
need more this

need less that
need me to be here, there, everywhere

Come ahead here, and see the light
should I, could I, would I
ever be the leader I needed as a young
teacher training to be my better self

The judgment makes me ruminate about where
true North is
Is the truth in me? Or have I lost it to the storms
that have come to flood these drains
washing away the small pieces that have
stuck preventing more of me
a cleansing cloaked in sixty seconds of tragedy

I am determined to remain, here in this drain
to create another passage

Writing this piece took courage, and sharing the poem with the school community was frightening. But a part of me felt relieved too. My story was out there for people to hear. It wasn't mine alone to carry.

One of the many things I admire about June is her unbending belief in justice coupled with her passion for life. She told the truth. The truth about herself and the truth about the world. "When we foster the maximal fulfillment of our own lives . . . then we make manifest the creative spirit of the universe: a spirit existing within each of us."[1]

Besides activating our creative spirit, the class also interviewed many of the people who knew and worked with June or published her writings: Alegria Barclay, Xochi Candelaria, Ruth Forman, Alexis Pauline Gumbs, Elizabeth Riva Meyer, E. Ethelbert Miller, Kelly Elaine Navies, Becky Thompson, and Adrienne B. Torf. Grounding their remarks in June's own writings, they shared how June's work inspired them, how she dealt with conflict, who she believed in, and how she wrote, taught, and navigated the world around her.

What I learned from those who love June Jordan is that you can be angry and demanding about your politics, can fight for your own dignity and that of others, while still inviting everyone in. It wasn't about who was chosen to be a part of the group, but about the boundaries of that participation and who was ready and willing to share.

Our poems written in response to June's poems were passionate and personal and painful. One long-time educator shared her experience as a mother to her autistic son. Another educator shared his realizations about patriarchy and sexual violence. I left the meetings with a sense of gratitude. I was grateful that everyone had been there to experience this community. It cemented in me the idea that "people are ready when they are ready," a saying from community organizing that my mentor and friend Matt Alexander—cofounder and long-time principal of June Jordan School—would always repeat.

I am reminded to be my best when I read June Jordan's work and feel her presence, strength, and integrity. She teaches me that everything I need is already inside of me and that I can choose what to do with it. As a leader, she inspired people by communicating her integrity through her poetic writing. She knew how to draw her boundary and still keep the door open to invite people in. She reminds us that leading is not about controlling people. Leading is about our truth and leading others to find their truths. The more we struggle with finding our own vision and purpose, the more we lose people on our journey toward liberation.

Our fall 2018 staff professional development time was not perfect. It was a Poetry for the People class in all its glory. People complained and gave opinions about other things they could be doing, and consistent attendance was a struggle. One day, Lauren could feel the tension in the room; instead of dismissing it, she addressed it at the end by saying: "I can feel you all have different and difficult relationships with each other right now. Just know that this happened in the Poetry for the People classes that June taught, and it was a regular thing for people to have conflict with each other. Keep showing up and doing your best and just know that there's nothing wrong with you." How refreshing it was to hear those words.

Finally, Lauren Muller brought June's creative lifeforce to us. Through her strength and personal commitment to spreading and teaching June

Jordan's work throughout her career, she was a true gift to me and to our community at a time when we needed inspiration and grounding. Even as Lauren's health was deteriorating from the radiation and chemotherapy, she showed up every week, ready to facilitate. I am grateful for the dedication she had for our work and for June Jordan's legacy. It felt right that during this challenging time, I had June's words, through Lauren, to guide me back to myself. And so did the staff and therefore the students.

I left June Jordan School for Equity after that school year. It was time to listen to the small voice in my head that was saying louder and louder to work on healing myself.

Every day, students and staff members walk past a beautiful mural of June painted by art educator Anne Grajeda. During the one-year anniversary of the shooting, we stood in a circle in the parking lot while a dear friend and former June Jordan staff member, Cuca Holsen, led a Call to the Four Directions cleansing ceremony. As we walked around the parking lot, the smoke from the sage dissipating across the pavement, I knew there would be many more groups of staff and students who would walk across that parking lot, into the halls of June Jordan School for Equity. All would leave knowing more about themselves and who they were than when they first entered. A truly revolutionary place will do that to you: make you realize that in this life, the most important learning we do is for ourselves. Our healing together was unconventional, at times painful, but also beautiful and full of love. In the words of June, "Love is lifeforce."[2] The pieces would fall together again, in a way that truly revolutionary places do, at the hands of those working the land.

Jessica Wei Huang has more than twenty years of experience as a classroom teacher and school leader. She currently works as a leadership coach and workshop facilitator. From 2004 to 2010, she was a classroom teacher at June Jordan School for Equity; she served as codirector and then principal from 2012 to 2019. Jessica holds a bachelor of foreign service from Georgetown University and a master of education from Stanford University. She has worked in public schools in San Francisco as well as international schools in Taiwan and Singapore.

Stay All the Way with Reggie and Ranya

Reid Gómez

I begin every class I teach in the Navajo language.
Yá'át'ééh, Reid Gómez yinishye. 'Ádóone'é nishłínígíí 'éí Naahiłii Lucumí Congo. Tł'ízí łání 'éí bá shishchíín. Naakaiiłbáhí 'éí dashicheii nááná. Naakaii 'éí dashinálí. 'Ákót'éego 'éí 'asdzání nishłį́ San Francisco, California, déé naashá.

I worked for the Advocates for Indigenous California Language Survival (AICLS) for a short but life-altering moment. They advocate speaking in your own language first, then following through with English. This language revitalization technique places the learner first and keeps their community at the center. For adult learners this practice is powerful, especially in those moments where it is impossible to leave English behind.

I grew up believing my family spoke a backward, degenerate language only we could understand. We didn't even call it a type of English—Black English or Navlish. We called it Gómez. I am an adult learner of Navajo. Once, after an event in my hometown of San Francisco, another urban skin told me how powerful it was for him that I began everything in Diné Bizaad. My writing was in English; my first words in Navajo. He is a Mescalero, and he told me he wished he had that power. It clears the room and puts things right, like sage. I told him, I know.

> The Navajo language is your elder. Nizaad, Diné bizaad ayóo jooba'. (Your Navajo language is kind to you.) Diné bizaad binahjį' háá'iidááah (The Navajo language is therapy). Diné bizaad bee da'ahííníítą' dóó 'ayóó 'áda'ahíínii'níí dóó bee saad bee hka'ahóníníígíí 'ałch'į' háádeiidzih dóó bee chánah daniidlį́į dóó bee k'é da'ahidii'ní.

(Through the Navajo language we are able to claim one another, love one another, encourage one another, comfort one another, and relate to one another.)[1]

When we speak in our own language, our possibility space becomes a galaxy. In this galaxy we exist; we have a future. We let the ancestors know. I told him: he has that power too.

Language is the structure that holds the people together.

In my work—in English and in the classroom—I believe in and create an elaborate story structure. Often there is resistance to that structure (its vocabulary/lexicon and its grammar, ordering of ideas sometimes thought of as logic). Often the resistance to the structure that is present is so complete the reader denies the structure's existence. From the AICLS I have learned the importance of creating our own immersion experiences—as language learners and speakers. Creating spaces where we "leave English behind" only becomes labor-intensive and fantastical because we are already submitting to and forced to move through another immersion space that claims the neutrality of the standard. This standard is provided by a powerful enforcement: the grammar of colonialism.

Our Collective Need to Redefine the Problem

This essay tells the story of a syllabus for a class on the grammar of colonialism: language planning and policy. The writing is deeply contoured by pain. Language is contentious. I struggle with what can be said in English, and what can be said in written English, every day. I begin as a woman, as a writer, and as a teacher. I begin with June and her "Poem About My Rights." June's oeuvre is vast, but my possibility space began the moment I heard a recitation of this poem at a reading I was attending to hear my sister and June's student, Ruth Forman, read her work. The line "Wrong is not my name" changed me forever and for good. Whenever I am lost or in pain I return to this poem, to these lines, and to June's audacious commitment *to be* in print, in the classroom, and in the mouths of other Black people.

> I am very
> familiar with the problems because the problems
> turn out to be
> me
> . . . I have been the problem everyone seeks to
> eliminate by forced
> penetration with or without the evidence of slime and/
> but let this be unmistakable this poem
> is not consent I do not consent
> . . . *I am not wrong: Wrong is not my name*
> My name is my own my own my own
> and I can't tell you who the hell set things up like this
> but I can tell you that from now on my resistance
> my simple and daily and nightly self-determination
> may very well cost you your life[2]

This poem, about my rights, protects me from every corrective linguistic measure that attempts to destroy my soul. Many don't understand this pain; they are unfamiliar with its root—speaking and being corrected. I name this pain and identify this root; I am the writer and speaker grown from it. Jordan's poem identifies our collective need to redefine the problem. We are a collective, and *not only* an individual, an I/we of ancestors, descendants of slaves (racialized Black, or red), colonized, and survivors who survive (because they have to).

Leanne Betasamosake Simpson describes this pain in relationship to shame. There is no topic sentence for pain or the way we hold it in our body, mind, soul, lineage, and dreams. Simpson writes, "One of the mechanisms settler colonialism applies to destroy Indigenous systems of reciprocal recognition is shame."[3] Shame "is a powerful tool of settler colonialism because it implants the message in our bodies that we are wrong. . . . The primary message in [negative stereotypes] is *you are wrong*, not even *you've done something wrong*, but *you are wrong*."[4] I cannot read these words and not hear June's voice speaking loudly across the distance—your name is not wrong. They are using the same phrasing. The dead speaking to the living. This is story. This is language. This is our ancestor. Our voice and expression are assaulted—relentlessly—generations of our ancestors were also assaulted. The world tells us we are wrong, and this results in the burden of individual and collective shame. We carry the idea that we are wrong with us everywhere we go. This concept is embedded in every word we speak, even when we speak to ourselves.[5]

The classroom is a place where we speak to each other. I am responsible for our community and our community agreements. I have a language plan and make our language policy. I do this work—speaking, making plans and policy—fully immersed in my degraded status as a degraded speaker. Following June, I attempt to create a space where we can be and speak without subordinating ourselves or our ideas to another's standard (grammar). Navajo author Blackhorse Mitchell describes writing (in this space, in this way) as a place to dream as one pleases.[6] My desire is to create a world where we are not wrong. In this world we identify the problems we want to address in the entanglement of racism/colonization, and not in ourselves as subject to that entanglement.

I have the ability to confront power through the syllabus. This essay is a story about several syllabi: June's and mine. My class, the grammar of colonialism, began as "the language class" at Kalamazoo College. The first work in the class is to rethink what it means to do language work. We do this by looking at language from three perspectives: the storyteller (Leslie Marmon Silko), the linguist (Keith Basso), and the poet (June Jordan). My goal is to shift the student's focus away from racializing speakers and writing practices to the way we (can and do) think about language. I've written about the way we are colonized as linguistic subjects in other work. The syllabus for this class makes my pedagogy and epistemology about language explicit in the inextricable relationship of form and content.

Power and the Production of Knowledge

We begin with Jordan's essays "White English / Black English: The Politics of Translation (1972)" and "Nobody Mean More to Me Than You and the Future Life of Willie Jordan." The students' first thoughts after my introduction in Navajo are Jordan's thoughts in Black English.

We read the novel *His Own Where*, which Jordan describes writing in "White English / Black English," as a curricular alternative to the parallel texts given to American Indian children which we study through educational ethnography and applied linguistics. *His Own Where* provides an exemplar. In addition to epitomizing what the students hunger for, it exemplifies the colonial project that we study in depth in the first half of the course, that I am asking them to survive and critique with the tools of the storyteller and the poet. Jordan's essays together also tell the story of a syllabus, and a class's relationship to the materials they are assigned and the language they will be recognized (heard and evaluated) and allowed to respond in (in oral and written form). When I am forced to define what we study, I often say we study power and the production of knowledge—namely, to use Jordan's words, the way language can "control and sentence to poverty anyone—because he or she is different and proud and honest in his or her difference and his or her pride."[7]

Jordan's essay "White English / Black English: The Politics of Translation" (1972) reinforces the point: "Language is political."[8] As Jordan explains: "The powerful don't play; they mean to keep the power, and those who are the powerless (you and me) better shape up—mimic/ape/suck—in the very image of the powerful, or the powerful will destroy you—you and our children."[9] And though the "two languages," Black English and White English, "are both communication systems with regularities, exceptions, and values governing their word designs [and] . . . equally liable to poor, good, better, and creative use . . . they are both accessible to critical criteria such as clarity, force, message, tone, and imagination."[10] Why is the failure to understand, to be fluent and easy with Black English, registered as a failure of structure, clarity, and grammar in "White" English?

Jordan answers: "The problem is we are saying language, but really dealing with power."[11] Jordan points out the way speakers are forced to "accept the terms of the oppressor, or perish: that is the irreducible, horrifying truth of the politics of language."[12] She frames the acceptance of another's terms, particularly "our enemy's terms," as a strategic failure. bell hooks's essay about language as a place of struggle, among others, is clear about the fact that what we do with English is unsettled. What I want to emphasize most is Jordan's claim that accepting another's terms is "a threat to mental health, integrity of person, and persistence as a people of our own choosing."[13] Protection from illness, pain, and shame is where and why I began with her refutation of the problem. We are told the problem resides in our very selves; my class, Jordan's essays, we speakers, readers, and writers have to—can—speak together. Our name is not wrong; we are not the problem.

If we accept, as I do, that "language is power, then as speakers, and language planning and policy makers, via the syllabus, we must think of our children,"[14] Jordan writes, "And, as for our children: let us make sure that the whole world will welcome and applaud and promote the words they bring into reality; in the struggle to reach each other, there can be no right or wrong words for our longing and our needs; there can only be the names that we trust and we try."[15] At this point in Jordan's essay she looks at the so-called "standard curriculum" and the language of that curriculum, namely the language of Shakespeare's *Romeo and Juliet*. What makes that language acceptable when the language of *His Own Where* is not? Jordan answers, "The powers that control the language that controls the process of translation have decided that *Romeo and Juliet* is *necessary*, nay, *indispensable*, to passage through compulsory, public school education."[16] Since I am one of the powers that control the language of the classroom, and I make our translation policy, I can decide that certain languages are necessary and indispensable. I can declare and support a future where our language and its speakers exist; even if that future is only ten weeks. I want to be clear every moment I can. The future centers our (Black Red) people and our (Black Red) English.

The title "Nobody Mean More to Me Than You and the Future Life of Willie Jordan" refers to a Black English aphorism crafted by Monica Morris, then a junior at SUNY, Stony Brook, in 1984. This essay tells the story of another syllabus. Jordan explains, "This story begins two years ago. I was teaching a new course, 'In Search of the Invisible Black Woman.'"[17] In this large class, an equal share of male and female Black students, and an additional five or six white students, "enthusiastically" discussed nineteenth-century historical narratives before moving on to literature by and about Black women from the twentieth century. When they read *The Color Purple*, they didn't like it. Before Walker they were enthusiastic and vocal; the day after Walker they were quiet. They didn't like her language. Jordan writes: "Black rejection was aimed at the one irreducibly Black element of Walker's work: the language."[18]

Jordan responded to her students' rejection of the very English they spoke with love. Her love for Black people, Black bodies, and Black expressions went straight into her pedagogy and her curriculum. Together they began to translate Walker's book into Standard English, and this led to the students' desire for Jordan to teach them how to read and write their own language. They came up with four rules and nineteen further guidelines. And, through that process of careful study and loving attention, "Black English no longer limited the students, in any way."[19] But Jordan had lost one student: Willie Jordan. She'd met Willie Jordan "in between 'In Search of the Invisible Black Woman' and 'The Art of Black English.'"[20] In addition to the two formal classes, they were engaged in an independent study, which he initiated, of South Africa. He was deeply intelligent, formal, "compulsively punctual, and always thoroughly prepared with neat typed compositions, [but] he had disappeared."[21] He was absent, without a note, a phone call, or an explanation.

Jordan is eloquent, clear, and honest: "There are few 'issues' as endemic to Black life as police violence."[22] Willie Jordan's brother had been murdered by the Brooklyn police. His brother, Reggie Jordan, was unarmed, twenty-five years old. Here I quote Willie Jordan's final essay, quoted in Jordan's piece dedicated to his, Willie Jordan's, future life:

> Reggie was shot eight times from point-blank range. The Doctor who performed the autopsy told me himself that two bullets entered the side of my brother's head, four bullets were sprayed into his back, and two bullets struck him in the back of his legs. It is obvious that unnecessary force was used by the police and that it is extremely difficult to shoot someone in his back when he is attacking or approaching you.[23]

We are colonized as linguistic subjects. As criminals or fugitives, Black and Indigenous bodies go missing and are murdered—not because we have done something, but because we are wrong. How do we speak to the violence of our lives if we are not allowed a language to speak with? If our speech is not even recognized as a language?

Willie's classmates, the students in The Art of Black English, decided to issue a statement in response to Reggie's murder. What language should they speak with? Standard or Black English? Jordan describes the long and painful deliberative process. She writes: "Now we had to make more tactical decisions."[24] In this moment the two essays my students read come together. We return to the first few lines of the "Nobody Mean More to Me" piece, and consider, "either we hide our original word habits, or we completely surrender our own voice."[25] And, we remember the final lines of the 1972/1981 piece "White English / Black English: The Politics of Translation," where Jordan declares, "No one has the right to control and sentence to poverty anyone—because he or she is different and proud and honest in his or her difference and his or her pride."[26] The death of Reggie Jordan takes its place in the long litany of the ancestors, and what Christina Sharpe characterizes as wake work: "and we join the wake with work in order that we might make the wake and *wake work* our analytic, we might continue to imagine new ways to live in the wake of slavery, in slavery's afterlives, to survive (and more) the afterlife of property."[27]

At this point in this essay, in the reading of Jordan's work, and in my class, we have entered the realm of formally addressing the ancestors in terms of their lives, and in the way those lives do, and do not, formally matter.

Black Lives Matter

I critique linear progress narratives aggressively, yet I cannot refute the poetic and metaphysical truth of Jordan's essay in my class. We share a reality within the when and where of Black and Indigenous lives (and *the way they matter*). My students have read *His Own Where* in the context of boarding school education. They learn the Safety Zone Theory and how it applies to Native America from 1492–2012—one year before the murder of Trayvon Martin. They are required to write policy papers and an op-ed piece about language. I teach Jordan's essays to students impatient to apply the knowledge we produce to their lives, while they actively face the very same lives, and life chances, faced by Jordan's students roughly thirty years later. Thirty years is a lifetime for many individuals, and a lifetime for all of my students—their own lifetime. Reggie Jordan was murdered in June's students' lifetime; Trayvon Martin was murdered in my students' lifetime.

In 2016, the award for the best paper published in *Language* (the flagship journal of the Linguistic Society of America) was "Language and Linguistics on Trial: Hearing Rachel Jeantel (and Other Vernacular Speakers) in the Courtroom and Beyond." Rickford and King write, "The central role of the Zimmerman trial in the birth of the influential #BlackLivesMatter movement and the central role of African American Vernacular English (AAVE) in the ignoring of Jeantel's testimony in that trial remind us of the central importance of language in the lives of individuals and societies."[28] A few key facts: "Black lives matter" was coined by one woman (Alicia Garza), reacting on Facebook to the systemic racism she saw in Trayvon's killing and Zimmerman's acquittal.[29] "Despite her centrality to the case, 'no one mentioned Jeantel in [sixteen-plus-hour] jury deliberations. Her testimony [Rickford and King analyze almost fifteen hours of trial-related recordings of Jeantel's language] played no role whatsoever in their decision."[30] Why? Jeantel speaks three to four languages—Haitian Kweyol, Dominican Spanish, AAVE, and Standard English—yet her language was characterized as "inarticulate, incoherent, and not credible." For some the sounds she made didn't even qualify a language, one person declaring, "she speaks Haitian hood rat."[31] Rickford and King spend roughly fifteen pages arguing the case of AAVE and confirming Jeantel as a speaker of said language. At this point in the essay, they point out the irony of Toni Morrison's 1975 talk about race as a distraction in American thought and culture, and her statement "Somebody says you have no language, so you spend twenty years proving that you do."[32] Rickford and King conclude that Jeantell was not believed for three reasons: "(i) dialect difference and unfamiliarity; (ii) Jeantel's underbite and voice quality; and (iii) attitudes, including dialect bias and institutionalized racism/prejudgment."[33]

Rickford and King's findings take me back to shame and blame. Language, the speaker, and her body provide two-thirds of the attribution of fault: Black English and the Black English speaker two-thirds wrong. They write, "The 'blame' for the jurors' and public's poor assessment of Jeantel's intelligibility and credibility was placed primarily on production properties of the speaker."[34] The perception that Jeantel, her very self, is wrong was so strong that even in several post-trial stories, specifically framed to vindicate her and improve her reputation, she is still framed as the problem, even when the segment celebrates her improvement. On Piers Morgan's show, Jeantel identifies her underbite as the problem, going so far to say that she needs her mouth (and clarifies to Morgan, her bones, not her teeth) to undergo a surgery that will take a year to heal.[35] If this is not an explicit attack on her body, I do not know what it is. In a segment introduced by George Stephanopoulos, one year later, with the words "she has turned her life around, thanks to hard work and some good Samaritans," Matt Gutman of *Sunday Spotlight* celebrates the transformation of Jeantel, stating that she was "outed as illiterate on national TV . . . bringing her rough dialect" into the courtroom, where she was "argumentative" and "defiant."[36]

Jeantel's so-called illiteracy and public outing (shaming) are highly relevant for my class. One of the ways we share power is my explicit discussion of my experiences as a colonized speaker and writer. One student and I would regularly lapse into argument. Ranya is from the Bronx. I am from Potrero Hill, San Francisco. Together we are Dominican, Congolese, Navajo, and Mexican hood rats: No one could understand us. There were many times these arguments led us astray, or might have seemed better attended to in the privacy of office hours or in between walks from this building to that one, but it was essential they happen in the context of the class—for students to see that we understood each other, not in terms of a shared feeling or conceptual approach, but in the language we spoke as Afro-Latina-Indigenous urban women. This language, and therefore we as speakers of this language, are disparaged. To some, student and colleague, it was gibberish—and here we were in heated debate about the Bronx, about police violence, and about what it means to be intelligent and not "stupid." At the end of one of these arguments, in full view of the class, Ranya asked: You mean I am not stupid?

Nobody mean more to me than you, Ranya Perez.

Where Africa Ends and America Begins

Teresa McCarty's theory of the safety zone comes into play at this moment in the class and in time. McCarty hypothesizes "a physical, social, psychological and pedagogical space in which federal officials and other colonizing agents, through educational policies and practices, have deliberately systematically sought to distinguish 'safe' from 'dangerous' Indigenous beliefs and practices."[37] What allows Jack in the Box to release its 2013 Super Bowl commercial, "Hot Mess," set to Pat Benatar's song "Heartbreaker," in the total absence of feminist rock or Black culture? Who decides when we have ceased to be a threat? Can we test the waters by listening to not only what is being said about us, but the terms they use to discuss us? What does it mean to face the aggressive silence, silencing, about the Murdered and Missing Indigenous Women, while we surveil and detain Indigenous youth making their way north, within the hemisphere?

Leslie Marmon Silko makes the point, in *Almanac of the Dead*, that it is impossible to know where Africa ends and America begins.[38] The ways we continue to be colonized through language (planning and policy) are present in June's class, and again in mine. We are talking about language, politics, and policies, but we are ultimately talking about the death of Black and Indigenous speakers. Questions of language, when thought through colonization, force us to examine the racial vocabulary and logic we've grown accustomed to thinking in. I have taught this class with Dominican, Shona, Odawa, Navajo, Lakota, Mixtec, Igbo, Zapotec, and Black English speakers. I've taught this class to descendants of slaves (plantation slaves, and mining slaves of the southern hemisphere, aka Latinos). Every time we find that Achebe, Ngũgĩ, hooks,

Jordan, and McCarty are having the same conversation—it becomes clear, it is difficult to tell where African ends and American begins. This is what I think in terms of the entanglement of racism and colonization.

In their paper Rickford and King present research that "demonstrates that speech perception and evaluation are significantly influenced by LISTENERS' attitudes, often by biases from factors like race, ethnicity, geography, and social status."[39] We are taught to perform, and affirmed for, such "linguistic profiling." I join Rickford and King in asking and believing that we can "make a difference in the world," particularly in the field of education, particularly in the construction of our syllabi (in the readings we select, in the languages we allow and affirm in the classroom, orally and in writing).[40] Jeantel and her story may seem distant from me and my students; I assure you she is not. I gave another version of this essay at a panel sponsored by the Committee on the Literatures of People of Color in the United States and Canada, titled "Black Literature Matters." After that presentation I returned to Kalamazoo College to teach the "language class" this story (and essay) is about. When I returned to class I began in Navajo and Black English, and I let Diana Ross give us the visual, tonal, and formal language to establish the metaphysical-theoretical agreement that we build our class on love, reminding my students that "this is my house, and I live here."

Every one of my classes has a theme song. I selected "It's My House" by Diana Ross for a set of woven reasons: We learn near Detroit, to tell the story of the concert at Central Park (the video I use as our theme video), and because language loss begins in the house. Our language revitalization needs to begin at home too. Whenever we are lost, we return to the theme: This is my house, and I live here. This house is built for love. See my name, I put it there. Gotta follow the rules to get me. We take responsibility for our language homes and what goes on inside them—because this is a poem about our rights. We stand on June's shoulders and continue the work Buddy begins in *His Own Where*, and we build this house together, with language.

The following week I was scheduled to participate in the collective leadership of a workshop on language diversity (and, in my mind, language rights). As I attempted this work, I remained deeply aware that Jordan's students chose to make their statement in response to Reggie Jordan's murder in Black English, aware that their "decision in favor of Black English had doomed [their] writings, even as the distinctive reality of [their] Black lives always has doomed our efforts to 'be who we been' in this country."[41] All of my work and writing are lifted by their language choice and rationale: "The students voted, unanimously, to preface their individual messages with a paragraph composed in the language of Reggie Jordan. 'At least we don't give up nothing else. At least we stick to the truth: Be who we been. And stay all the way with Reggie.'"[42]

June's students wrote:

YOU COPS!

WE THE BROTHER AND SISTER OF WILLIE JORDAN, A FELLOW STONY BROOK STUDENT WHO THE BROTHER OF THE DEAD REGGIE JORDAN. REGGIE, LIKE MANY BROTHER AND SISTER, HE A VICTIM OF BRUTAL RACIST POLICE, OCTOBER 25, 1984. US APPALL, FED UP, BECAUSE THAT ANOTHER SENSELESS DEATH WHAT OCCUR IN OUR COMMUNITY. THIS WHAT WE FEEL, THIS, FROM OUR HEART, FOR WE AIN'T STAYING SILENT NO MORE.[43]

My work on language diversity (and, in my mind, language rights) turned into a year and half of soul-destroying pain shaped by racism and classism taking the form of active and passive resistance. I could say what I wanted to say, as long as it was what others wanted to hear, in the terms they were accustomed to hearing. One of the major obstacles was that we were saying language, but I was talking politics. My language (politics) violated some fundamental agreement we had been assumed to have made. That agreement kept the students on one side, and us (the educated/educator) on the other. I was lost—on the wrong side. I turned to my sister Ruth Forman to pull me out. Ruth sent me back to June. And, as the ancestors do, June pulled me all the way out. Her students continue the work of pulling in this essay, in June's essay, and in these relations we make working in language together. In a refusal to speak to this in any other terms than my own, knowing I too need to stay all the way with Reggie, and Ranya, I resigned my leadership and participation in the language-diversity work on the campus.

Reid Gómez: Writer, dancer, and percussionist. Congo; Mexican; Diné. Reid is from San Francisco, California, and attended the University of California, Berkeley, from 1986 to 1990, and again from 1992 to 1999. She wrote with Ruth Forman and calls her sister. Assistant professor, gender and women's studies, University of Arizona. Collective author of *Say, Listen: Writing as Care* by the Black|Indigenous 100s Collective (np:, 2024) and *The Web of Differing Versions: Where Africa Ends and America Begins* (forthcoming, University of Minnesota Press, 2026).

"I choose / anything / anyone / I may lose"

June Jordan, Faith, and Holy Risk

Dani Gabriel

June Jordan absolutely rearranged my life with poetry that was electrified and urgent. She wrote "Argument with the Buddha" shortly before I became her student, and it embodies everything that makes her work so critical to me: It is a real hard look at faith, and risk, and, of course, love. For me, then, grappling with systems of oppression and identity, this poetry was the key and the way through. For all of us now, grappling with a devastating pandemic on top of systems of oppression and questions of identity, this poetry might in fact be a way through.

June was very well versed in world religions. I still have my giant copy of Huston Smith's *World Religions* from her poetry class. To study religion in the context of poetry was an opportunity I didn't fully appreciate at the time. It seemed logical to study these things together. Only many years later, when I pursued religious training, did I come to realize what a privilege it was, and how I had had the opportunity to learn some of the deepest truths of the world's faith traditions through a medium that illuminates them like no other can. This is the context for June's argument: she's arguing with her friend the Buddha, someone she knows well and appreciates deeply.

She agrees with the Buddha about a lot of points around suffering, but says, "We disagree / about desire."[1] This poem makes desire into a holy thing. Desire is about connection, and it becomes sacred. "I choose / anything / anyone / I may lose," June writes, knowing that the "may" is actually "will," and that we are all rapidly losing, right now in the present tense.²

We are all experiencing loss. The loss of dear ones, the loss of jobs, the loss of any sense of security we might have been holding onto. And here's June, choosing anything or anyone she might lose. Daring to love in the face of danger. Acknowledging the realness of the choice and the risk, and being bold enough to do it anyway. In a situation where your people are being brutally oppressed, do you give in and let go of the good people around you? No. In a situation where all is uncertain, do you give up love? For June, the answer is no. Or maybe, hell no. You choose the dangerous path, the one of love.

In this poem, as in all of June's work, it's not a Hallmark-card kind of love. June never shied away from controversy or hard things. There's no neat ending, there's no easy landing. In fact, in the end there is the unknown. She writes "and after that // nothing / for sure."³ And still this love persists. This love, this choice, is about getting down into suffering with others. It's the kind of empathy and solidarity that illuminates and heals. I find this over and over in June's writing, and I experienced it as her student.

One day after class June offered to help me with a poem. I was not catching on to the rhythmic aspect of poetry very quickly. I had a good handle on content and form, but my words just weren't flowing. June had me look at the words and how they were working together and helped me get the poem to move. This was challenging for me both because I kind of didn't get it, but also because the poem was about a real trauma I had experienced. We made some progress. But then she just stopped, and looked at me, and shook her head. She acknowledged the horror of what I was writing about in a way that was direct, was compassionate, and kicked off a healing process that took many years. This process was interwoven with poetry throughout, and would not have been possible without June's willingness to get in it with me.

So today when I have to make choices, in the middle of a killer pandemic that has swept the world, this guides me. As I face my fears of losing family and friends, I offer pastoral care to members of our local homeless community as well as a church community. In my ministry

I seek to acknowledge others' suffering and to be present to it, and to them. "I choose and cherish / all that will perish."[4] I choose to be present in this time and place, and to all it brings. I am working on being unafraid to be present to suffering, and I choose, in the midst of it, to love.

In "Argument with the Buddha" June writes, "I breathe / head to head / with suffering."[5] This, for me as a Christian minister, is where it's at. This is where I first encountered the very real, slightly dangerous character named Jesus: going head to head with suffering. My experience of the Gospel and of Jesus himself centers in his getting into the suffering with us, with love, with humor, and sometimes with rage. What June does with this poem, in many ways, is lift up a radical theology that could coexist with a Christian message about the One who is incarnate, present, all in with us in our suffering.

Jesus wept. Jesus raged, and was disappointed, and was confused, and was overwhelmed. Jesus experienced suffering and death like all of us, and still Jesus loved. Jesus was constantly choosing the hard path, the risk, the certain end of loving his friends. He knew what he was getting into, and he chose it. For me, however, I am always mindful of the resurrection. The Christian story has a certainty to it. This poem is minus the promise of resurrection, however. What I celebrate as an ultimate rebirth we will all experience, this poem leaves open. And still, in the unknowing, the poet chooses love. It's still worth it. We're still worth it.

And who are we, when we go head to head with suffering? When we get in it with others? Maybe the dust of divinity gets on us too. When we take the risk to love that which we may lose, we are participating in an act of faith that is bigger than we are. It's bigger than this time and place, bigger than this pandemic, bigger than the systems of oppression that threaten to grind us down and erase us. When we engage, when we "renounce renunciation," we are claiming our lives and our possibilities.[6] We risk losing it all to proclaim the value of love and the worth of each other. I, for one, am all in.

Dani Gabriel is a queer/genderfluid poet and writer. Dani has four full-length poetry collections, including *Low Rent Prophet* (Nomadic Press, 2021; distributed by Black Lawrence Press) and *Love Poems in the Apocalypse* (Main Street Rag Publishing Company, 2022). Dani received an MFA from Mills College. They were the poet laureate of El Cerrito, California, from 2018 to 2020. You can find out more about their work at www.allthepossible.com.

Between the Knuckles of My Own Two Hands

Learning from June Jordan

Sriram Shamasunder

2001 and 2002, the last years of June Jordan's life, were my first years in medical school. I had been in Poetry for the People, the course June conceived of and taught at UC Berkeley. During my final undergraduate years after taking the course, I was a teaching assistant, running one of the small groups of about fifteen students.

I am a child of Indian immigrants and, like many, was a premedical student. I meandered into Poetry for the People to fill a humanities requirement. A kid with shaky confidence, I had my head down early in undergrad, taking science classes. I stayed in Poetry for the People for two years after I fulfilled the requirement less because I thought I was a poet but more because the class made me feel like I might have something to say. I liked that as a young person, the class aimed to have me craft something that might matter to someone. June was our professor, both tender and fierce, but mostly someone I admired at a distance.

This changed in my last few weeks at UC Berkeley before medical school, when we studied Arab and Arab American poetry. A disagreement between Jewish students defending Zionism and those supporting Palestinian liberation grew from a murmur to a rumble throughout the semester. In one of our last classes of the semester, a teaching assistant (in front of a class of 250–300) publicly accused June of failing to stand up on behalf of Palestinian people. June didn't show up for class next week, without a word.

On the weekend, I went by her house in the morning. We all knew she had breast cancer. We knew she was struggling with it, but not the extent. She was surprised to see me, but she let me in her house in North Berkeley. I stepped through her front door. The sun lit up the kitchen and made specks of dust visible until I tried to bring them into my palm. About twenty bottles of medications were laid out on the kitchen counter, to treat cancer, and fight nausea and pain.

We sat at her kitchen table. I tried to find the words to encourage her to come back to class. I stumbled as I tried to convey that the whole class knew her commitment to the Palestinian struggle. June remained unmoved. She was worn. The endless stream of medical appointments and chemotherapy and the spread of medications on her countertop had blurred into questions about legacy, and impact.

She began to talk. June shared that the entirety of her career had been brought to a halt by the political stance she took in the paper *The Village Voice* in 1982, when she wrote "Apologies to All the People of Lebanon" about the Israeli military massacre in the refugee camps in Sabra and Shatila. That same year she wrote the poem "Moving Towards Home," with those iconic words that pushed so many of us to extend beyond our birth demographic to make common cause with the most vulnerable, the most persecuted:

> I was born a Black woman
> and now
> I am become a Palestinian[1]

In the eighties, her writing life and career as an author took a beating for her defense of Palestinians. She paid significantly for taking that stand. In some ways she received the backlash we witnessed Congresswoman Omar endure when she was labeled anti-Semitic in 2023. Except June at that time didn't have a social media platform to fight back. Major publications just ceased to publish her work. If you look at June's bibliography, there is a significant gap between the mid-eighties and the mid-nineties. Publishers refused to work with her. This may in part be the reason she is not as well read as her friends and contemporaries such as Alice Walker and Toni Morrison.

Her willingness to risk stature for solidarity was questioned by a young woman from a younger generation who seemed to be unaware of her personal sacrifice. All of it was hard to stomach.

That afternoon, as June got up and moved about her house, cleaning up and doing some chores, we continued to talk. I played with her beautiful black puppy, and he climbed on my Indian kurta shirt. Muddy paw prints marked all over the white kurta.

I had a white T-shirt under that shirt, so she asked me to give her the paw-stained kurta top so she could clean it. The stain didn't come out immediately. She insisted she keep the kurta, clean it, and bring it back to me at our next class. That all made me hopeful that she would return to class.

The next week she returned. She had a poem and my kurta top. She read the poem to the class: "It's Hard to Keep a Clean Shirt Clean." The central metaphor grappled with a commitment to certain values, and visions, and inevitably having the original ideal sullied by the messiness of life. To be in the world, rather than an observer, required a pact with the not-perfect, the profound wedded to the practical. And when we clean ourselves off and get up, none of us are the same, or can claim purity.

Soon after June wrote that poem, I moved away to New York for medical school. We somehow ended up talking a couple times a week across coasts. June navigated the world of oncologists and chemotherapy and MRI scans. I had started slowly wading into that world. It was bewildering to both of us. During our conversations, she recounted her life. I asked questions and she expanded, seemingly grateful to reflect.

Those conversations included June, as a young woman, sitting next to Malcolm X in Harlem. She recalled Malcolm X schooling her on how to convey a message. When a reporter finished questioning Malcolm X, he would later turn and ask June what was asked and when, and how he had responded, in order to guide the conversation down a path that would best serve his message.

She spoke about her friendship with Fannie Lou Hamer, the great civil rights leader who put her body on the line to register black folks to vote throughout the South. June at the time had a deep aversion to all white people. A hatred even. Period. Fannie Lou Hamer said to June, "Ain't no such a thing as I can hate anybody and hope to see God's face."[2] In our conversations, June said that shifted her. June was struck by the way Fannie Lou Hamer could face vicious threats and murderous hate and return love—first and foremost, for her own salvation.

She recounted her experience with Ralph Ellison when she was in her twenties. Ellison had become disenchanted with the power of words to change any one life and publicly taunted a group of luminary poets, including T. S. Eliot, that their life of words did not make one iota of difference in the context of the violence of the mid-twentieth century. June didn't have the words to say at the time that she wrote for victims to redeem possibility in their lives rather than for any perpetrator of violence or oppression. Only later did I find that experience recounted in the piece "Of Those So Close Beside Me, Which Are You?" in her book of essays *Technical Difficulties: African-American Notes on the State of the Union*.

Each conversation unveiled a different time of her life, and the arc of purpose and love that lives at the center of a life worth living. We also spoke of my life, my recent breakup with a woman from Berkeley, June's love for tennis. What struck me was the quality of her listening, her range to be loving or indignant or vulnerable.

As June got sicker, the conversations spread out and became less frequent, until she passed as I entered my second year of medical school. Now when I reflect on that year of conversations, it was some combination of revealing a committed life and passing a torch that June showed me. She did that for so many of her students. We look to our elders to demonstrate another way of being in this broken world. Another way of extending our circle of commitment to the person in front of us, or Palestinian people. *And and Both*. June gave us that.

Now nearly fifteen years after medical school, I have started and run an organization, the HEAL Initiative, that trains and transforms frontline health workers from nine countries around the world, including Indigenous communities in the United States. We have worked in Haiti after the earthquake in 2010, and in Liberia during Ebola in 2014. Mostly we work on the nonglamorous work of building the capacity of local health professionals to serve their communities. It is an international solidarity. We get asked from time to time why we work internationally when there is so much need in the United States. There is no *the United States* or *abroad*. We answer, we do *both*. June taught us that.

Those quiet conversations with June so many years ago from New York to Berkeley in the last year of her life have very much shaped my own. I had a daughter four years ago. We gave her the middle name June. It's a nontraditional name for a little Indian girl. But it reminds me consistently of living life with enough personal risk to grow the circle of whom we might stand up for, and bringing the next generation (and the next) into that commitment.

Sriram Shamasunder is a professor of medicine at University of California, San Francisco. He has worked as a doctor in Oakland, Navajo Nation, Liberia, Haiti, Burundi, and rural India. Sri is the director of the HEAL Initiative, a health workforce program in Navajo Nation and nine countries around the world. He was a Fulbright-Nehru scholar to India and received the UCSF Chancellor's Award for Public Service in 2023. He is a published poet and former student of June Jordan.

PART THREE

The Awesome, Difficult Work of Love

A Place of Rage

A Conversation

Angela Y. Davis, Pratibha Parmar, and Leigh Raiford

This conversation, which opened the 2021–2022 Critical Conversation Series "Catching Up with June: Celebrating the Life and Legacy of June Jordan," was sponsored by the African American Studies Department at the University of California, Berkeley. Professor Leigh Raiford interviewed Angela Y. Davis and Pratibha Parmar, both of whom worked closely with and were friends with June Jordan since the 1980s. The following, edited by Becky Thompson, is a condensed version of this conversation.

Leigh Raiford: June Jordan, who was born 1936 in Harlem, New York, and joined the ancestors in 2002 in Berkeley, California, authored more than twenty volumes of poems, essays, libretti, art catalogs, and works for children. In the breadth of her commitments, Jordan asserted that freedom cannot be qualified. She called us in to stand together against all manner of terror and injustice. She was an innovative teacher always attuned to the whole being of her students. From 1988 to her passing in 2002, June Jordan was a member of the African American Studies Department at UC Berkeley, where she created the long-running Poetry for the People program.

Our conversation is a celebration of June Jordan and an opportunity to learn together the depth of her radical commitments, the incisiveness of her pen, and the expansiveness of her vision for liberation. Gathering is at once grounding and generative, a reminder of the Black feminist foundations of our work at UC Berkeley, and an opportunity to renew our commitment to Black studies as life studies. We begin with the film *A Place of Rage*, directed by Pratibha Parmar, as we are celebrating thirty years since its release. *A Place of Rage* offers a fierce, trenchant assessment of the social movements of the 1960s from the vantage point of the 1990s culture wars. The film features interviews with three of the most influential Black feminist intellectuals of our time, Angela Davis, Alice Walker, and June Jordan. Along with Third World feminist filmmaker and our colleague at UC Berkeley Trinh Minh-ha, Davis, Walker, and Jordan highlight the centrality of Black women's labor and the necessity of intersectional movements for the liberation of all people past, present, and future.

This film stands as one of the few film opportunities we have to hear Jordan in her own words, and to hear her laughter. *A Place of Rage* is also a portrait of solidarity, that agreement of feeling or action of mutual support within a group from which friendship might bloom. I'm thrilled to be in conversation with two of June Jordan's comrades, friends, familiars: globally recognized filmmaker and human rights activist Pratibha Parmar, the director of *A Place of Rage*, and activist and scholar Angela Davis, featured participant in the film.

I want to start by asking how you both came to know June and her work.

Pratibha Parmar: I came to know June first through her writing, particularly her book *Civil Wars*, which was given to me as a birthday gift by Paul Gilroy when we were postgraduate students at Birmingham University. I'd never heard of June Jordan before. When I read *Civil Wars*, I was blown away by the complex ways in which she had addressed thoughts that I'd had but had limited language to be able to express. I was also drawn to her inquiry into crucial political moments, both seemingly small scale and much more global, and how she did that through deeply personal lens. It was compelling reading: how a poet addresses the political; how a poet addresses the social; what kind of language a poet uses to describe and explore social justice and change. With that book, I entered into a political kinship with June.

Many years later, in 1987, I had an opportunity to meet her when she came to London to do a poetry tour. I had just returned from India, where I had been with my mother, and June was in town only for a day. A feminist magazine, *Spare Rib*, asked if I would interview her at her hotel. She was quite held back, as June could be. When I began to talk to her about her work, particularly the essay that she had written about her collaboration with Buckminster Fuller, the futurist architect, suddenly the whole conversation opened up. Shaheen, my partner, is an architect, and at the time she was working with a group of Black women in London to envision a Black women's community center. So these discussions about justice and environment and space were quite pertinent in my life. June had addressed these in the most brilliant of ways in her visionary project Harlem Skyrise. That initial mutual interest bonded us as we began tracing in our conversation genealogies of oppressions and interconnectedness on a global scale. I needed that connection at that time—to speak with someone who offered a container for related ideas I was exploring. Then, over the decades, our friendship and family relationship grew.

Angela Davis: I knew about June Jordan, had read and taught her work, and was influenced by her long before we actually met, long before we became friends. We had many friends in common, but strangely, we had never seen each other face-to-face. There's a photograph that is now circulating widely on the internet which June always had in her house. That photograph was a picture of the Black women's writing group in New York that she was a part of. Toni Morrison is in the photo, and Ntozake Shange, Alice Walker, Louise Meriweather, Vertamae Smart-Grosvenor, Nana Maynard, Audrey Edwards, and June Jordan. I didn't know Audrey Edwards, but I knew every other member of that group with the exception of June. Toni Morrison, who was my editor and became my very close friend, told me over and over again, Angela, you just have to meet June. And you know, virtually everyone could not believe that we'd never met.

When we finally met, it was because June was considering moving to the Bay Area when UC Berkeley was about to hire her. Toni gave her my phone number. I'll never forget the first time I spoke with her. If you knew June, you'll remember her very distinctive voice. It was both very powerful and, at the same time, somewhat childlike. And so my first reaction when I answered the phone was: Who is this child calling me? Who is this child asking to speak to me? But in any event, she told me she was scheduled to give a job talk for African American Studies. She invited me to attend. I attended, met her for the first time, and then our friendship developed from there. This was in the 1980s. During that period, Black women writers were our representatives, they were speaking us. In many ways they were our political spokespersons. And June was one of that group of Black women writers whose visions helped to shape the movement to come.

LR: I was thinking about the group the Sisterhood, which then became the West Coast outgrowth of the writers' group. It served as an interface between the academy and public media, with Black women writers at the center. In talking about your early connections with June, might you two talk about the poems that June dedicated to you—"In Paris" and "Solidarity"—and how those poems came to be? Could you speak some about the evening in Paris when it was raining and you couldn't catch a taxi (which June also wrote about more in her essay "Waiting for a Taxi")? That was when you met. Is that right?

PP: That was when we met, Angela, in Paris.

AD: I thought we had met before. I thought we had met in London? Did we?

PP: Yes, yes, of course, you are right—we had met before, when a group of us came to visit you in a hotel in London. Yes, we did meet before then.

AD: On South Africa's Women's Day.

PP: That's right. And we all came and piled into your hotel room. But we hadn't met properly, in the way we did in Paris, where we hung out for the weekend. We happened to be in Paris because June had come to London. This was two years after I met her. I used to work in feminist publishing and wanted to ensure that June's writings were published in the UK, since they weren't yet available, so I facilitated the publication of her books. I will never forget this. I remember when June said I should officially be her agent, and I was quite clear and said, "I'm not your agent, I just want to make sure that your work is available." She insisted, "No, I've spoken to my friend, Angela. And she says, you are effectively my agent. And you have to, you know, take that on." I was really only doing it as an act of solidarity.

Fast-forward two years. June came to London to do a book tour. She voiced a desire to go to Paris. En route to Paris she said, "Well, I have a friend who's also going to be in Paris at the same time." That happened to be Angela. You may remember which district we went to, Angela, since you had lived in Paris, where we went to a Moroccan restaurant. It was raining really hard and no taxi would stop for us. We finally did manage to get back to our hotel. It was quite a moment. The next morning, literally the next morning, June knocked on our hotel bedroom door. She had a little tray with a jug of water and a page from a yellow legal pad rolled up on the tray. She said, "Here's your breakfast gift." It was astounding. It was the poem "Solidarity," about the four of us waiting for a taxi. She literally overnight, after that experience that we had shared the night before, had written this poem. It was incredible to see how June transformed pain and anger and rage into something beautiful with her words as a poet.

AD: Yes, I remember that period. When one looks at what was happening in France and Paris and all over the country, including in some of the so-called overseas territories, a consciousness of racism was finally emerging. At that particular time, we were Black women and could not get a taxi in Paris. I remember around the same time talking to someone from, I think, Martinique who had the same problem. And I said, this is no different from New York. That person said, "Well, no, I think we were not standing in the right place," which was an indication of the degree to which a consciousness of racism was so long in coming in France. When I look at the developments now, when I read some of the materials that Black feminists in France are writing, I think about June, and I think about how she might have responded today.

Pratibha, you're absolutely right, June lived through her poetry. She understood the world through her poetry. And she wrote poetry about everything. I've never been so impressed before, by a person, with perhaps the exception of Toni Morrison, who could write constantly, regardless of what the circumstances were, you know—who didn't, as I do, need the right kind of conditions to sit down and formulate ideas. Those ideas, those amazing insights about the world were always there. Her existence was a poetic existence.

LR: One of the things that I love so much about the poem "Solidarity" is the way she's asking questions, to us and to the world, through her poetry. "Who would build that shelter? Who will build and lift it high and wide above such loneliness?" How do you understand June's conception of solidarity in her writing and in her personal relationships? That conception seems to be the crux of her politics and her poetics.

AD: It's taken me a while to recognize the extent to which her poetic engagement with the world was her political contribution. I had many conversations with June trying to convince her to participate in this or that event or join this or that organization. I was never really successful. We both really found sisters in each other with respect to our political views, but we expressed that commitment very differently. It has taken me a while to recognize that regardless of the importance of organizing and organizations and a kind of didactic expression, what we are struggling against and for in this moment, in the long run, is important—but it's not really going to change the world in ways we thought it would. The arts engage with life and the world by acknowledging the role of the senses and visuality. In the final analysis, that is what has the capacity to help us engage in radical transformation.

My sense of what it means to be active in and committed to a collective process has changed over time. There was a time when I was convinced that collective work had to happen literally in a collective context, so that it could not happen unless one were in active communication with groups of political people. June helped me understand that creating the collective can also happen in the process of producing art. June's art, her poetry, was saturated with the sense of the power of masses of people. Although she was not the one who wanted to go out and try to put those groups of people together. And the ways in which she navigated the relationships between politics, aesthetics, political commitment, and artistic commitment are so revealing.

Today, precisely as a consequence of her contributions and those of others, we're beginning to see the value of the realities that are often embedded in such stereotypes as the angry Black woman. It used to be that the figure of the angry Black woman was to be dismissed. But now we're beginning to recognize that there is a kernel of truth there, and that anger is about resistance. There's a reason why we can say that Black women have been involved in every single important movement and have actually given leadership. But, of course, that leadership has not been acknowledged. Thanks to young activists we have a very different sense of what leadership entails now. It does not have to be masculinist, individualistic, and all the other things that we attach to the male figures who have publicly represented Black movements. We know that collective leadership is possible, and June's work was collective. Even though she did it alone and was often wary of having anyone else tell her what to do, she taught us how to express rage in a collective, productive way. And thirty years after the filming of *A Place of Rage*, we're now seeing the very concrete fruit of the work that she laid out for us then.

What I so deeply appreciated about June was her capacity to be herself regardless of the context. Whether she was playing with friends, reading, teaching, or giving an interview about Palestine, I really loved that ability to sustain herself, no matter where she was, or who she was with. I think of myself as very different. When I teach, I reach for those sets of knowledge and experience I think that are necessary to be an effective teacher, which is not the same as the ones I draw upon as an activist, which are not necessarily the same as what I draw upon in my friendships. I was not accustomed, because of my training, to revealing my personal life to the public. I'm thinking back to the filming of *A Place of Rage*. I felt somewhat awkward, whereas June was brilliant, absolutely brilliant. She knew how to ground herself in that aesthetic vision, I would say, and everything else flowed from that.

PP: It's so interesting, Angela, that you said you had different ways of expressing your political activism. That was precisely why I wanted to make the film. That weekend in Paris is when the idea for the film was born in my mind. I saw and experienced the both of you in the same space. I knew both of you came through similar political struggles, the Black Power movement, the civil rights movement, movements for social justice and change through different means and ways of expressing it. Neither one or the other was any less or more, but these were different ways of approaching change. You say that June was able to be freer and you felt more awkward, and maybe that's what you felt. But by the time we were filming, you were so open and willing. When I asked you if I could film you running to show one of the ways you take care of yourself, Angela, that wasn't just because that would make for the most beautiful, stunning visuals. (And now, everyone on the internet tries to rip off memes of you running.) It was because you embodied the cultivation of self-care which was generative in terms of your inner resilience and your grace. I felt that so strongly about you. That's why I wanted to capture those images. And you were willing and open to do that, allowing me that kind of intimacy into your life. There were wonderful images, but also modeling to so many of us who are engaged in political struggle how we have to learn to take care of ourselves. The film tried to capture this holistic vision of who you both were.

If, looking back on the film, there is a moment of pause, it would be the archival footage of you being arrested by the FBI, and then the global international movement to free you. During the "Free Angela Campaign," you were so near to the electric chair. But the global movement freed you. That is so moving to me to this day, because I'm so grateful that you're still with us, and you're still in the world and continue to have the impact that you have. But that was a chilling moment for me when I look back on the film. I still think about that.

AD: Thank you so much, Pratibha. You know, in many ways, the world is catching up with June. And perhaps also catching up with an awareness of the relationship between one's personal and political life, one's capacity to engage in self-care. June was an absolutely passionate tennis player. I don't think there were shots of her playing tennis in *A Place of Rage*. When I think of her, I think of the absolute joy with which she played tennis. She tried to convince all of her friends to learn how to play tennis, because that was where she felt so free and alive. It's quite remarkable to think back to that period. And as I said before, I miss June every day.

What really struck me about June was her sense of global solidarity, as comes through in her poem "Solidarity." If we look now at the Black Lives Matter movement and the role that the Palestinian struggle has played in allowing that movement to mature and be aware of itself in relation to people all over the world, June was calling for solidarity with Palestine, when everyone else was afraid to utter a word in solidarity with the Palestinians. The thing I'm saddest about is that she was not able to witness the flowering of this sense of the connections between the Black movement and the Palestinian movement. Whenever I'm asked to speak, I always point out that June Jordan led us in this direction long before most of us were even willing to listen to what she was saying.

LR: One of the things that is so powerful in *A Place of Rage* is that it demonstrates the legacy of Black women's organizing in the civil rights and Black Power movements. But it's also rooted in a commitment to international intersectional feminism. Since we're talking about internet memes, there is a clip from the film that's been circulating recently where June talks about the two most important struggles of our time—gay liberation and Palestine. I'm also struck by her attention to environmentalism and the ways in which the terror of imperialism, of colonialism, are wrought not only against humans, but the nonhuman world. We are literally all in this together. In the late eighties, early 1990s, it was something that smelled and tasted so right. But it was very hard to really understand and embody that.

Can you two talk a little bit about what was at stake in the articulation of a truly global intersectional politics in that moment? What was at stake in that? What were the difficulties of articulating such a politics?

PP: When I met June, up to that point within the UK, women of color and the Black women's movement had been coming together on common issues. We had had many successful campaigns around certain social issues, had organized in our communities, had supported each other, had spoken out against racism within the white women's movement. But there came a moment when those solidarities began to fragment. Conversations around hierarchies of oppression started to emerge around identities, about who was more oppressed than who. That was utterly demoralizing. As I was trying to find a way through these debilitating arguments, I reached out to June's writings. When I met her, she spoke to the global connections that women across the world need to be making. Recently I was rereading this interview I did with her in 1987, "Other Kinds of Dreams," where she said our allegiances cannot just be constrained by our gender or race or our sexuality. Our allegiances need to be much broader; otherwise, we are not going to survive. That is still so relevant to the moment that we are experiencing right now. June was incredibly bold. She spoke about Palestine when it was unpopular, and she was severely criticized and ostracized publicly for doing so. In the film she says there is a litmus test for our time and poses the question, "What are you going to do about Palestinian rights? And what are you going to do about LGBT rights?" That encapsulated June, because she never compartmentalized. For her it was always much more about global interconnectedness of oppressions. As a poet, she was able to make these connections textural and emotionally evocative and in ways that spoke to many of us at the time and to this day.

AD: I'm remembering how politically difficult conditions were at that time. This was the Reagan–Bush era. This was the period of the consolidation of global capitalism. The welfare state was in the process of declining. The conditions that were unfolding were precisely those that led to what we call mass incarceration in this country. The prison industrial complex was in the process of being erected. And we hadn't figured out how to mount the kind of resistance that would have been required at that time. Let's remember also that this was the period of the decline of the socialist community of nations. Capitalism was being represented as triumphant. And we were attempting to find our way, groping, as it were, toward an understanding of the condition such that we would be able eventually to create solidarity movements. The movement for solidarity with South Africa was very powerful, perhaps the most widespread and obvious mark of solidarity. June was talking about solidarity with Palestine.

I can remember, June traveled to Lebanon and wrote. She always wrote poetry about everything she did—the big expressions of desire for radical change in the world, as well as the small experiences that she had with her friends. It would be important to reread her work during that period, precisely in order to get some insight about where we were and how we were feeling. Many people were depressed that we had to deal with Ronald Reagan and the Bushes. And we really did not know where we were going. And at the same time, there were all of these other movements that were emerging, that were so important: the environmental movement, the women of color, feminist movement, the LGBTQ movement.

I don't know if anyone else of that period was able to adequately recognize the potential of these movements that were so frequently dismissed as special interests and movements that only involved relatively small but particular sectors of the population, but certainly had nothing to do with the grand struggle for democracy. June knew precisely of that: if we fully understand why it was so important to struggle for LGBTQ rights, if we know why it was so essential to express solidarity with Palestine and speak out against the Israeli occupation of Palestine, then we will understand what the struggle for radical democracy really was. I find myself returning to that period remembering how perceptive June was, and how more of us should have been willing to follow the leadership that she was offering us at that time. But we can do it now; because the problems remain. And I'm so happy to hear that you have an Abolition Democracy Initiative at UC Berkeley. We were just beginning to try to figure out what those relationships were, then.

When we were about to create Critical Resistance, I tried to get June involved in the organizing committee. But that's not what she did. I've learned since that I cannot argue for the same kind of participation on the part of others who can express themselves far more powerfully through their words, through their music, through their poetry. I've learned now that I have to follow them, rather than ask them to follow me. Even though she was not directly involved, I can remember many times referring to her poems and her way of grasping that moment. They were, in many ways, a beacon for us as we tried to do the organizing that would ultimately lead us toward greater understanding of the relationship between the carceral state issues of sexuality, of racial capitalism, and the destruction of the environment.

LR: I'm thinking about the darkness of that moment in the late eighties and early 1990s. And how enthralled people seemed to be with the movements of the sixties as this high watermark of progress of democracy, and a kind of romantic, almost like fetishization, of the forms of activism and protest of that earlier moment. This is also why *A Place of Rage* is so unique. It's able to offer exactly the kind of critique of those earlier movements for the ways that they frame and put forward the great Black male leader, that they excise or marginalize feminist, queer, and sometimes internationalist politics in a particular kind of way. I'm thinking of the seeds of terror that were emerging in that moment.

The title of the film is so powerful, asking us: What is the place of rage in our movements? In our looking back to the movements of the sixties and seventies, we were no longer allowed to really express rage. Rage had to be contained. We had to sort of express gratitude, maybe indignation, but not rage. I'd love for both of you to talk about the title of the film and the importance of rage—not just the beauty of June's words, but also the rage and anger that is so fundamental that she marshaled.

PP: The title of the film comes from June speaking about an event that happened when she was a young girl living in Bedford–Stuyvesant. Her best friend Geoffrey was chased by the police onto the roof of their building and beaten beyond recognition. When she was talking about this in the interview, she said, *You know, it hardened me in a place of rage.* And at that point, I knew that would be the title of the film. The working title I had been working with was *Through Their Eyes*. I wanted to make the film through multiple narratives, from the point of view of these women speaking to those movements through the prism of their lives. June also spoke of the metaphorical idea of a place of rage. Not only did it harden her to witness police violence against her young friend, but also feeling rage about the US and its history—the bloodshed, and the genocide as a racist settler-capitalist nation, that is, to this day, a place of rage. Rage is actually healthy and respectable and needed. There is this idea that we need to speak with more civility, we need to be modulated in how we engage in political discourse. But this modulation can be an attempt to flatten our anger and our rage, which is righteous, and it is what we need to get on the streets. When Black Lives Matter happened, the rage that was displayed was righteous rage, which contributed to a changing discourse around police violence and the carceral state in the US.

AD: June always knew how to express that rage, so that the rage didn't turn inward. I also think about Audre Lorde's essay "The Uses of Anger." I learned so much from June about how to productively express one's rage. And I saw her do that in so many different contexts, particularly because she was such a brilliant poet. Also, she was so compassionate and felt deeply for everyone undergoing any form of oppression.

I'm remembering the earthquake that happened in 1991. I was speaking at the University of Wisconsin–Madison. And I was staying at the residence of the university president, Donna Shalala, whom June had introduced me to because June had taught at the university. I was there when it seemed like the world ended. I can only remember seeing images about the Bay Bridge coming down. I have these images in my mind of the bridge floating in the Bay and everything absolutely destroyed. We know that it wasn't that bad for everyone, although many people, especially farmworkers, in the area of Salinas suffered. What June did—she was so bold and so courageous—was she went down to the places where people were suffering and talked to them about the impact of the earthquake. She wanted to do something immediately. And, of course, there are poems about that as well. I think that we all have so much to learn from the way June lived her life and produced the work that we rely on so much today that helped to shape what we now call Black feminism and helped to shape what we call the evolution of feminism. But also, she felt a deeply personal responsibility to do something to express that rage, regardless of the circumstance.

PP: I really miss June so much. I miss her words, and I miss her incisive perceptions and commentary on what she called "the relentless laughter of evil." She believed change was possible. She had this beautiful vision, and envisioned a different kind of world through her writings and her poems. I think about that envisioning during really dark times when you feel that as movements or as individuals we have no power. That was precisely because—what you said, Angela—because of her huge heart, and her compassion, and her belief in humanity. I agree, Angela, everyone needs to just periodically go back to June's writings and see the depth of her vision for a different kind of world.

LR: It's so inspiring to get the charge and be set back to that path. My last question: What do you miss most about June? And what do you think are her most important lessons for our moment?

AD: Artists, cultural workers—people involved in some way with cultural activism—have a great deal to learn from June. And precisely at this moment we've seen during the pandemic, the emergence of this broad consciousness regarding the structural character of racism, the police murders of George Floyd and Breonna Taylor, this is a different conjunction, a very different juncture from the one June experienced. But I think she was the artist who most perfectly encapsulated how the artist responds under conditions such as this, as we see the proliferation of visual art around issues of police violence and mass incarceration; as we see music—hip hop, of course, but also jazz—flourishing as they address the question of racism and repression. June is the one who can show the way. For me, she always worked as if she had a responsibility to people throughout the world, to engage in the kind of work, whether it was poetic work, whether it was political work, to demand change. At this moment, we need her leadership even more than we might have needed it then.

So let's remember that we're just now catching up with June and her vision. This is especially the case with respect to international solidarity. One of my critiques of what is happening at the present moment is that while we have the technology to produce the most phenomenal kind of global solidarity, we're lagging behind the actual potential.

And so we need to be in connection with what's happening in Brazil and the flourishing of Black feminism in Brazil, the extent to which Black women are giving leadership to the campaign against racism there. I could go on and on. But I think that this is some of that global solidarity that was at the very center of her being and she felt it. It was not something that was ever a question for her. And I think we need that kind of sensibility at this moment.

PP: Angela has summed that up so beautifully. One of the ways that June and I bonded was our commitment to global solidarity. I miss that connection. I was a child of immigrants who immigrated as refugees to the UK when I was twelve. I had no language with which to speak or understand what was happening to us, for instance how and why my mother was exploited as a seamstress in sweatshops. It was Angela's book *If They Come in the Morning* that politicized me, gave me the language to understand the connections between class and race exploitation. And that was not specific to any one nation-state. It was happening across the world. One of the questions I often get asked is, "How come you as a South Asian woman connected with the freedom movements, the Black rights movement, and the civil rights movement?" I only get this question within the US, and I say that actually, those movements, and these women and Angela's influence and impact, were global. The ripple effect of the Black Power movement and the civil rights movement, and their influence on movements for liberation and on freedom fighters in India and elsewhere, was massive. These movements were not confined to the US, although they engaged with the US state. They actually inspired so many of us across the globe.

AD: Let's also not forget that you are a part of the Black movement in the UK. I remember when we first met in the context of a large group of women back in the eighties. Someone asked me if I wanted to meet with a group of Black women activists, and I said, yes, of course I do. I may not have revealed my surprise, but it was my first encounter with the notion of Black as political. The majority of the women in the room were South Asian. For people who may not know the history of Black feminist organizing in the UK, the Black movement did not simply consist of people of African descent, but of people of Asian and Middle Eastern descent. It was a political notion of Blackness, it was an anti-imperialist notion of Blackness. And I think we still have a great deal to learn from the ways in which Black became a far more capacious way of knowing and acting in the world, and June loved that. And, you know, nowadays with everything focused on identity in this narrow sense, we forget that, you know, Du Bois pointed out that the connection between Black people in the US and Black people in Africa was not biological, or the important connection was not the ancestry connection, it was the anti-imperialist commitment, which was the more powerful connection.

LR: Right. I keep coming back to the question of living room and of shelter. It's is not about any specific identity. It's the right to live. It's the ability to express something so core and fundamental and so expansive, simultaneously, moving between two poems that I opened with—"Solidarity" and "In Paris." We should change the title of this conversation to "Catching Up with June," because that's what we're doing right now.

Angela Y. Davis is professor emerita of history of consciousness and feminist studies at the University of California, Santa Cruz. An activist, writer, and lecturer, her work focuses on prisons, police, abolition, and related intersections of race, gender, and class. She is the author of many books, from *Angela Davis: An Autobiography* (Random House, 1974) to *Freedom Is a Constant Struggle* (Haymarket Books, 2016).

Pratibha Parmar is a globally recognized, award-winning filmmaker and human rights activist who brings a passionate commitment to illuminating untold stories. Her film credits include *Alice Walker: Beauty in Truth* (2013), *Khush* (1991), and *My Name Is Andrea* (2022). Pratibha is author, coauthor, and editor of several groundbreaking books and essays on creativity, race, class, and gender, including *Warrior Marks* (Routledge, 1993).

Leigh Raiford is professor of African American studies at the University of California, Berkeley, where she teaches, researches, curates, and writes about race, gender, justice, and visuality. Raiford is the author of *Imprisoned in a Luminous Glare: Photography and the African American Freedom Struggle* (University of California Press, 2011) and *When Home Is a Photograph: Blackness and Belonging in the World* (forthcoming, Duke University Press, 2026).

In Response to "Apologies to All the People in Lebanon"

adrienne maree brown

the first time i read this poem i had to read it a few times. it was appalling. it devastated my heart, my private pain landscape lit up with that powerless fireshame of being a u.s. american. palestine, being murdered by israel, the war marking the region, the foggy self-defense narrative infecting the world. it felt like it was written that morning, written every morning i have read it again, including this one.

it comforts/ed me to know that june jordan knew what it was to not know, not want to know. to have on a national veil, to let it hang heavy enough to press closed the eyelids and quiet the questions, the protestation.

palestine took time for me to understand too. now i am learning about india. socialization is a mask with no eyes, you have to have a moment of pulling the whole thing off, apart, to see the innocent blood on your own fingers.

> I didn't know and nobody told me and what
> could I do or say, anyway?[1]

it comforted me to see her reckon with being a poet and artist when warriors were called for. to have to find a way to wield the words, sharp and deft, practical and true. in doing so, she invited us all to leave the frivolous, to learn who we are, and then make it powerful when it shouldn't be beautiful.

i remember, meaning i will never forget, learning that the military was not the valiant ground of heroes i was raised in, but a moral conundrum. a fat tick of violent anticipation. a guarantee that war was always coming. i remember learning about the genocidal treatment of indigenous people, of the Nakba, of slavery, of the FBI and CIA, of capitalism and climate catastrophe and forced migration and cages on the border full of children—all the hidden histories that are technically current.

> There was the Mediterranean: You
> could walk into the water and stay
> there.
> What was the problem?
>
> I didn't know and nobody told me and what
> could I do or say, anyway?[2]

it felt like this poem, these lines, this brilliant repeated line which captures the tone of denial, were holding my heart to the light. you were naive, once, but . . . but there's no way you could be now. after a certain age, a certain exposure, you must choose.

will you look at the bodies, see your fingerprints, turn, and face it, and try with words and actions to stop, to change the mess? or continue your denial? run away?

> I'm sorry.
> I really am sorry.[3]

june jordan looked, and then took all our hands across time and space and walked us to where the blood was still sticky. now we know, we've been told, and we can change, and say we are sorry, even when words are too small for the work, we really are sorry.

adrienne maree brown is the editor of *Pleasure Activism: The Politics of Feeling Good* (AK Press, 2019), author of *Emergent Strategy: Shaping Change, Changing Worlds* (AK Press, 2017), and coeditor of *Octavia's Brood: Science Fiction from Social Justice Movements* (AK Press, 2015). She is the cohost of the *How to Survive the End of the World* and *Octavia's Parables* podcasts. adrienne is rooted in Detroit.

After June Jordan, a Poem About Police Violence[1]

Jehan Bseiso

Tell me something what you think would happen
If everytime
they kill a black boy
Trayvon Martin, Michael Brown, Dontre Hamilton

If everytime
They kill a Palestinian boy
Farouq Abdul Qader, Shadi Arafa, Mahmoud Olayan

What do you think would happen?
If everytime they kill.

#Happened:
Eric Garner choked to death just for selling cigarettes.
#Happened:
Tamir Rice shot for packing a deadly toy gun.
#Happened:
Ahmad Abdullah Sharak, bullet coated steel rubber in the head for walking in Ramallah.

A bunker in North Carolina will not protect the police from people.
A separation wall across Palestine will not make the dispossessed forget.

I just called (from Gaza) to say I love you.
BLM to BDS
From Ferguson to Jerusalem
Across race and barbed wire,
we hold one breath.

Jehan Bseiso is a poet, researcher, and aid worker. Her poetry has been published in several online and offline platforms. Her coauthored book *I Remember My Name* (with Samah Sabawi and Ramzy Baroud; Novum, 2016) is the Palestine Book Awards winner in the creative category. She is the coeditor of *Making Mirrors: Writing/Righting by and for Refugees* (with Becky Thompson; Interlink, 2019) and is on the production team of the Palestine Festival of Literature. Jehan has been working with Médecins Sans Frontières / Doctors Without Borders since 2008.

For the Sake of a People's Poetry
June Jordan and Walt Whitman

Donna Masini

Before June Jordan was my friend, she was my teacher. In 1984, in a small workshop at the Poetry Society of America, she insisted I read—and write a paper on—Walt Whitman. Why Whitman? I wanted to know. Why *me*? This wasn't school. And how come nobody else had to do this? June laughed that unforgettable laugh. June was not democratic in every regard. I'm glad she insisted I read Whitman. I am very glad she did not have me begin with *Democratic Vistas*.

"For the Sake of a People's Poetry," Jordan's essential essay on Whitman, first appeared as the foreword to *Passion: New Poems, 1977–1980*, which begins with the often-quoted dedication, "to Everybody scared as I used to be." In a voice "intimate and direct," as she says of Whitman, the foreword begins:

> In America, the father is white: It is he who inaugurated the experiment of this republic. It is he who sailed his way into slave ownership. It is he who availed himself of my mother: the African woman whose function was miserably defined by his desirings, or his rage. It is he who continues to dominate the destiny of the Mississippi River, the Blue Ridge Mountains, and the life of my son. Understandably, then, I am curious about this man.
>
> Most of the time my interest can be characterized as wary, at best. Other times, it is the interest a pedestrian feels for the fast-traveling truck about to smash into him. Or her. Again. And at other times it is the curiosity of a stranger trying to figure out the system of the

language that excludes her name and all of the names of all of her people. It is this last that leads me to the poet Walt Whitman.[1]

Listen to that syntax—those rhythms and repetitions. Jordan *wields* language. Organic and thrilling, these syntactic repetitions enact the repetitions of history. Not only a great poet, she is an exquisite essayist, deploying a trenchant, flexible rhetoric. Through her syntactic strategies, her modulating tones, leaps, rhythms, we experience Jordan's wit, her fierce and searching intelligence. The essay ends: "Walt Whitman and all of the New World poets coming after him, we, too, go on singing this America."[2]

Now turn the page: With her first lines—"What will we do / when there is nobody left / to kill?"[3]—we're launched into a book of poems in which the poet addresses, challenges, begs to inform us, has decided she has something to say about "40,000 gallons of oil gushing / into the ocean,"[4] about "what you think would happen if / everytime they kill a black boy / then we kill a cop,"[5] about rape and silence in "Rape Is Not a Poem"[6] and "Case in Point."[7]

She speaks to us. Like Whitman, she includes and addresses us. In our name she writes to Fidel and the People's Republic of Angola, to Fannie Lou Hamer; writes for South African women, in a poem presented at the United Nations. This New World poet decided she had something to say about unemployment, the Shah of Iran, and Ana May Pictou Aquash "slain on The Trail of Broken Treaties."[8] She had something to say about Sojourner Truth, the moon landing, bisexuality, Vieques, phone machines, and a moment in which even the police can see "the mustard seed / the trembling river and the totem trees . . . they do not shoot."[9] And in the classic "Poem About My Rights," she addresses the politics of rape with her exquisite gift for metaphor:

> Which is exactly like South Africa
> penetrating into Namibia penetrating into
> Angola and does that mean I mean how do you know if
> Praetoria ejaculates what will the evidence look like[10]

Relentless, inclusive, challenging, she tells us: *We are the ones we have been waiting for.*[11]

It becomes clear that Jordan is the New World poet Whitman called for in his somewhat meandering and problematic *Democratic Vistas*, much as Whitman had responded to Emerson's call. One way to describe her aesthetic is to quote her on Whitman:

> In the first place, there is nothing obscure, nothing contrived, nothing an ordinary straphanger in the subway would be puzzled by. In the second place, the voice of those lines is intimate and direct at once: It is the voice of a poet who assumes that he speaks to an equal and that he need not fear that equality; on the contrary, the intimate distance between the poet and the reader is a distance that assumes there is everything important, between them, to be shared.[12]

Like Whitman, June contains multitudes. She encompasses, in this essay, in the poems that follow, economics, aesthetics, the marketplace, linguistics, love, racial/sexual/literary politics, and a scarcity model vs. populist model. Populist: It's become a degraded word, connoting white, nationalistic, reactionary. The word now makes us question who decides who "the people" *are*. This problem is there already in Whitman, especially in *Democratic Vistas*, his critique of democracy. Perhaps I'd never read all of it. In fact, until writing this essay, I'm not sure I read any of it. It is, let's speak plainly, turgid, convoluted, hardly inclusive—and marked by new and important ideas. Whitman expresses his disgust, his near despair, at the hypocrisy, the "hollowness at the heart," the "materialistic and vulgar" in American democracy, all that is thwarting the great American Experiment.[13] This being the difficult post–Civil War time of reconstruction and reckoning, things looked pretty dismal to the generally optimistic Whitman. He placed his hope in a Future Literature that was, he believed, contingent upon the nation's imagination moving beyond old world "feudalism," beyond a literature that was the product of, and in the service to, an educated elite.

Whitman called for a New World poet. And, in order that "the process of reading is not a half sleep, but . . . an exercise, a gymnast's struggle," he called for a muscular, supple, and democratic *reader*.[14] I don't have space here to athletically address the problematic in Whitman, which is more obvious in *Democratic Vistas* than in the poems. For now, let's accept his own proudly proclaimed capacity for contradiction, and note that either Whitman or Jordan could have written this:

> In the poetry of The New World you meet with a reverence for the material world that begins with a reverence for human life, an intellectual trust in sensuality as a means of knowledge and of unity, an easily deciphered system of reference, aspiration to a believable, collective voice . . . an emphatic preference for broadly accessible and/or "spoken" use of language.[15]

When Jordan responds to Whitman's call, she, this "lyric catalyst for change," does so in song and sonnet, in surprising shifts of tone and texture, in complex rhythmic modulations—formal and structural techniques she learned, she says, as a painstaking student of English Literature. (These are not just prosodic devices she taught us, but tools, strategies for investigation and discovery.) I often suggest Jordan to students who are stuck in dead rhetoric, talking their opinions, "being the good guy." I watch as they begin to notice, to *feel* how Jordan rides a rhythm to find out what she means, to take herself—and us—somewhere unexpected. They begin to understand the ways in which language embodies our arguments, feelings, thoughts, contradictory impulses. By the end of the ride, we are always somewhere new, not only at the level of thought—but in our nerves. And the thing about Jordan is, she's never "the good guy." She interrogates herself, her motives and contradictions, puts herself—and her readers—on the line. *We* are responsible. "I have evolved," this New World poet says,

> from an observer to a victim to an activist passionately formulating methods of resistance against tyranny of any kind. . . . I have faced my own culpability, my own absolute dirty hands . . . in the continuation of injustice and powerful intolerance. I am discovering my own shameful functions as part of the problem . . . I no longer think "They" are this or that, but rather, "We" or "I" am not doing enough.[16]

Recently, a gifted Palestinian graduate student decided he could not attend our MFA graduate reading. So sickened, so outraged by the

2018 massacre of Palestinians in Gaza, he was too depressed to read his poems. I wrote him about Jordan, her indefatigable courage, even in the face of calamity. Write, June said. No matter what is happening, write. Write something every day. Like Whitman confronting the horrors of the Civil War, June tried always to show up, to address what she saw happening. Believed she could address—or attempt to address—the unspeakable. Believed it was possible. Not just possible, a responsibility. This is courage, in the root sense of that word. It takes *heart*. June was on the front lines. Always. This New World poet. And it wasn't always easy. I tried to write my grad student about all this, about what his poems could do for him, for *us*. But he was not ready. Jordan, as she herself said, had had to evolve. "So back in 1964," she says, "I resolved not to run on hatred but, instead, to use what I loved, words, for the sake of the people I loved."[17]

Here is our New World poet:

> I think that I am trying to keep myself free, that I am trying to become responsive and responsible to every aspect . . . I think that I am trying to learn whatever I can that will make freedom of choice an intelligent, increasing possibility. . . . Toward the close of the sixties . . . I decided that I wanted to aim for the achievement of a collective voice, that I wanted to speak as a community to a community, that to do otherwise was not easily defensible, nor useful, and would be, in any case, at variance with the clarified political values I held as my own, by then.[18]

And here is our New World poet:

> I choose to exist unafraid of my enemies; instead, I choose to become an enemy to my enemies. And I choose to believe that my enemies can either be vanquished or else converted into allies.[19]

In his poems, Whitman wrote and imagined out of his best self. He spoke to us, men and women of a generation or ever so many generations hence. Because Whitman seems to have had a firm belief in the plentiful ever-renewing natural resources of this country, he was better able than we are now to assume there would be a recognizable world in a hundred years. Jordan, writing a hundred years later, wrote her urgent, necessary poems in spite of all we now know. June Jordan became the New World poet Whitman had called for.

A version of this essay was read as a panel presentation on "For the Sake of a People's Poetry" at Cave Canem's "A Tribute to June Jordan," CUNY Graduate Center (2018).

Donna Masini is the author of *Did You Find Everything You Were Looking For?* (W. W. Norton, forthcoming), *4:30 Movie* (W. W. Norton, 2018), *Turning to Fiction* (W.W. Norton, 2004), *That Kind of Danger* (Beacon, 1994), and a novel, *About Yvonne* (W. W. Norton, 1998). Her work has appeared in *Best American Poetry*, *American Poetry Review*, *Poetry*, *Ploughshares*, and *The Paris Review*, among others. A recipient of NEA and NYFA grants, a Pushcart Prize, and residencies at Civitella Ranieri, Bogliasco, and Yaddo, she is a professor of English at Hunter College.

Truth-Telling as an Emancipatory Act
What June Jordan Taught Me About Liberation

Elizabeth Riva Meyer

I met June Jordan in 1989, decades before I became a trauma therapist. At no other time in my life had someone straight-up asked me to speak my truth. I was a young undergraduate, and California was new to me. An invitation to oppose silence and, instead, root my voice in the telling of lived experience drew me to June. Her classes at the university were outstretched arms saying, "Come as you are. Drop nothing at the door." She was one of the first to teach me, through embodiment and absolute imperative, just how to name. And she will forever hold that coveted spot like a lover or sage you pray to meet in your waking life.

I grew up a white person in the Southern United States—Memphis, Tennessee, to be exact. I don't recall any type of overt truth-telling or lessons in how to name abuse, and especially not when considering the legacy of racial terrorism and systemic dehumanization of Black people. I do remember silence, secrecy, and a language based in splitting, to cope with what I now understand as the shadow self: that part of you sequestered and blocked off from consciousness, because to awaken and become familiar with what you imagine to be so bad about yourself is intolerable. We all do it to survive on some level, until we learn integration. White America has survived and terrorized in this psychological state of splitting; collectively we can't look at our ugly, imagine ourselves as bad, name our violations, sit with our sins, so we bury them. We blame. We project. We other. We kill the ones our minds create as "outsiders" and justify these acts of physical and psychic murder with false narratives of our innocence, in every effort to not face the violence and legacy within.

Even though no one ever told me we were keeping secrets, I knew we were; you can feel those things.

Coming from the city where Martin Luther King Jr. was murdered holds a civic and national trauma all its own. That act of racial violence and assassination stains my city permanently; it is coded into the cells of Memphians. That memory rests atop the centuries-old message that Black lives are disposable, unworthy of humanity, and to be used for profit and killed without remorse. As a child, I had no words for this felt sense of what we now call historical trauma. But I registered how easily a human being could be revered, uplifted, or invisibilized and confirmed as nothing by another. I could feel the ghosts, Black and white, hovering beside us or in communion during the slightest exchange. Maybe the murmurings differed in terms of sentence structure or language, but the sensation was always the same: an anxiety, a nearby experience of someone imagining they could be subjugated, erased, annihilated in the blink of an eye.

Mixed into this historical backdrop was the transmission of intergenerational trauma viscerally passed down to me: Jewish fright that translated into rumination, worry, and a cellular belief that *you are the ones they are coming for* combined with psychic pain and sensitivities categorized as mental illnesses that hijacked life and dampened the spirit of several family members. I have often wondered if the magnitude of suffering was intrinsically tied to the Southern geography I come from, not only what the land itself holds, but the psychological state you are invited into when history has not been named and digested by multiple generations.

These stories were foundational to the structuring of my psyche. They made me porous to others' suffering, highly perceptive to unspoken and injurious dynamics, and wired to read and decode what could not be talked about or tolerated in a room. It's no surprise that today I find myself in portables and imaginary spaces on a school campus intentionally carved out to support people in naming the unspeakable and co-conspiring to truth-tell, as acts of liberation. Today, the city is

Richmond, California. And the relationships I co-create with elementary and middle school students, caregivers, and staff are the real-life opportunities for breaking silence and attending to historical wounds.

Similarly, this is what June had offered me: an assignment to wake up and get real with myself. My initial place of refuge and sanctity was "The Politics of Female Childhood," June's first class held on the University of California, Berkeley, campus. I had never considered my girlhood as something to be examined, as something politicized due to my gender identity. June asked us to consider the sociopolitical dynamics of our childhoods—the way power was wielded by adults and particularly in response to us being female. June asked us where it hurt. She was interested in the pain and invested in us learning to speak truth to interpersonal power dynamics and structural oppression that birthed and perpetuated those very pains. Our instruction was to speak the unspeakable, possibly the undesirable, and always something authentic and of weight. This psychological and spiritual exercise in truth-telling morphed into two poetry classes the following semester that June taught in the African American and women's studies departments and that were ultimately grounded in the formation of Poetry for the People. Here, we met writers including Cornelius Eady, Adrienne Rich, Joy Harjo, Ntozake Shange, and Janice Mirikitani. We traversed the deeply personal, where the telling was radical and honest, to land us unforgettably in stories that quaked with truth. I found freedom with June and in the heartbeat of this collective that served as a witness, a psychological link, and a hub of activism.

One of the resounding aspects of trauma is the isolative experience of being left alone to cope with overwhelming sensations, thoughts, and feelings that are unmanageable for a sole psyche. Poetry for the People became a communal container; the poems themselves became sacred places for the words to fall, to be held and tightened to form the closest real-life experience possible for the listener. June knew that the act of writing brings cohesion, that structuring a poem creates a home for your once-before isolative experience, that the outrage can now live somewhere and be transformed. June also knew that vocalizing those very truths—out loud and among many—is a way to join forces and incite the use of wordsmithing as a form of collective revolution and healing. We aired our voices on the radio, told our hurts to strangers in crowded reading halls, and published a blueprint for teaching poetry to the people. We knew our actions aligned with a call to bring light to the damage.

As a poet for the people, June dove right into the underbelly. She did not stay away from or fall asleep to or delude herself from the sicknesses that collectively haunt us; she wove cultural trauma into her writings as wake-up calls and links to present-day atrocities. June used personal experience, relationship, and a practice of stretching across lines to bring issues of national and international horror to the forefront and to the table. She meant business. For June, words were precisely chosen ammunition, accessible to us all and purposefully crafted for liberation. When June wrote, she fought. And she fought for the people; she constantly gave voice to anyone denied their God-given humanity and rights. And she always made it clear that the fight was in service of humanizing a condition or relationship, and wrapped into that service was her forever ask about power: who had it, who didn't, and "who in the hell set things up like this."[1] I say all this to be explicit about the comradeship I feel in direct relation to June's primary teaching: a cry for truth above all else, as life force, self-determination, political freedom, and accountability to one another.

June Jordan's writing personalizes violence to expose the generational human damage that occurs when oppressive systems irresponsibly and abusively govern our lives. There is nothing narcissistic about this linking; Jordan's purpose is to connect intimate experiences of her stripped humanity and "wrongness" to systemic acts of dominance and dangerous dissociation perpetrated worldwide. In "Poem About My Rights" she makes us see and feel the psychological impact of racial and gender-based trauma, and we cannot turn away. She does her Jordanesque thing by tracing the harrowing consequences of anti-Black and misogynistic violence around the globe and then back to her family and singular self:

> Do You Follow Me: We are the wrong people of
> the wrong skin on the wrong continent and what

in the hell is everybody being reasonable about
and according to the *Times* this week
back in 1966 the C.I.A. decided that they had this problem
and the problem was a man named Nkrumah so they
killed him and before that it was Patrice Lumumba
and before that it was my father on the campus
of my Ivy League school and my father afraid
to walk into the cafeteria because he said he
was wrong the wrong age the wrong skin the wrong
gender identity and he was paying my tuition and
before that
it was my father saying I was wrong saying that
I should have been a boy because he wanted one/a
boy and that I should have been lighter skinned and
that I should have had straighter hair and that
I should not be so boy crazy but instead I should
just be one/a boy and before that
it was my mother pleading plastic surgery for
my nose and braces for my teeth and telling me
to let the books loose . . .[2]

The mapping of these interlocking wounds is undeniable, and as fierce as the reclamation of voice and selfhood that follows. Jordan insists upon her sovereignty. And again, we cannot turn away—her daily living, fighting breath an opposition to anyone believing they dictate her rights or her freedom:

> *I am not wrong: Wrong is not my name*
> My name is my own my own my own
> and I can't tell you who the hell set things up like this
> but I can tell you that from now on my resistance
> my simple and daily and nightly self-determination
> may very well cost you your life[3]

This righteous practice of claiming independence from systems that violate and harm was central to June's writing and teaching. She invited me to find my points of reference, to personalize stories of dominance and freedom that could communicate the meaning-making of my grandmother's suicide, my sister's unrelenting rituals, my dislocation from an erotic sense of self, and the villainization of Arabs and their brown skin as national Gulf War dialogue. That's what June taught me: to put words to the private so I could make them public, stand with others, and let a multitude of voices be truth. She also taught me that these traumas were never untethered or free from the destructive belief systems of divide and conquer, but instead resultant of them.

As a mentor, June urged us to be deeply honest about our lives. To never cut corners or morph our messages for the liking or need of another. To revere the complexity of our singular identities and be human with the mess and glory of it all. To make sure that when we speak about the personal we always and forever link it to the political, as the two never exist outside of one another. To truth-tell as if our lives and the lives we fight for depend on it. To listen—the kind of listening where you're 100 percent invested in the teller's story and perspective, not a version you make up that comforts your narrative. To gather and make sure strength in numbers prevails. To use words as our weaponry. To recognize the power and purpose of the collective. To write poems that call out, uncover wounds, create fire, make love, love you back, warn, protect, and slay. June never let us forget that our job as writers and activists is to trace the root of the pain, outline the systemic failures that oppress and kill, and let voice tell the story that will ultimately collectivize and free us. June was a trauma-informed justice-and-liberation warrior.

To be trauma-informed means to always be historical in your thinking, seeing, sensing, and analysis of who you and another human being are in relationship to one another. We are never just two people in the present moment in love, in conversation, in conflict, or at war; we are two people, at a full table, in the company of ancestors and ghosts. Through us, they speak. They pain. They grieve. They humble us. And they light the way.

And how do we then listen to who shows up at the table? How do we recognize and wake up to the harmful legacies that underlie and inform present-day interactions and when unchecked erupt as injury and retraumatization? How do we soften and deactivate the knee-jerk response to push away and silence the rage, outcry, terror, and even wisdom that these generational visitors bring? The external work—of being in right relationship with one another—cannot honestly take place if we do not notice, track, and self-interrogate the cellular conditioning and destructive messaging we unconsciously act out with one another. We each must begin deeply at home in ourselves, coming to terms with and digesting the wounds of familial and collective legacies. As a white mental health clinician who provides care in communities of color historically neglected and traumatized by systemic racism, I am responsible for processing and metabolizing the ancestral violence passed down and housed within my body and psyche. Depth-oriented, collective trauma work is political work, because we are consciously and adamantly welcoming and refusing to split off from the truth of lived experience, and we are forming a collective consciousness that does not collude with the delusion of the perpetrators' stories. When June spoke of truth-telling, she was inviting us into this tiered psychological approach that requires fierce self-awareness, relational risk-taking, and a commitment to act as each other's comrades and kin as we community-build, behold, and rally.

And so, the act of therapy must be a political undertaking. It must be political because it is about human life. And it must be deeply relational because the sanctity of our lives and our very freedoms are bound up in how we choose to witness, affirm, and speak truth to one another. Therapy is an action we take and make intimately with another. You and the other have this sublime opportunity to be in a relationship that is attempting to wake up. Truth-telling is an act of emancipation, and when done in relationship with others, these acts are revolutionary. Together, we are breaking familial, cultural, and societal codes of relating that attempt to control who we can be inside ourselves and in the company of others. When I humanize my practice of therapy and challenge archaic, oppressive rules of what "mental health treatment" has historically been, I invite myself as a practitioner into the room, fully human and as an active participant. If I deny history in the room, I deny pieces of myself and pieces of another. I silence. I choose power over agency and creative meaning-making. I act as if I am the one in charge, as if I dictate what healing can look and feel like. I stamp further into memory the message that I/we cannot bear what is here and what desperately wants to be known. Legacy needs room to breathe, to tell us where the hurt is, to loosen from what no longer serves, to recall trusted medicine, and to lead us through and out.

Like poets, therapists attend to ancestral wounding.

Anytime I sit with a student, or the number multiplies and I am with a family, we step into territory that requires listening in a way most commonly, and at times even strategically, denied. In a world that asks us to swallow, gaslight, and abhor the uglies within and the violent history between, naming what keeps harm cycling is an act of resistance and an act of liberation. And if we consciously choose to relate to one another in ways most denied in a nation that asks us to cosign an ahistorical understanding of our relational dynamics and needs, then we create a potential for truth-telling. We risk for the sole purpose of our collective humanity. June never gave up on love—the action-oriented expression of unadulterated passion and connectivity as healing force, in direct opposition to violence. For her, the practice and art of love was a politic, and one I boldly join.

When I sit with the young children who visit my playroom, I track the convergence of two people and the storytelling alive in the moment of dream, of national proportion, of a working-through that is bigger than the two of us. When I, a fifty-two-year-old white, Southern, queer, Jewish woman, spend time together with an eleven-year-old Black heterosexual boy who is West Coast born, history revisits. Cultural dynamics, power dynamics come alive, speak through us in play as well as conversation. And the therapeutic relationship and field become a playground for either awakening or a recurring and oh-so-known deadening. We can rewrite the narrative of abuses and denials, or we can recreate the pattern that has kept pain and suffering incubated, oppressive, and destructive. June would ask me to fight for the rewrite, but not until we have sufficiently, beautifully, and with as much consciousness as possible dived into the risky waters of naming our truths.

Children have told me their pain in the most stupendous ways; saying their acts of self-recognition and awakening have been poetic would be understated. The stories are countless, and each one hallmarks the child as the narrator of their own tale. Each one cements what we know, what June knew: that telling the truth of your lived experience out loud can only bring you closer to freedom.

And sometimes the poetry comes before the actual words, in the searching. Sometimes the things we ache for must be birthed through the body—a trusting of preverbal memory and sensation. Poets know these places; they are the in-between where we find grief and muse.

Body memories are evoked when people converge and, therefore, multidimensional fields of reckoning are present. And we must make room, if we are truly listening and hope to get somewhere that is not bound in niceties or nonverbal oppressive codes of conduct or a tired homeostasis. Therapeutic attunement, like the poet's relationship to her words, is formed through a deep listening, an attempt to bring shape and specification to what has not lived out loud before. June wanted precision, specifics. Because there is power in exactitude and in claiming what is.

The children do this naturally. They tell me their truths in ways I could never prescribe. Their ease in using fantasy and imaginative play to communicate what unconsciously lies beneath the surface amazes me. They guide me. Although the individual stories are distinct, the underlying desire remains the same: to experience mirroring that reflects the significance of one's internal world and disconfirms the terror of being left alone to manage the unmanageable. When I surrender and respond to a child's symbolic howl for connection and security, my hope is to psychically transmit a message of belonging and safety. And from this place of being seen and held as beloved in the mind of another, truth-telling in verbal and nonverbal forms of communication takes shape.

The boy who lies on the floor of my office. His right hand reaching out for my left. In the dark. No words. And it's the middle of a school day. His fingers cup mine, to secure the moment, internalize the message: *I can choose this. This want is mine. My hand can want another hand. I am safe.* This is poetry. Specific. Personal. This is where our lives must be of worth to one another. I am reminded of how June lived out the personal as political and the political as personal. And in this room, this boy's bravery to ask for what he wants is his rally cry. Because in tending to his hurt, he makes himself vulnerable, humanizes his need, and moves in the direction of truth. He asks our relationship to serve as a buoy, and together we celebrate the power of connection. I let him ground and savor the experience of someone holding space for his emotional reality. We begin the rewrite.

Truth-telling is confessional. First, you must break that code of silence internally and risk coming to terms with parts of yourself that have been bracketed off from consciousness. Revelation even in the most subtle form is always an aspect of truth-telling.

The undoing of silence is a corrective emotional experience, one we so desperately need on a collective level.

I hear June's hymn in all our tellings: "I am not wrong. Wrong is not my name / My name is my own my own my own."[4]

These stories we tell are meant to be heard. Oracle. Revival. Serum. Telling them just to ourselves becomes verbatim and a form of imprisonment. There is something about putting pen to paper, form to want, and speech into air that allows the truth to expand and convert not only the teller, but the listener; transformation occurs, and all parties are elevated. June is in these rooms. She is alive and awake in these tellings. Because she knows more than anyone:

> These poems
> they are things that I do
> in the dark
> reaching for you
> whoever you are
> and
> are you ready?[5]

Elizabeth Riva Meyer has worked in schools and community-based care as a trauma therapist for over eighteen years. Joining June Jordan's Poetry for the People as an original member in 1991 remains one of the most influential periods of her life, with truth-telling as a core tenet and political act. This teaching weaves into her practice: supporting families in tending to intergenerational wounds and systems-inflicted harm. A growing passion includes mentoring younger clinicians, helping them strengthen their use of self to listen below the surface.

Finding "Living Room" with My Drone

Zeina Azzam

> Under a picture of Gaza City's port, captured by his drone, journalist Yaser Murtaja wrote, "I hope the day that I can take this image when I am in the sky instead of on the ground will come!" [In April 2018, Murtaja] was killed by Israeli forces while covering the . . . protests . . . near the Gaza Strip's eastern border.
>
> —*Al Jazeera, "Yaser Murtaja, and His Dreams of Travelling"*

Be my eyes:
Show me the boys and girls on rooftops
filling their lungs with cool air,
teach me the way fishing boats line Gaza's harbor
in a pattern, like small islands fanning out to sea.
You could make me believe how this sea
goes from turquoise to green to deep blue,
starting from the curving beach and moving
toward sunset, like one vast wave.
I could finally know the contours of a cloud,
travel with the sun in the sky
on a bright arc that starts in Gaza.

Make my dream:
You could help me say for once in my life,
I am a bird soaring above my homeland.
I will fly far away to take pictures, write stories
about people who make art and music and build bridges
then come back to tell my wife and child I missed them,
a hummingbird always returning to its birthplace.

They say journalists in war zones have so much courage
but I want to release the adrenaline, the lump in my throat,
the vest that has knighted me as a member of the press
like two swords, one on each shoulder, sharpened—
I know I could be the sacrifice, I could be the story.

What I wanted was to document the Great March of Return,
to report about Palestinian lives, photograph the tear gas,
burning tires, the flags and bandages and blood
and the marching, the resisting, the falling, the weeping,
the screaming, the bullets of the snipers, the silence of the bullets,
for the world that was watching, in silence.
Remember my words:

اسمي ياسر مرتجى	My name is Yaser Murtaja
عمري 30 سنة	I am 30 years old
ساكن في مدينة غزة	I live in Gaza City
عمري ما سافرت!	I have never traveled before in my life!

Ever since I read June Jordan's poem "Moving towards Home," I have been haunted by her words: "I need to speak about home / I need to speak about living room."[1] Jordan's poem lifted up this idea of "living room"—room for living and breathing and being free from oppression and war—as she wrote about the Sabra/Shatila massacre of Palestinian refugees and Lebanese civilians, which unfolded in Beirut, Lebanon, in 1982. The horrific event was yet another tragedy to mark the Palestinian experience of dislocation and dispossession, and it clearly had a profound impact on Jordan. She spoke out courageously for human rights, for rights to a home and to living room "where my children will grow without horror . . . where I can sit without grief without wailing aloud / for my loved ones."[2] Her enduring and beautiful words toward the end of the poem resonate deeply: "I was born a Black woman / and now / I am become a Palestinian . . . // It is time to make our way home."[3]

As one of the Black writers and thinkers who, early on, was public in her support for Palestinian rights, Jordan paid a political and personal price for voicing her opinions. It is on the shoulders of brave artists and literary figures like her that countless and diverse activists for Palestine stand.

June Jordan understood the Palestinians' yearning to return home to a safe place. This has been the demand of over three-quarters of a million Palestinians who were forced from their homes in 1948 by Zionist militias. That act of violent ethnic cleansing, the Nakba, continues to this day in the occupied West Bank, including Jerusalem. In Gaza, since Israel's most recent war that started in October 2023, Israel has been conducting a genocide.

Indeed, the Gaza Strip has borne the brunt of Israel's colonial policies since 1967. It is noteworthy that Gaza's land area, 140 square miles, is home to fully 70 percent of 1948 refugees and their descendants. Israel's punishing economic blockade, initiated in 2007, and its recurring military assaults on Gaza's population (2008–09, 2012, 2014, and 2021) made life in the enclave extremely arduous and dangerous. The United Nations had regularly reported on severe challenges such as Gaza's contracting economy and soaring unemployment, its collapsed health care system, and the lack of potable water. It characterized the area as becoming "unlivable."

This bleak scenario kindled Gaza's civilian-led protests of the Great March of Return, beginning in March 2018, to demand the right to go home. In response, Israeli snipers killed over two hundred innocent Palestinians and injured tens of thousands more in the fenced-in space of the demonstrations—including children and the elderly, health care workers, journalists, and women and men from all sectors of society.

One of those shot dead was thirty-year-old journalist Yaser Murtaja, despite his clearly marked press vest. Murtaja was known to send his camera drone high above Gaza so he could have a view of his homeland from the sky. It was the only way he could see it: as a Gazan he was not permitted to travel outside of Gaza. In his own way, Murtaja was searching for June Jordan's "living room"—this elemental need, this room to breathe bigger, see wider, hope freely. His young life was cut down brutally, like the lives of those in the Sabra and Shatila refugee camps in 1982, and those in Gaza who, since 2023, have been killed in stupefying numbers.

Assassinations of journalists have recurred often during Israel's wars on Gaza, and especially the one that began in October 2023. In fact, nearly two hundred Palestinian journalists and media workers were killed during this most recent war, and many others were injured or arrested by the Israel Defense Forces. The International Criminal Court considers attacks on journalists as war crimes.

I felt it was important to include Yaser Murtaja's words in Arabic, next to the English translation, because he spoke and wrote these compelling statements in Arabic, his own language. It is one small way to ensure that his voice will still be heard.

Zeina Azzam is a Palestinian American poet, editor, and community activist. Her poetry books include *Bayna Bayna: In-Between* (Poetry Box, 2021) and *Some Things Never Leave You* (Tiger Bark Press, 2023). She volunteers for organizations that promote Palestinian human rights and the civil rights of vulnerable communities in Alexandria, Virginia, where she was poet laureate from 2022 to 2025. Her poems appear in a number of online and printed literary journals and anthologies including *Pleiades, Split This Rock, Making Mirrors: Writing/Righting by Refugees* (Interlink, 2019), and *Gaza Unsilenced* (Just World Books, 2015). She holds a master of arts in Arabic literature.

Love Like a Mango, Obvious

Will Horter

Recent events have given me more time than I'd like to ponder those moments when my life dramatically shifted. January 19, 1986—the eve of the first Martin Luther King Jr. national holiday—was one such turning point. That was the day I met June Jordan, and witnessed a violent preview of the methods elites would use to maintain power in America.

June's "Poem About My Rights" had become an anthem for the ragtag group of anti-apartheid activists pushing my Ivy League college to divest from companies profiting from apartheid in South Africa. We, the Dartmouth Community for Divestment (DCD), were a small, diverse group of students, faculty, and locals appalled by the horrors of apartheid. We faced off against powerful forces: trustees that controlled mines in South Africa, and students more interested in the next frat party than justice in Africa.

These forces collided on that snowy January night in Hanover, New Hampshire. June and her prophetic words were a witness to the power struggle that foreshadowed America's cultural polarization. At countless times at rallies and the endless, almost painful, consensus-based meetings around the shanties we'd built on the college's sacred Green, the last line of "Poem About My Rights" was like a tuning fork for us. Not only did she make the horrors of apartheid palpable, her poem became a rallying cry, merged the personal and political into a ferocious warning to elites: Change was coming.

> I can't tell you who the hell set things up like this
> but I can tell you that from now on my resistance
> my simple and daily and nightly self-determination
> may very well cost you your life[1]

As we discovered that night, Dartmouth's privileged elites, and elites nationally, didn't like the coming change and were prepared to fight back, dirty.

The struggle wasn't just political; it was personal. Like most college students, I was searching for my identity—trying to figure out how society worked, how to live a moral life in an unjust world, all while seeking my niche on a campus where power and privilege dominated. As a socially awkward nondrinker on a frat-dominated campus, I felt out of place. I felt I didn't belong and feared I was an imposter—a feeling I later learned was common among students from nonprivileged backgrounds. June's words resonated, helping turn our feelings of estranged "otherness" into a rallying cry for resistance:

> Do You Follow Me: We are the wrong people of
> the wrong skin on the wrong continent and what
> in the hell is everybody being reasonable about[2]

Her poetry captured the existential angst of acting honorably in an unjust world where power too often goes unchecked:

> and in France they say if the guy penetrates
> but does not ejaculate then he did not rape me
> and if after stabbing him if after screams if
> after begging the bastard and if even after smashing
> a hammer to his head if even after that if he
> and his buddies fuck me after that
> then I consented and there was
> no rape because finally you understand finally
> they fucked me over because I was wrong[3]

A few months earlier, we had convoyed into Hanover with three partially built shanties on a flatbed truck, expecting them to be dismantled immediately. Instead, they endured, becoming symbols of student activism in Reagan's America and the global fight against apartheid. We expected our shanties would stand for only minutes before we were hauled away in handcuffs, so we were shocked when they survived the first night. Even more surprising was when our shanties became global news. No one expected shanties on the bucolic central Green of the most conservative Ivy, the home turf of the right-wing *Dartmouth Review*. Those drafty shanties became my adoptive home most winter nights. Rent was free, food was plentiful. Looking back, they were the most comforting home I've had—until they weren't.

On the eve of the inaugural Martin Luther King Jr. Day, we gathered to hear June speak. June described the atmosphere in the room in her essay "Alternative Commencement Address at Dartmouth College, June 14, 1987":

> I found myself part of an enormous, exhilarated crowd of students, faculty, and administrators happily assembled for their Dartmouth celebration of the legacy of Dr. King. The large room in which we sat breathed simplicity, cleanliness, and goodwill. I heard no aggrieved and no accusatory tones of voice. I saw no conflict in that close-packed multiracial gathering.[4]

June electrified the room, weaving civil rights history with stories of her upcoming musical about the Ku Klux Klan. I cried, I laughed, but most of all, I felt powerful—part of the global movement for truth and justice that couldn't be denied.

June described her sense of tranquility after her speech:

> That evening . . . I took a measuring look around my quintessential Yankee quarters at the historic Hanover Inn. This frugality, this New England exactitude, this sturdy adherence to traditions as palpable as the spotless flowered wallpaper or the tiny cake of Ivory soap, this was bedrock America, I thought, where I might find comfort and fall asleep, without fear.[5]

I, too, felt peaceful that night as I went to sleep at a friend's place. I had no fear and for the first time, I felt I was on the right side of history. That feeling didn't last.

Before sunrise, I learned how power and privilege truly work in America.

The phone startled me awake at 3:00 a.m. The voice on the other end said our shanties had been destroyed. I dressed so quickly, I put my sweater on backward. Rushing back to the Green, I learned twelve vigilantes—ten from the infamous right-wing *Dartmouth Review*—had smashed our shantytown with sledgehammers and crowbars. Two of my friends were inside. Though unharmed, they were shaken by threats. What had been a place of comfort and community hours before was now violated and destroyed.

As I stared at the wreckage, a stanza from "Poem About My Rights" flashed through my mind.

> they fucked me over . . .
> which is exactly like South Africa
> penetrating into Namibia penetrating into
> Angola and does that mean I mean how do you know if
> Pretoria ejaculates what will the evidence look like the
> proof of the monster jackboot ejaculation on Blackland[6]

We witnessed "monster jackboot ejaculation" brought home to Hanover, New Hampshire. Our shanties had made progressive students and activists from Vermont and New Hampshire feel "safe," like we belonged. However, to Dartmouth's powerful elites, and, as we later learned, the rising right-wing movements nationwide, our shanties symbolized something to be crushed by any means necessary—including violence masked as a stunt.

The twelve vigilantes, calling themselves the Dartmouth Committee to Beautify the Green Before Winter Carnival, had been detained in the campus police office, so we headed over.

When I entered the basement office, I immediately heard their laughter. The dirty dozen—after assaulting two young women and smashing an international symbol of antiracist resistance—were laughing, slapping each other on the back as if it were a frat prank, not an investigation into a violent felony.

The sledgehammer-wielders' privilege protected them, and they knew it. June captured this in her "Alternative Commencement Address":

> Those twelve disciples of pure white snow could not tolerate those shanties. They could not and would not abide by civilized rules of conflict. They felt no shame. They knew no reason for restraint. In New Hampshire, one of the few states to reject Martin Luther King

Jr. Day as a legal holiday, those disciples had no need to worry about repercussions: they were safe.[7]

What the vigilantes considered "trash" was our inspiration. The culture wars were beginning.

As I listened to their laughter, the last lines of "Poem About My Rights" took on new meaning.

> but let this be unmistakable this poem
> is not consent I do not consent . . .
> and I can't tell you who the hell set things up like this
> but I can tell you that from now on my resistance
> my simple and daily and nightly self-determination
> may very well cost you your life[8]

June's words helped transform my pain, despair, anger into resolve. That moment changed my life. Since then, I've dedicated myself to confronting arrogant power wherever I found it.

The shanties' destruction shocked June too. In her "Alternative Commencement Address," June recounted her horror upon discovering the wreckage:

> The next morning, I arose quite early. It was cold. From my window, facing the Green, something seemed wrong. I could no longer clearly see the South African anti-apartheid shanties the Dartmouth students had erected there. Hurriedly, I dressed, packed and went downstairs to the street. Across from me at the intersection, a young white woman held up a crudely torn cardboard and magic marker sign: HONK IF YOU HATE APARTHEID. It was very cold. She must have been freezing. And she stood there, stubbornly lifting that sign above her head. It occurred to me that she might be crying. Something about the flush of her cheek suggested that. One car after another car and then another car and then another car slowly passed by the student, in silence. Nobody hated apartheid. It occurred to me that I might be crying. I wanted to run anywhere: to stand there beside the student or really just run away, away from Dartmouth, away from New Hampshire—or else towards the incoming traffic and into it. I wanted to stop the cars with my body. I wanted every car in

the United States to raise an uproar. I wanted the horns of those cars to reach to Pretoria and shake down that infamy right there, right here, in Hanover, New Hampshire. But instead, I stood still and watched that young white woman and I listened and I waited until, finally a car horn broke into that chill silence. And then another one, and then two cars honked their horns. I could hear them. I could see them. We were outnumbered but we were here.[9]

Since then, in many David vs. Goliath struggles for justice, I've found comfort in June's words: "We were outnumbered, but we were here."

From Idol to Mentor

Months later, I did something I had never done before (or since)—I wrote June a fan letter, pouring out my gratitude for her inspiration. Her response revealed another aspect of her genius: her ability to help people find, craft, and share their voices. She became my one and only pen pal, my inspiration as an activist, and my biggest booster as a developing writer.

On my way to southern Africa to join the anti-apartheid fight, I stopped in New York to work on Jesse Jackson's presidential campaign. There, I met Patrice Perkins, who—unbeknownst to me—was partnered with Adrienne Torf, June's collaborator on *Bang Bang über Alles*. The next thing I knew, I was adopted into June's social group.

When the campaign ended, I left for southern Africa, where I met many unsung heroes fighting for freedom against apartheid and imperialism. When I asked how I could best help, they each said, "Go home and fix your country."

So I moved back to Oakland, reconnected with June, and tried to figure out how to fix my country.

June's Love Connection

Over time, our relationship evolved from mentor–mentee to friends; with it, our conversations transitioned from politics to love and connection, although as with her poetry, the distinction was always ambiguous.

My return to the US wasn't smooth. Jobs for new grads were scarce, and I was struggling to find my footing. I couldn't figure out how to channel my growing understanding of injustice into something meaningful. June guided me with a mix of sharp insight and unwavering encouragement. She urged me to apply to law school.

June's support extended beyond the intellectual or political. She paid attention to the whole person, even the parts I didn't prioritize. When I mentioned I was lonely and inept at dating, June urged me to pursue love with the same courage I brought to fighting injustice. June had a way of rooting her advice in love, framing it as part of the larger struggle for liberation.

She also appointed herself my matchmaker, the one area that I resisted June's advice.

Law school was hard; it drained me. To recuperate, I headed to British Columbia for the summer to recuperate. When I told June I'd fallen for Claudia, a fellow Jamaican, she was overjoyed.

Four months after meeting Claudia, we got engaged, and June couldn't have been happier. By the time we married, June's health had declined, and she couldn't attend the wedding in Ocho Rios, so she sent us a poem:

Poem for Will Horter and Claudia Campbell on the Occasion of Their Joining Together—August 21, 1993

Love
like a mango obvious
succulent
but hard
to devour entirely
Love
like a mongoose unlikely
in combat
but cunning
and often enough
a winner

Love
like a half moon kiss rising
close above a coconut tree
lifted out of cold sand
and the sound of waves
washing the world away
Take all of this love
and make it
good
a perfect fruit consumed
beneath

Love	a perfect moon
like the green hills	and lead the waters of your
of Jamaica	trust
while hungry people kill	into high tide
and die below bloody tin roofs	with all the fullness of your perfect
of a misbegotten city	matrimony.

While honored that June had created a poem for us, my thirty-year-old self didn't grasp what she was saying. I understood the mongoose and mango references, but the poem's deeper meaning eluded me, until recently.

June as Muse

June was a force who never let you forget the importance of your voice. She had a way of showing up, even when life threatened to pull you away from the things that mattered most. Before law school, she helped me find opportunities to publish my writing, nudging me toward a future she believed in even when I wasn't sure myself. Her faith in the written word—and in me—was unshakable.

But life has a way of pulling us in different directions. I lost touch with June when I traveled north to be closer to Claudia while finishing my third year of law school. The demands of building a new married life in Canada, then the pressures of work, distracted me while June was battling cancer.

Though we spoke occasionally, I stayed away more often than I should have. I never saw her in person again before she passed, but her voice stayed with me, echoing through every turning point in my life.

When Claudia and I discovered we were pregnant, I was terrified. How can you bring a child into such a chaotic world? A friend suggested I write letters to my unborn child, documenting my choices, explaining what I had done to forestall the chaotic world she had inherited. Kind of a climate-chaos version of the "Letters from a Father to His Daughter" that Nehru wrote about parenting through the partitioning of India.

But when my daughter Asha was born four months prematurely, her survival uncertain, all my plans were scrambled. In my shock, it was June's encouragement that came back to guide me. Faced with the overwhelming confusion of those days, I turned to writing, channeling my fears and hopes about my daughter's future, and the world she would inherit, into messages for family and friends. What began as updates for loved ones became something deeper—a rediscovery of my voice.

June's poetry was my touchstone during that time. Whenever I found myself staring at a blank page, unsure how to capture the weight of what we were living through, her words brought me back to center. Writing those updates—what I called "hope messages"—was as much for me as it was for others, a way to stay grounded in love and resilience. Her poetry was often a tuning fork, bringing me back into harmony with myself, reminding me of the power of speaking my truth, no matter how imperfectly. As Asha grew stronger, so did my writing.

This gift June gave me, she also shared with countless others. At the Poetry for the People gala at Berkeley, I witnessed firsthand how June helped people of all backgrounds find their sacred voices. Her students' poems transported me into diverse lives defined by beauty, joy, anger, and longing that defined their lives.

June's longing and desire for connection wasn't just for her friends or students but for her country. June wielded every tool at her disposal—her voice, her time, her essays, poems, columns, and teaching—to expose the forces that threatened it: bigotry, racial and police violence, misogyny, oppressive regimes, and war.

Her words were often harsh, and her disappointment and anger deep, but her love for her country and her longing to heal its deepest wounds pulsate brightly in all her efforts.

I have tried to emulate that. It's been a difficult, but hugely satisfying journey.

I frequently got lost along the way, and June's poetry, essays, and silent counsel in my ear always helped me find my path.

While struggling through my separation from Claudia, I reread our wedding poem. June's advice became clearer: She was counseling me to tame my mongoose-like tendencies, urging us to embrace the inherent contradictions in relationships and savor the pleasures of the moment. Love, she seemed to say, requires trust—not just in others but in the messy, beautiful process of connection itself.

It's advice I wish I had been ready to hear sooner, but even now, it feels like a gift.

I miss you, June, but you are never far away.

Will Horter is an activist, writer, dad, and friend. As a campaigner for his entire adult life, his strategies are based on building relationships through grassroots organizing and precise political intervention. His work has changed the landscape of environmental and democracy campaigning in British Columbia. His current work as CEO of Action CoLabs involves building a powerful ecosystem of partner organizations working together to shape culture and shift power. Like tennis, campaigns aren't won by lobbing the ball up the middle of the court; to win, you have to hit to the lines.

June Jordan

When All Things Are Dear That Disappear

Wesley Brown

W. H. Auden expressed upon the death of William Butler Yeats that Ireland's calamitous history had hurt him in poetry. It could be said, as well, that conscienceless power hurt and angered June Jordan into poetry and political engagement. So, as we stagger into the 2020s, unable to see for looking, we are in desperate need of rekindling our attention to the writing of June Jordan to remind us that the national sickness we are experiencing at the present moment is not an aberration. And her words, having been indispensable to us while she was physically in our midst, are equally important now.

For me, the poem "On a New Year's Eve" speaks directly to the necessity of remembering what has systematically driven the worst human impulses in our nation's distant and recent past, while remaining vigilant in making room for the delight hidden in plain sight.

The opening lines,

> Infinity doesn't interest me
>
> not altogether
> anymore[1]

suggest that, for June Jordan, the experiences or events beyond our capacity to measure are not nearly as wondrous as the ephemeral and seemingly inconsequential moments.

> like the children
> running
> hard on oneway streets . . .[2]

Jordan then catalogues the sacredness of what is, by its very nature, temporary:

> first bikeride round the house
> when you saw a squat
> opossum
> carry babies on her back
> opossum up
> in the persimmon tree
> you reeling toward
> that natural
> first
> absurdity
> with so much wonder still
> it shakes your voice[3]

As for the breathtaking spectacles of the natural world, such as snow, the stars, rain, and mountain peaks, Jordan's focus is not where we would expect.

> let the world blot
> obliterate remove so-
> called
> magnificence
> so called
> almighty/fathomless and everlasting/
> treasures/
> wealth
> (whatever that may be)[4]

And it never ceases to quicken my breath through the simplicity of her language, which articulates, as a children's story would, the history of the forest from the perspective of the trees.

> it is this history
> I care about
> the one we make together
> awkward
> inconsistent
> as a lame cat on the loose
> or quick as kids freed by the bell
> or else as strictly
> once
> as only life must mean
> a once upon a time[5]

And what could be a more visceral and unimpeded embodiment of freedom than the bell releasing children at the end of a school day?

June Jordan also offers a reminder that while straining our bodies and voices . . .

> preaching on
> that oil and oxygen
> that redwoods and the evergreens
> that trees the waters and the atmosphere
> compile a final listing of the world in
> short supply[6]

. . . we must resist the seductive free fall into the diction and actions of the powerful. And in the final lines of the poem, she reminds us that our efforts to advocate on behalf of the only earth we will ever have must also attend to the heart and bone of what is precious and vulnerable within ourselves.

> but all alive and all the lives
> persist perpetual
> in jeopardy
> persist
> as scarce as every one of us
> as difficult to find
> or keep
> as irreplaceable

as frail
as every one of us . . .

and
. . . . . .
I know

all things are dear
that disappear

*all things are dear
that disappear*[7]

As someone who was fortunate enough to know June Jordan, I have treasured and continue to treasure her persistent and irreplaceable presence when voiced out loud, on the page, or through the urgency of what was so much a part of everything she was driven to do. And that is the only thing allowing me to accept the last lines of the poem when thinking of June Jordan:

*all things are dear
that disappear*[8]

Wesley Brown is the author of three novels—*Tragic Magic* (Daunt Books, 2025), *Push Comes to Shove* (Concord, 2009), and *Darktown Strutters* (Cane Hill, 1994)—the short story collection *Dance of the Infidels* (Concord, 2017), the novella *Blue in Green* (Blank Forms, 2022), and five produced plays. He wrote the narration for a segment of the PBS documentary *W. E. B. DuBois: A Biography in Four Voices* and coedited *The Methuen Drama Anthology of Women Playwrights, 1970–2020* (Bloomsbury, 2020). He is a former visiting professor in the arts division at Bard College at Simon's Rock and professor emeritus of English at Rutgers University.

"Something Like a Sonnet"

Reading June Jordan, Finding My Voice, and Becoming an Oral Historian

Kelly Elaine Navies

> This is the difficult miracle of Black Poetry: that we persist, published or not, and loved or unloved: we persist.
>
> —June Jordan, "The Difficult Miracle of Black Poetry in America"

People often ask me how I came to be an oral historian. The answer is that the path was laid before me by teachers and elders, such as my parents, as well as the late Barbara Christian and the late June Jordan, who instilled in me a passion for history, poetry, and the oral tradition. My first teachers were, of course, my mother and father, Constance Elaine Gregory and Richard D. Navies I, both of whom were natural storytellers, deeply rooted in a knowledge of their history and the struggles of African American people.

The dialect poetry of Paul Laurence Dunbar rolled off my mother's tongue with ease, and in a honeyed, musical voice she would tell stories about a grandmother who floated on air and a great-grandmother born into slavery in Asheville, North Carolina. On long-distance road trips, Daddy would proudly repeat the story of his great-grandfather Lit Navies, a landowner in Mississippi who had a confrontation with the sheriff and had to leave town to escape a lynching. This ancestor ended up in Arkansas, where he apparently had another run-in with whites, and this time they succeeded in lynching him. These stories were just the beginning—I became conscious of a lineage of words, history, struggle, and sound. Their voices are the bass line and heartbeat to the ancestral soundtrack of the work I do as the museum specialist in oral history at the Smithsonian National Museum of African American History and Culture.

The last semester before I transferred from UCLA to UC Berkeley in 1988, I took a course from none other than Ntozake Shange—it was she who introduced me to June Jordan. I still have the paperback copy of June's *On Call: Political Essays* that I purchased for this class. On the cover, June is pictured with Francisco Campbell in an area of Teotecacinte, Nicaragua, that had recently been bombed by the Contras. I had seen June Jordan's name among the books on my father's shelves but had never read her work. At age twenty, I don't think I had ever read a book that covered such a wide array of topics, from the conflicts in Nicaragua and South Africa to interracial marriage and the life and work of Phillis Wheatley. It was that particular essay, "The Difficult Miracle of Black Poetry in America, or Something Like a Sonnet for Phillis Wheatley," that had the most impact on me. In this piece, June takes on the story of Wheatley, the first Black poet published in America. Wheatley was kidnapped from West Africa as a young child, was enslaved by the Wheatley family of Boston, and was writing poetry by fourteen years old. Jordan starts: "It was not natural. And she was the first. Come from a country of many tongues tortured by rupture, by theft, by travel like mismatched clothing packed down into the cargo hold of evil ships sailing, irreversible, into slavery."[1]

Like everyone else, I had been introduced to Wheatley as one of Black History's iconic "Firsts." But I had choked on her colonial phrases and enslaved mentality, even as I respected the literary accomplishment of one who had been stolen from Africa and sold into slavery as a child. Jordan's piece exploded those surface responses to Wheatley's work with a scathing revisionist stance: "How could you, belonging to no one, but property to those despising the smiles of your soul, how could you dare to create yourself: a poet?" and "How should there be Black poets in America?"[2]

You see, June cut through the layers of misinterpretation, right to the core of the story, and saw the true miracle that Wheatley represented. The miracle was not that she could read and write poetry even better perhaps than those who had taught her—the miracle was that she wrote, *poetry*, in an alien land, under oppressive circumstances. Recalling the poem "Sympathy" by Paul Laurence Dunbar, Jordan addressed the quandary, the magic of a caged bird, an enslaved human being, singing, or in this case, writing poetry. And Jordan did it by turning her brilliant and, yes, scholarly analysis into lyrical prose and poetry. In this way, June resurrected the true spirit of Wheatley that had lain dormant beneath centuries of dry accolades and face-value readings of her work. Jordan outlined the narrative of Wheatley's short life, from her historic first book of poetry, published when she was still enslaved, to the few short years she lived after her white owner, Suzannah Wheatley, died, and she married a Black man, John Peters. She continued to write poetry, but this poetry, the poetry of a free Black woman married to a free Black man, was never published.

This subversive essay stirred something in me, reminded me of my mother's soulful voice and my father's rebellious one. It showed me that our history cannot be fully interpreted or understood without poetry. How else to capture the silences and omissions, the depth of misery and the resilience? In "Something Like a Sonnet," Jordan responds to her own rhetorical question, "How should there be Black poets in America?" as a conscious and intellectually free Black woman. The juxtaposition of June's liberated voice, beside that of the enslaved woman Phillis Wheatley, underscores June's thesis that Wheatley—who died in poverty, though legally free, at the young age of thirty-one—left us before we could know what her voice was really like as a freed woman.

After absorbing Jordan's perspective on Wheatley and becoming enamored of the music of its language, I have found the genres of poetry and history are forever linked in my consciousness and understanding. My approach to the work I do as an oral historian is suffused with a love of poetic language, rhythm, style, and sensibility. When I conduct an oral history, my concerns are similar to June's in her essay: "What were you thinking/doing/experiencing that hasn't been documented?" I seek to bring out the stories that people carry inside them but do not generally share, unless asked in the right way. What struggles and journeys lie beneath the surface? In one interview I conducted, a

Black man shares a story he hasn't spoken of to anyone in over sixty years: He recalls swimming in a Baltimore water hole on the white side of town. "He wasn't supposed to be there," he says quietly, "and they killed him."[3] Using few words, spaced between thin breaths, he tells a shocking story of a Black child murdered by whites for swimming on the wrong side of town. Why, after all these years, does he decide to tell this story? I record, feeling the shift that has occurred in the telling. Once released, these truths are free to land on the hearts and minds of anyone who takes the time to listen.

Jordan ends this brilliant essay with a poem about Wheatley written in the form of a sonnet:

> Chosen by whimsy but born to surprise
> They taught you to read but you learned how to write
> Begging the universe into your eyes:
> They dressed you in light but you dreamed
> with the night.
> From Africa singing of justice and grace,
> Your early verse sweetens the fame of our Race.[4]

June Jordan's essay influenced my evolution as a writer, historian, and oral historian. It gave me a blueprint for weaving poetry into the writing of history, and, perhaps more significantly, showed me how to bring a poetic sensibility to historical research and analysis. Further, by highlighting the ways in which the history of African Americans has often been suppressed by traditional historical documentation and analysis, it nudged me toward and prepared me for the subversive work of oral history. The discipline of oral history evolved from a need to discover a perspective of history beyond that available from written documents alone. The paper trails that are the foundation of traditional historical documentation and scholarship more often leave evidence of the lives of the privileged and powerful. For example, when researchers and writers began to draw upon ancient oral traditions and listen to the recollections of the formerly enslaved in oral history projects, such as the Works Progress Administration interviews almost one hundred years ago, our understanding of the era of slavery and the lives of the enslaved expanded and pushed scholars to ask more relevant questions. As an oral historian, I seek to facilitate the telling of stories that have often been overlooked or even suppressed by traditional historical sources. I am always thinking I don't want these voices to be lost to time and misinterpretation, like the voice of Phillis Wheatley, or the enslaved women experimented upon by "pioneering" gynecologist J. Marion Sims, and so many others whose stories we will never know. In this way, each oral history I record and preserve is an act of rebellion against a tradition of colonizing scholarship that glorifies the oppressor at the expense of the oppressed.

As much as these stories document trauma, they also document those moments of joy that have sustained African American people. For example, I've recorded the recollections of two sisters who attended the triumphant Marian Anderson concert at the Lincoln Memorial in 1939, dressed in their Easter Sunday finery. Their voices were still filled with pride seventy-five years later. Their story says, *We were there—you may not have seen us in any movie or book about that day, but we were there.*[5]

In the fall of 1988, I finished Shange's class on a whole new level of consciousness from when I began, eager to continue my study of African American history and poetry in UC Berkeley's African American studies department. Serendipitously, my arrival on Berkeley's campus in the fall of 1989 coincided with that of June Jordan. I immediately signed up for her class, The Politics of Female Childhood. Here, I met the woman in the flesh, and she was funny, direct, soft, and fierce, all at the same time. She had this way of challenging you with her all-knowing eyes, dead serious one minute and the next erupting into the silliest girlish laughter. Her curriculum embodied her entire philosophy of writing, and really, of the meaning of life itself. We read the autobiographical essay "Such, Such Were the Joys" by George Orwell and the novel *Brown Girl, Brownstones* by Paule Marshall—works that are seemingly unrelated, but essentially different takes on self-exploration, class analysis, and marginalization. Then, she would challenge us to write about our own female childhoods with provocative prompts like "Good vs. Bad" and "Love or Fear." She also had us read passages from the Bible, like 1 Corinthians 13:11: "When I was a child, I spoke as a child."

I wrote about how I learned that girls and boys were different when I got in trouble for taking off my shirt during recess in elementary school. The boys could take off their shirts when they were hot and sweaty—why couldn't I? I wrote about discovering the nuances of colloquial Black language when I learned that "bad" was a compliment. When I got my first afro, my mother's best friend had said, "That's badddd!" I started to cry before they quickly explained what she meant. Often these prompts led to much more serious and heart-wrenching revelations. But June didn't stop with our in-class readings, which took place with our seats arranged in a circle.

After we had bared our souls with one another over a period of transformative weeks, she surprised us about midway through the semester by telling us our final project would be to share these stories with the public, on the radio! And that we did. We produced an hour-long show for the local public station, KPFA. What would Phillis Wheatley have said if she had the opportunity to take such a class? What flood of poetic catharsis would emerge from a prompt such as "home" or "mama"?

After this course, I took her course on African American poetry. In this course, we read in the rich tradition of African American poets, from Langston Hughes to Cornelius Eady, and wrote poetry inspired by their works. As we studied the poetry of Gwendolyn Brooks and its themes of motherhood, I wrote a poem called "Somebeginningsofmywomanme" that began:

> All I know
> come from
> stories I heard
> an' a faded photo of three
> of my ancestors/me
> she Black/fresh earth after morning rain
> an'
> comely
> mama say she float on air
> while chantin juju an' pickin wild dandelions

During this same semester, fall 1990, I took a course from Barbara Christian called Images of Black Women in Literature. While we studied the works of Ann Petry, Alice Walker, Toni Morrison, and others, she gave us an optional assignment to write a paper about a maternal ancestor who had lived in the nineteenth century. Optional, of course, because many people cannot write about their nineteenth-century maternal ancestors, because they don't know anything about them, particularly African Americans. I decided to rise to the challenge, go "in search of my mother's gardens," and write about the ancestor my mother had been telling me about all those years, the mother of the woman who she claimed had floated on air. I decided that I would write my paper based on oral histories with my grandmother's siblings, all of whom remembered this particular ancestor, their grandmother.

Thus, from this cauldron of literature, poetry, and history, steeped in themes of motherhood, womanism, and defiance and immersed in the scholarly and creative worlds of June Jordan, Barbara Christian, Alice Walker, and other Black women writers, I became an oral historian and poet. When I am engaged in the act of what I call "soul listening," capturing the story of an elder, the words and worlds of these mentors are my compass, showing me the way and urging me to pass it all on to the next generation of daughters.

Kelly Elaine Navies is an oral historian, writer, and poet. As museum specialist in oral history, she coordinates the Oral History Initiative at the Smithsonian National Museum of African American History and Culture in Washington, DC. Her writing and poetry may be found in several publications, most recently in *Affrilachia: Testimonies* (University Press of Kentucky, 2024) with photographer Chris Aluka Berry. As an undergraduate in the African American studies program at UC Berkeley, she was a founding member of June Jordan's Poetry for the People.

Wild Grapevines

Kelly Elaine Navies

Now I know more
of the beginningsofmywomanme
over one hundred years
She walked
grandmother of my mother's mother
many miles
over land stolen from the Cherokee
looking for herbs
to heal her children
baby would you like some Sassafras tea?
She might say
with a smoky mountain twang
or don't you wanna piece of granmas hot bread chile?
before walking another
high country mile
from wombs of many sisters
she pulled forth new life
and this gift she passed on
to Annie
mother of my mother's mother
the one mama saw
risin from the ground
while callin on spirits
with the holy sound
of her voice
strong Annie
married a weak and angry man
who tried to beat the wings
off her back

but the singing wind tells me
that Annie will always fly
cuz her seven daughters
left the mountains
swingin on the ends of wild grapevines
one of the seven gave birth to my mama
who then gave birth to me
who gives you this poem
so you will see
that the beginnings of mywomanme
speak to
the beginnings of us all
our women we

Choosing My Mind Between the Mosquitos and the Moon[1]

Ruth Nicole Brown

I have a set of instructions:

Do something with that which you don't see

I'm telling you

(it's here).

It's a lot of us, together.

Can you feel it

yet?

      Some nature in nature.

                        I have a few notes from the meeting:

              She's worried about what everyone else is saying.
                  She's trying to avoid getting in trouble.
               She's play fighting not really fighting fighting.
                          Now wanting to drop it
                                      after
                                She started it.

Her desire to be a doctor
doctor is supposed to motivate.
Does problem-solving
lead to more problems?
Punishment includes its
own critique about all
the problems it
(re)produced.

Can you feel it

yet?

Black girlhood: New natures.

In solitude and reflection she contemplates Black girlhood outsides. She was searching for a more Toni Cade Bambara-esque correct path when brought into mediation for correction. She is not the first.

Outside was no escape.

Still, she delights in Black girlhood energies surround sound. She remains quiet and listening. There is a different presence at the table than usual, a breeze. The preference she abides for networks of collective beings and unexpected mediums, who know to nuance pink when backed by friable wall surfaces, are all kin. She remembers tracing the veins of a leaf and how deep it is to be in what Denise Ferreira da Silva theorized as knowing (at) the limits of justice.[2] She wants to practice this inside as then practice for outside—till the boundaries are not the source of power from which responsible student is measurable by dogmas of controllable goodness.

Not easy to read nor to see, freedom she keeps telling us, is not possible without her and those ants.

Prior to getting in trouble, she walked. She observed the cardinals and koi and relished the small universes transforming every thingbeing her eye fixed on into something else. As was she. The police were still there. They watched her incessantly. She looked back at them and felt both human and suspect. A deer appeared through the grasses. Ears alert to her rhythm. She jumped in fear and then laughed.

That is how she loves. Feeling.

Outside widens her sense of time and space. It has made her want to learn genomic biology and chemistry. Here she is tracked on their list with other decided subjects, she who also cannot be known as having been called Black girls. Unannounced anti-capitalists they keep going and returning. There is a responsibility she recognizes but did not create. The climate begs for change.

PART THREE: THE AWESOME, DIFFICULT WORK OF LOVE | 247

She questions carbon, "What do you know about release?"

Filling my eyes with flowers of no name,
contemplate

this communication for
17 billion years from now:
you should not mess
with Black girls
with the same kind of concern
you have for
nuclear waste.

---

*   The portions of text in italics are the first lines of each stanza from June Jordan's poem "Out in the Country of My Country." This creative work is a demonstration of speaking nearby (following Trinh T. Minh-ha in "Speaking Nearby").

Testing my heart with precipice and crest . . .

the how is between blue and green. An egret stopped flight just to tell me to tell you never get so correct you forget coral reef. The paperwork certainly misinterprets your quiet as silence, inducing a shame to which you do not belong. Remember, **they never ask** a password to speak, again. Sing wren. Song sparrow. This is how to transform victimhood circumstances into critical thought. And so do you.

Choosing my mind between mosquitos and the moon

we overthrow entire systems.

PART THREE: THE AWESOME, DIFFICULT WORK OF LOVE | 249

Chasing my face among displacements of a stream

Singular heart beats to a bassline of those who also refuse
                              the violence of becoming
                              the violence of restoration
                              the violence of expulsion

                    What else can a twelve-year-old humanist do?

Before you go, overturn it. To turn it all the way out.

Ruth Nicole Brown is an artist-scholar whose life work is dedicated to the celebration of Black girlhood. Inaugural chair and full professor of African American and African studies at Michigan State University, her study of Black girlhood emerges from over a decade of practice, including face-to-face conversations, rituals of dance and movement, and active relationship-building with Black girls and women in Saving Our Lives Hear Our Truths, which is lovingly referred to by the acronym SOLHOT. Author of *Black Girlhood Celebration: Toward a Hip-Hop Feminist Pedagogy* (Peter Lang, 2009) and *Hear Our Truths: The Creative Potential of Black Girlhood* (University of Illinois Press, 2013), Ruth Nicole was awarded the Whiting Public Engagement Fellowship for SOLHOT's premier project, Black Girl Genius Week.

A Note on Praxis and Black Girls

Dominique C. Hill

> What I wanted to do was I wanted to live my life
> so that people would know unmistakingly that I am alive, so
> that when I finally die people will know the difference for sure
> between my living and my death
>
> —*June Jordan, "Many Rivers to Cross"*

I want you to know and remember, June Jordan is an embodiment of praxis. In "Many Rivers to Cross," Jordan disclosed her struggles to find footing as a mother, writer, and contracted employee alongside the story of her mother's transitioning from life to death. While confessing the dearth of choice, heaviness, and impediments to full living, she named her rivers. And when she went home to live with her parents, she stepped into a river. Lodged within her narration is the labor of crossing rivers as well as the theory and practice of living. Taking up Jordan's river crossings, this auto/poetic essay revisits the metaphor "many rivers to cross," also a song written by Sam Cooke, to pronounce praxis a legacy of Jordan's. Further, this essay in content and process engages the tool of truth-telling, a necessary action in the challenging and necessary labor of love.

I. A Portal to Praxis

Ancestors, also known as portals to answers, don't always come while sleeping. Sometimes they come through people. Sometimes they come while we are trying to do something differently. June Jordan came when I wanted sooo bad to get it right—"it" being how to translate theory into something real, of real use.

The year was 2009. With one year of doctoral studies under my belt, an insistence that I needed to study with Ruth Nicole Brown, and a commitment to researching Black girls' educational experiences in ways that did right by us, I signed up for Brown's course on girlhood. After all, upon reading up on her work through the Black girl creative space of Saving Our Lives Hear Our Truths (SOLHOT), I intuited I needed to learn from her. During my initial encounter, it was the truth serum I was not yet ready for and eventually faced. It demands realness, especially of its homegirls—those responsible for maintaining the tone the girls set, bringing snacks, building the arsenal for us to work from, and ensuring we have what we need to create and be with each other. Brown was charting an important journey declaring Black girlhood studies an academic field of study and centering Black girlhood celebration. Though the words weren't foreign, together they didn't so easily run off the tongue. Importantly, she made it abundantly clear that this invitation to see Black girls in their complex genius started long ago and that there were no outside saviors in such work. It was there in African American Girlhood that I was introduced to the soldier, artivist, Black girlhood studies conduit, always poet, June Jordan.

I don't know if it was her father's ambivalence and avoidance of her mother, the pain of being regarded as a failure, coming to terms with family, heartbreak, or a combination or none of these that forged new visions of living for Jordan. What I learned, though, through her well-documented and sensed rivers, is that death sometimes looks like living, coming alive sometimes requires death, and intergenerational relationships unconsciously teach this lesson. I trusted Brown. I went to Illinois without fully being able to name *why*. Have you ever been called to a place but unsure of why? I could not give it language then, could not make sense of why I knew I had to study with Brown or why I needed SOLHOT, but I yearned to know and to meet praxis. I wasn't ready, more like I wasn't (yet) open enough, to name my rivers. And praxis helped me see myself differently.

II. The Unnamed River

When I met Jordan through the Black girl celebratory space of SOL-HOT and the course African American Girlhood, I did not know I was disallowing myself to feel things. Had no clue I was approaching a crossroads around what I defined as my work. Neither did I know June Jordan by name (but I felt, and learned, her under a different name). Do you know how it feels to want something so badly *and* not be doing a damn thing about it? Not doing much more than wanting? Insisting the problem is "out there?" I started my Black girlhood work with the unconscious belief that the work I needed to do was theoretical. That the primary (possibly only) issue was with the wording. I had a language problem, I thought. If different words were used to describe Black girls, if I continued my work with Black girls in and beyond formal school spaces, if my language showed no signs of pathology, the work was done, right?! Wrong. The rivers before me were many, but the one that consumed much of my time was my insistence to hide my *usedta be* from my *now*, and my *now* me from who I hoped to become. Then, I wasn't open enough to see the bracketing I'd done on myself. The continuous self-partitioning I participated in to show up as together as possible. The irony. When Jordan got a hold of me, however, when I opened myself to the work of living in full presence, I understood language to be symptomatic, a sign of a sickness beneath the surface. Language manifests as fever, broken skin, bad breath—an indicator something is damaged at the root.

III. I[M]am Possible

Impossible/ beyond description
ill eligible
Is that my address?
Wrong Towers, apartment number "impossible to explain"
To get to/in/out of?
On, "not yet exactly" avenue?
Is that why Black girls be
ill eligible?

Regarded as wrong?
Cuz they be impossible to explain?
Not yet woman as they are and yet oh so seen—
as grown, fas, as nothing of substance
but more than enough to chew off, bite off, break off—
enough to make folk come alive again
Is living on "not yet exactly" ave—
Why Faith Fennidy got removed from Christ the King,
for her Black hair being wrong?
Why before her there was Tiana, Lamya, Vanessa, Mya and Deanna
and others?
Why Black girls go missing from rooftops, villages, playgrounds?
And is it because she be Black and girl that everyone is being
reasonable?
Is living on "not yet exactly" avenue why no precautions were taken
and left Ayanna murdered?
Is it because she be Black, girl, and wrong that everyone is being
reasonable?
And that still is not consent
She does not, we do not consent.
We, who grew up on the ave, who broke form,
impossibly here,
remote from interpretations,
not yet exactly anything other than absolutely possible.

Celebrating Black girls, not disappearing them/us into woman woes and concerns—claiming Black girlhood as sacred, intergenerational, identity-affirming and not identity-specific—requires a comfort with self I did not always have. When I entered SOLHOT, when I met Jordan, I arrived at that river. Prior to my arrival at this river's shore, I had no idea my work would take a deeply internal road. Nor that I would evolve into me, a Blackqueer body alchemist and vulnerability guide. Soon after opening myself to Jordan, I stood face-to-face with the realization that if I could truly see myself whole, then other girls had a chance in my eyes. If I could look at my scarred skin and see art, then I could do the same when looking at Black girls, including the one who often sized me up in the mirror. If I could see myself in them, I could also feel them.

If I could *be* with Black girls—not posing only as the serious woman who took issue with education or the graduate student hiding her overcommitment to doing school well, but instead allowing myself to move and question and laugh and cry—then I could simultaneously live in my skin and be (w)holy. If I could hold true to being the girlwomangod who stuck/still sticks her tongue out while she dances, knows how to do school well and (still) chooses to do it wrong, then maybe when I received access to "power" rooms, those rooms filled with folks perfecting machinations designed to fix Black people, I would be too busy co-constructing other rooms. I would be impossibly standing with you, as you. In her book-length poem *Who Look at Me*, written especially for Black youth and about Black survival and imagination, Jordan taught us that since our Blackness renders us impossible, and structural and culturally manufactured demarcations might encourage and seemingly require us to splice ourselves into pieces, living in our skin may prove difficult—and yet, we do live. Therefore, I am impossible and yet somehow standing with others traversing the laborious and necessary task of being true to who we are despite the impossibility and genius of it. Jordan understood, taught, warned, anything less than living will cost us our lives. And surely, anything less than living as we are, in our skin—is defeat. In the spirit of Jordan, I invite rumination: What work are we refusing? What rivers haven't we crossed?

Dominique C. Hill is a creative and vulnerability guide whose scholarship interrogates embodiment with foci in Black girlhood, education, and performance. Hill's art and scholarship illuminate tensions between race and gender, identity and structures, and reality and possibility. Hill is the coauthor of *Who Look at Me?!: Shifting the Gaze of Education Through Blackness, Queerness, and the Body* (with Durrell M. Callier; Brill, 2019), which interrogates the gaze afforded Blackness and queerness in education. Hill's pedagogy and praxis of Black feminism is informed by Jordan's cultural work, audacious living, and approach to education beyond the confines of schools. Hill is an assistant professor of women's studies at Colgate University.

Become a Menace

Afaa M. Weaver 尉雅風

To the unsheathed knife,
be the sheath
To the blinding light,
be the shade
To the screaming wind,
be the still air
To the disappearing night,
be the sun's kiss
To the piercing horn,
be a cry of pain
To the loaded gun,
be invisible
To what falls to break,
be an open heart
To the hand that crushes,
be a caress
To hatred
be love
To love
be truth
To an ending
be a beginning.

Afaa M. Weaver's new collection is *A Fire in the Hills* (Red Hen Press, 2023). He recently won the Paterson Poetry Prize and the Wallace Stevens Award. Afaa is a chancellor at the Academy of American Poets.

Afterword

June Jordan

An Eternal Summer

Imani Perry

There are writers at whom we marvel, a small and special cohort. But among them is an even smaller number with whom we think as we pursue every endeavor—especially our own writing and even more importantly, our own efforts at decency and virtue. June Jordan is in that tiny, precious group. Perhaps that is why we tend to call her June instead of the more distant and formal Jordan. We fall in love with her, in all her political conviction and sweet sensitivity, and want to hold her close.

She is like that favorite teacher, the one who as children we painstakingly wrote cards to, hoping to impress her with our penmanship and poetry. Every piece she wrote is didactic without arrogance. She instructed with a gentle hand, standing in dilemma, challenging us to problem solve. I regularly teach two essays of hers, "Report from the Bahamas" and "Nobody Mean More to Me Than You and the Future Life of Willie Jordan."

The former I bring into the classroom for its honesty about multinational corporations, tourism that rests upon the firmament of colonialism, and the uneasy relationships between here and there, with here and there referring to distinct class positions, citizenships and gender politics. In that piece, June models honesty about her own privilege and yet is rigorous in thinking beyond herself to the life of Olive, the domestic worker who cleans her room.

I love "Nobody Mean More to Me Than You" because it is a love letter to Black language while simultaneously confronting what it signifies in a white supremacist world, how it marks us. She goes even deeper, reminding us that language is never a static fact; it is a tool of relation and communication. Therefore language demands improvisation and negotiation, just like jazz. The essay is pedagogical as well, showing a teacher who, operating at her best, allows for the whole student to emerge and bloom. June is a facilitator for that process, sensitive to both the heartbreak of violence and the joy of community.

The poems and essays in this volume attest to how June remains our faithful teacher from the grave and on the page, a model of truth, witnessing, analysis, and a magisterial vulnerability that isn't offered for the sake of entertainment (reading her isn't just for pleasure or an anguish that absolves us of political responsibility.). No, her vulnerability asks us to be truth tellers too. She issued calls, and on the foregoing pages you read beautiful responses. This is important political work in this era of climate catastrophe, mass killing (of people and histories), and convenient subterfuge, a dying-while-destroying imperialism, and the marketization of everything as Arundhati Roy describes it. I beg you to hold fast to this book and return to it and June Jordan's corpus whenever your courage falters and your spirit is low.

I met June Jordan only once. It was at a dinner filled with dignitaries. In my early twenties, I sat between her and Toni Morrison (awestruck) and across the table was Derrick Bell. I don't remember what she said, but I remember how it felt to be around her. She was delicate, coppery, and listened more than she spoke. Her liquid eyes danced and her smile was so bright it seemed to illuminate the whole room like summer sunlight. That is what it looked like, I thought then (and still do), to live in the full confidence of one's calling and convictions, unfettered by conventional should-haves and must-do's. That is the glow of freedom dreaming. Still standing in her light, we remember her and honor her—years past her departure—an eternal summertime of the soul.

Acknowledgments

Thank you to everyone included in and touched by the Blueprint Collective, by Poetry for the People, and by June Jordan.

This collection was made possible by falling angels. Falling, as in gliding, surprising, audacious, with outstretched arms. From her hospital bed one day before she traveled to the next realm, Lauren Muller was still divining next steps, from the same San Francisco hospital where Lauren visited June before she threw out a thousand batons. Thank you to Barbara Ransby, consummate activist/scholar who guided us to Haymarket. All praises to Maya Marshall for your heavy lift, your humor, your talent, your divine interventions. Seriously, you made this publication possible. Appreciation to Abbie Phelps, Reed Floarea, Jameka Williams, Sam Smith, and Jim Plank for ushering this collection into the world. Thank you especially to Adrienne Torf, whose piano, advice, and kindness have been constant. To Ethelbert, who stuck close through so many moons and led us to Chester Higgins's glorious photo on the front cover. To Genevieve Harriford for tree-hugging in high winds. For three decades being family. To Alexis Pauline Gumbs for your luminous first words and Imani Perry for the last. Thank you to Caroline Reger for your many skills and patience in the first years of this project. And blessings to Ariel Muller, for your sister love for Lauren and her legacy, 'til the end and still. Lauren's family and colleagues celebrate her life with the Lauren Muller Beloved Scholarship for City College of San Francisco students.

Through Black Lives Matter, the pandemic, terror in Gaza, and rising repression in the US, the contributors have hung in there, now gracing these pages with tributes and celebrations, wisdom and questions, poetry and prose to buoy us. June . . . your writing, teaching, and activism all live—in olive trees, on billboards, in classrooms, and in our wild and sustaining imaginations.

Notes

Foreword: A Definition of Love
1 June Jordan, "The Creative Spirit: Children's Literature," in *Revolutionary Mothering: Love on the Front Lines*, ed. Alexis Pauline Gumbs, China Martens, and Mai'a Williams (PM Press, 2016), 12.

Black Alive and Looking Straight at You
1 Originally published in *Power and Possibility: Essays, Reviews, and Interviews* (University of Michigan Press, 2016). Reprinted with permission. Thank you to Charles Watkinson for late-night approval.
2 June Jordan, "Where Is the Love?," in *We're On: A June Jordan Reader*, ed. Christoph Keller and Jan Heller Levi (Alice James Books, 2017), 346.
3 June Jordan, "Break the Law," in *Some of Us Did Not Die: New and Selected Essays of June Jordan* (Basic/Civitas Books, 2002), 80.
4 June Jordan, "Waking Up in the Middle of Some American Dreams," in *Some of Us Did Not Die: New and Selected Essays of June Jordan* (Basic/Civitas Books, 2002), 117.
5 June Jordan, "Requiem for the Champ," in *Some of Us Did Not Die: New and Selected Essays of June Jordan* (Basic/Civitas Books, 2002), 121.
6 June Jordan, "New Lives," in *Some of Us Did Not Die: New and Selected Essays of June Jordan* (Basic/Civitas Books, 2002), 282.
7 June Jordan, "Notes Toward a Black Balancing Between Hatred and Love," in *Some of Us Did Not Die: New and Selected Essays of June Jordan* (Basic/Civitas Books, 2002), 285.
8 June Jordan, "On the Occasion of a Clear and Present Danger at Yale (1975)," in *Civil Wars: Observations from the Front Line of America* (Simon & Schuster, 1995), 93.
9 June Jordan, "Report from the Bahamas," in *On Call: Political Essays* (South End Press, 1985), 47.
10 Jordan, "Notes Toward a Black Balancing," 285.

It Began as a Romance
1 June Jordan, "On a New Year's Eve," in *Directed by Desire: The Collected Poems of June Jordan*, ed. Jan Heller Levi and Sara Miles (Copper Canyon Press, 2005), 206.
2 June Jordan and Adrienne Torf, "Poem to Take Back the Night," in *Collaboration: Selected Works 1983–2002* (ABongo Music, 2003), track 13.

3   June Jordan and Adrienne Torf, "Song of the Law Abiding Citizen," in *Collaboration: Selected Works 1983–2002* (ABongo Music, 2003), track 6.
4   June Jordan and Adrienne Torf, "To Free Nelson Mandela," in *Collaboration: Selected Works 1983–2002* (ABongo Music, 2003), track 7.
5   June Jordan and Adrienne Torf, "Freedom Now Suite: Part 3," in *Collaboration: Selected Works 1983–2002* (ABongo Music, 2003), track 3.
6   June Jordan and Adrienne Torf, *Bang Bang über Alles*, 7 Stages Theatre, Atlanta, Georgia, June, 1986.
7   June Jordan and Adrienne Torf, "Freedom Now Suite: Part 2," in *Collaboration: Selected Works 1983–2002* (A Bongo Music, 2003), track 2.
8   June Jordan, "Poem for a Young Poet," in *Directed by Desire: The Collected Poems of June Jordan*, ed. Jan Heller Levi and Sara Miles (Copper Canyon Press, 2005), 501.
9   June Jordan, "A Powerful Hatred," in *Life as Activism: June Jordan's Writings from The Progressive* (Litwin Books, 2014), 142.

How She Sang the Blues

1   Alexis De Veaux, "Creating Soul Food: June Jordan," *Essence*, April 1981, 140.
2   De Veaux, "Creating Soul Food," 147.
3   De Veaux, "Creating Soul Food," 147.
4   Alexis De Veaux, "A Conversation with June Jordan," *Essence*, September 2000.
5   June Jordan, *Soldier: A Poet's Childhood* (Basic/Civitas Books, 2000), xv.
6   De Veaux, "Creating Soul Food," 140.
7   De Veaux, "Creating Soul Food," 140.
8   De Veaux, "A Conversation," 102.

June Jordan and the Renaissance of Poetry as a Performing Art

1   Brockport Writers Forum, "June Jordan at the Brockport Writers Forum," interview, posted October 19, 2017, by Brockport Writers Forum, YouTube, 14:47, www.youtube.com/watch?v=Ii4y8MKcrwk&t=441s.
2   Robert Lowell, "Robert Lowell Reads Skunk Hour," reading, posted August 17, 2010, by awetblackbough, YouTube, www.youtube.com/watch?v=hSlcc2b02yc&t=55s.
3   John Ashbery, "John Ashbery reads 'Self-Portrait in a Convex Mirror' (full poem)," posted July 28, 2013, by Zachary Pace, YouTube, 29:01, www.youtube.com/watch?v=zrvXX9QVAT8&t=363s.
4   Adrienne Torf in conversation with the author, August 21, 2019.
5   Allen Ginsberg, "'Howl' read by Allen Ginsberg, 1975," posted May 6, 2015, by Vince.Plants, YouTube, 26:18, www.youtube.com/watch?v=x-P2fILsLH8.
6   June Jordan, "From *The Talking Back of Miss Valentine Jones*: Poem # One," in *Directed by Desire: The Collected Poems of June Jordan*, ed. Jan Heller Levi and Sara Miles (Copper Canyon Press, 2005), 195–96.
7   June Jordan, "June Jordan Reading Her Poems," posted January 23, 2019, by thepostarchive, YouTube, 49:14, www.youtube.com/watch?v=TzbGbhbR6c0.

8   Jordan, "From *The Talking*," 196.
9   Ntozake Shange, *for colored girls who have considered suicide / when the rainbow is enuf* (Shameless Hussy Press, 1974).

"A Report from the Bahamas"
1   Keiko Tamura, *Forever Foreign: Expatriate Lives in Historic Kobe* (National Library of Australia, 2007).
2   June Jordan, "Report from the Bahamas," in *On Call: Political Essays* (South End Press, 1985), 47.
3   Jordan, "Report from the Bahamas," 47.

"Elegy for a Soldier"
1   "Elegy for a Soldier" from *Desesperanto: Poems 1999–2002*, © 2003 by Marilyn Hacker. Reprinted with permission of W. W. Norton & Company.

Letters to My Friend, for June Jordan
1   June Jordan, "Foreword," in *Civil Wars: Observations from the Front Line of America* (Beacon Press, 1981), xi.
2   Jordan, "Foreword," xii.

¡Puño en Alto! ¡Libro Abierto! / Fists, Up! Books, Open!
1   June Jordan, "Third Poem from Nicaragua Libre: Photograph of Managua," in *Directed by Desire: The Collected Poems of June Jordan*, ed. Jan Heller Levi and Sara Miles (Copper Canyon Press, 2005), 336.
2   Fernando Cardenal, "The Whole Country Was a Huge School," *Envío* 289 (2005), https://www.revistaenvio.org/articulo/3026.

The Waters Are Wide: We Can Cross Over
1   June Jordan, "Many Rivers to Cross," in *On Call: Political Essays* (South End Press, 1985), 19.
2   June Jordan, "Of Nightsong and Flight," in *Directed By Desire: The Collected Poems of June Jordan*, ed. Jan Heller Levi and Sara Miles (Copper Canyon Press, 2005), 145.
3   June Jordan, "These Poems," in *Directed by Desire: The Collected Poems of June Jordan*, ed. Jan Heller Levi and Sara Miles (Copper Canyon Press, 2005), xxxiii.
4   June Jordan, "Jordan on Certain Kinds of Theory," in *We're On: A June Jordan Reader*, ed. Christoph Keller and Jan Heller Levi (Alice James Books, 2017), 260.
5   June Jordan, "Alla Tha's All Right, but," in *Directed by Desire: The Collected Poems of June Jordan*, ed. Jan Heller Levi and Sara Miles (Copper Canyon Press, 2005), 285.
6   June Jordan, "Free Flight," in *Directed by Desire: The Collected Poems of June Jordan*, ed. Jan Heller Levi and Sara Miles (Copper Canyon Press, 2005), 287–88.
7   June Jordan, "Problems of Language in a Democratic State," in *Some of Us Did Not Die: New and Selected Essays of June Jordan* (Basic/Civitas Books, 2002), 229.

8   June Jordan, "Nobody Mean More to Me Than You and the Future Life of Willie Jordan," in *On Call: Political Essays* (South End Press, 1985), 123–39.
9   June Jordan, "Report from the Bahamas," in *On Call: Political Essays* (South End Press, 1985), 47.
10 June Jordan, "Moving Towards Home," in *Directed by Desire: The Collected Poems of June Jordan*, ed. Jan Heller Levi and Sara Miles (Copper Canyon Press, 2005), 400.
11 June Jordan, epigraph to in *We're On: A June Jordan Reader*, ed. Christoph Keller and Jan Heller Levi (Alice James Books, 2017), front matter.
12 Dominique Christina, "Karma," reading, posted July 20, 2013, by Dominique Christina, YouTube, https://youtu.be/qPPelxEMRQY?si=-8XfCKVZm3hYTEx6.
13 Sara A. Rashed, "Welcome to America," in *Making Mirrors: Writing/Righting by and for Refugees*, ed. Jehan Bseiso and Becky Thompson (Interlink, 2019), 100.
14 Jehan Bseiso, "No Search, No Rescue," in *Making Mirrors: Writing/Righting by and for Refugees*, ed. Jehan Bseiso and Becky Thompson (Interlink, 2019), 31. Bseiso's epigraph sounds just like something Jordan might have written, as she located the reader so often in her poems through her epigraphs. See, for example, her epigraph for "In Paris," "dedicated to Pratibha Parmar," and her poem "Ghaflah": "In Islam, Ghaflah refers to the sin of forgetfulness." June Jordan, "In Paris" and "Ghaflah," in *Directed by Desire: The Collected Poems of June Jordan*, ed. Jan Heller Levi and Sara Miles (Copper Canyon Press, 2005), 430, 520.

"Some of Us Did Not Die": Remembering June Jordan

1   E. Ethelbert Miller, *Fathering Words: The Making of an African American Writer* (St. Martin's Press, 2000), 82.
2   June Jordan, "Tribute to Paul Robeson," in *Affirmative Acts: Political Essays* (Anchor Books, 1998), 235.
3   June Jordan, "Ah, Momma," in *Directed by Desire: The Collected Poems of June Jordan*, ed. Jan Heller Levi and Sara Miles (Copper Canyon Press, 2005), 194–95.
4   June Jordan, "Love is Not the Problem," in *On Call: Political Essays* (South End Press, 1985), 53.
5   Adrienne Rich, "Foreword," in June Jordan, *Haruko / Love Poems* (High Risk Books / Serpent's Tail, 1994), ix.
6   Rich, "Foreword," ix.
7   June Jordan, "These Poems," in *Directed by Desire: The Collected Poems of June Jordan*, ed. Jan Heller Levi and Sara Miles (Copper Canyon Press, 2005), xxxiii.
8   June Jordan, "Moving Towards Home," in *Directed by Desire: The Collected Poems of June Jordan*, ed. Jan Heller Levi and Sara Miles (Copper Canyon Press, 2005), 399–400.
9   Suheir Hammad, *Born Palestinian, Born Black* (Harlem River Press, 1996), xi.
10 June Jordan, "A New Politics of Sexuality," in *Life as Activism: June Jordan's Writings from The Progressive*, ed. Stacy Russo (Litwin Books, 2014), 54, 55, 58.
11 June Jordan, "Poem About My Rights," in *Directed by Desire: The Collected Poems of June Jordan*, ed. Jan Heller Levi and Sara Miles (Copper Canyon Press, 2005), 309–12; June Jordan, "Poem Against the State (of Things)," in *Directed by Desire*,

222–30; June Jordan, "Grand Army Plaza," in *Directed by Desire*, 312–13; June Jordan, "The Test of Atlanta 1979–," in *Directed by Desire*, 390–92.
12 Jordan, "Poem About My Rights," 309–310.
13 Karla Hammond, unpublished interview, 1981, E. Ethelbert Miller Archive, Gelman Library, George Washington University.
14 Jordan, "Poem Against," 229–30.
15 Jordan, "Poem Against," 230.
16 Jordan, "Grand Army Plaza," 312.
17 Jordan, "Grand Army Plaza," 313.
18 Jordan, "Nicaragua: Why I Had to Go There," in *On Call: Political Essays* (South End Press, 1985), 65.
19 Jordan, "Test of Atlanta," 391.
20 June Jordan, "Poem About Police Violence," in *Directed by Desire: The Collected Poems of June Jordan*, ed. Jan Heller Levi and Sara Miles (Copper Canyon Press, 2005), 272.
21 June Jordan, speech, Emory University, January 21, 1997, Atlanta, GA, unpublished.
22 June Jordan, "Letter to Ethelbert," in Miller, *Fathering Words*, 176.

Bit by Bit
1 June Jordan, "Eyewitness in Lebanon," in *Life as Activism: June Jordan's Writings from The Progressive*, ed. Stacy Russo (Litwin Books, 2014), 183.

america
1 Dima Hilal "america" originally published in *Scheherazade's Legacy: Arab and Arab American Women on Writing* (Bloomsbury, 2004). Reprinted with permission of the author.

Elphinstone, Bombay, 1993
1 June Jordan, "Nicaragua: Why I Had to Go There," in *Some of Us Did Not Die: New and Selected Essays of June Jordan* (Basic/Civitas Books, 2002), 199, 200, 201.
2 Jordan, "Nicaragua," 209.
3 Jordan, "Nicaragua," 210.

"The Bombing of Baghdad": Building Connections in a Time of War
1 June Jordan, "The Bombing of Baghdad," in *Directed by Desire: The Collected Poems of June Jordan*, ed. Jan Heller Levi and Sara Miles (Copper Canyon Press, 2005), 535–36.
2 Jordan, "Bombing of Baghdad," 536.
3 Jordan, "Bombing of Baghdad," 536–37.
4 Jordan, "Bombing of Baghdad," 538.
5 Jordan, "Bombing of Baghdad," 538.
6 Jordan, "Bombing of Baghdad," 537.

7 June Jordan, "Study #1," in *Directed by Desire: The Collected Poems of June Jordan*, ed. Jan Heller Levi and Sara Miles (Copper Canyon Press, 2005), 524; June Jordan, *June Jordan's Poetry for the People: A Revolutionary Blueprint*, ed. Lauren Muller and Poetry for the People collective (Routledge, 1995), 63.

8 "She Had Some Horses" from *She Had Some Horses*, © 1983 by Joy Harjo. Reprinted with permission of W. W. Norton & Company.

9 Joy Harjo, "She Had Some Horses," in *She Had Some Horses* (Thunder's Mouth Press, 1983), 63–64.

10 Jordan, "Bombing of Baghdad," 538.

11 Brown University, Costs of War Project, 2018.

12 Jordan, "Bombing of Baghdad," 538.

13 Jordan, "Bombing of Baghdad," 538.

14 Jordan, "Bombing of Baghdad," 539.

Maestra

1 June Jordan, "Campsite #21," in *Directed by Desire: The Collected Poems of June Jordan*, ed. Jan Heller Levi and Sara Miles (Copper Canyon Press, 2005), 540.

2 June Jordan, "Bridget Song #1," in *Directed by Desire: The Collected Poems of June Jordan*, ed. Jan Heller Levi and Sara Miles (Copper Canyon Press, 2005), 524.

3 June Jordan, "Third Poem from Nicaragua Libre: Photograph of Managua," in *Directed by Desire: The Collected Poems of June Jordan*, ed. Jan Heller Levi and Sara Miles (Copper Canyon Press, 2005), 336.

4 June Jordan, "Nobody Mean More to Me Than You and the Future Life of Willie Jordan," in *On Call: Political Essays* (South End Press, 1985), 126.

5 June Jordan, "Free Flight," in *Directed by Desire: The Collected Poems of June Jordan*, ed. Jan Heller Levi and Sara Miles (Copper Canyon Press, 2005), 289.

6 June Jordan, "From 'Creation is Revolutionary,' Interview with Karla Hammond (1978)," in *We're On: A June Jordan Reader*, ed. Christoph Keller and Jan Heller Levi (Alice James Books, 2017), 230.

Dear June

1 "June Jordan's Guidelines for Critiquing a Poem," in *June Jordan's Poetry for the People: A Revolutionary Blueprint*, ed. Lauren Muller and the Poetry for the People Collective (Routledge, 1995), 36.

A Blueprint for June's Love

1 June Jordan, "Introduction: Some of Us Did Not Die," in *Some of Us Did Not Die: New and Selected Essays of June Jordan* (Basic/Civitas Books, 2002), 8.

2 June Jordan, "Scenario Revision #1," in *Directed by Desire: The Collected Poems of June Jordan*, ed. Jan Heller Levi and Sara Miles (Copper Canyon Press, 2005), 599.

Choosing a Praxis of Liberation

1. June Jordan, "On a New Year's Eve," in *Directed by Desire: The Collected Poems of June Jordan*, ed. Jan Heller Levi and Sara Miles (Copper Canyon Press, 2005), 206.
2. June Jordan, "Introduction," in *June Jordan's Poetry for the People: A Revolutionary Blueprint*, ed. Lauren Muller and the Poetry for the People Collective (Routledge, 1995), 3.
3. June Jordan, "Problems of Language in a Democratic State," in *Some of Us Did Not Die: New and Selected Essays of June Jordan* (Basic/Civitas Books, 2002), 232.
4. June Jordan, "Study #1," in *Directed by Desire: The Collected Poems of June Jordan*, ed. Jan Heller Levi and Sara Miles (Copper Canyon Press, 2005), 524.
5. Jordan, "Problems of Language," 229.
6. Jordan, "Problems of Language," 232.
7. June Jordan, "Poem in Memory of Alan Schindler, 22 Years Old," in *Directed by Desire: The Collected Poems of June Jordan*, ed. Jan Heller Levi and Sara Miles (Copper Canyon Press, 2005), 545.
8. Jordan, "Poem in Memory," 545.
9. Jordan, "Poem in Memory," 545.
10. June Jordan, "For Michael Angelo Thompson," in *Directed by Desire: The Collected Poems of June Jordan*, ed. Jan Heller Levi and Sara Miles (Copper Canyon Press, 2005), 171.
11. June Jordan, "Argument with the Buddha," in *Directed by Desire: The Collected Poems of June Jordan*, ed. Jan Heller Levi and Sara Miles (Copper Canyon Press, 2005), 508.
12. Jordan, "Argument," 508–9.
13. Jordan, "New Year's Eve," 206.
14. Jordan, "Argument," 509.
15. June Jordan, "Introduction: Some of Us Did Not Die," in *Some of Us Did Not Die: New and Selected Essays of June Jordan* (Basic/Civitas Books, 2002), 13.
16. Jordan, "Some of Us," 14.

On the Spirit of June Jordan

1. Sam Chaltain, "June Jordan: The Beautiful Struggle," Sam Chaltain, April 15, 2016, http://www.samchaltain.com/the-beautiful-struggle.
2. Alexis Pauline Gumbs, "m/other ourselves: a Black queer feminist genealogy for radical mothering," in *Revolutionary Mothering*, ed. Alexis Pauline Gumbs, China Martens, and Mai'a Williams (PM Press, 2016), 20.
3. June Jordan, "The Creative Spirit: Children's Literature," in *Revolutionary Mothering*, ed. Alexis Pauline Gumbs, China Martens, and Mai'a Williams (PM Press, 2016), 11.

Standing at the Gates

1. June Jordan, "The Creative Spirit: Children's Literature," in *Revolutionary Mothering: Love on the Front Lines*, ed. Alexis Pauline Gumbs, China Martens, and Mai'a Williams (PM Press, 2016), 11.
2. Jordan, "The Creative Spirit," 11.

Stay All the Way with Reggie and Ranya

1. Evangeline P. Yazzie and Margaret Speas, *Dine Bizaad Binahoo'aah: Rediscovering the Navajo* (Salina Bookshelf 2009), 266.
2. June Jordan, "Poem About My Rights," in *Directed by Desire: The Collected Poems of June Jordan*, ed. Jan Heller Levi and Sara Miles (Copper Canyon Press, 2005), 310–12.
3. Leanne B. Simpson, *As We Always Have Done: Indigenous Freedom Through Radical Resistance* (University of Minnesota Press, 2017), 185.
4. Simpson, *As We Always Have Done*, 186.
5. Simpson, *As We Always Have Done*, 186.
6. Reid Gómez, "The Meaning of Written English: A Place to Dream as One Pleases," *American Indian Culture and Research Journal* 41, no. 4 (2017): 108.
7. June Jordan, "White English/Black English: The Politics of Translation (1972)," in *Civil Wars: Observations from the Front Line of America* (Beacon Press, 1981) 72.
8. Jordan, "White English," 62.
9. Jordan, "White English," 63.
10. Jordan, "White English," 66.
11. Jordan, "White English," 66.
12. Jordan, "White English," 66.
13. Jordan, "White English," 68.
14. Jordan, "White English," 72.
15. Jordan, "White English," 68.
16. Jordan, "White English," 71.
17. June Jordan, "Nobody Mean More to Me Than You and the Future Life of Willie Jordan," in *On Call: Political Essays* (South End Press, 1985), 124.
18. Jordan, "Nobody Mean More," 125.
19. Jordan, "Nobody Mean More," 133.
20. Jordan, "Nobody Mean More," 127.
21. Jordan, "Nobody Mean More," 133.
22. Jordan, "Nobody Mean More," 135.
23. Jordan, "Nobody Mean More," 138.
24. Jordan, "Nobody Mean More," 135.
25. Jordan, "Nobody Mean More," 123.
26. Jordan, "White English," 72.
27. Christina Sharpe, *In the Wake: On Blackness and Being* (Duke University Press, 2016), 18.
28. John R. Rickford and Sharese King, "Language and Linguistics on Trial: Hearing Rachel Jeantel (and Other Vernacular Speakers) in the Courtroom and Beyond," *Language* 92, no. 4 (2016): 949.
29. Rickford and King, "Language and Linguistics," 949.
30. Rickford and King, "Language and Linguistics," 950.
31. Rickford and King, "Language and Linguistics," 957.

32 Toni Morrison, panel discussion, "Public Dialogue on the American Dream Theme," Portland State University Black Studies Center, May 30, 1975, Portland, OR, available at https://soundcloud.com/portland-state-library/portland-state-black-studies-1.
33 Rickford and King, "Language and Linguistics," 972.
34 Rickford and King, "Language and Linguistics," 976.
35 Rachel Jeantel, interview, *Piers Morgan Live*, July 15, 2013, CNN.
36 "Rachel Jeantel's Transformation," *Sunday Spotlight*, July 13, 2014, ABC News.
37 Teresa L. McCarty, *Language Planning and Policy in Native America: History, Theory, Praxis* (Multilingual Matters / Channel View Publications, 2013), 90.
38 Leslie Silko, *Almanac of the Dead* (Penguin, 1991), 421.
39 Rickford and King, "Language and Linguistics," 976.
40 Rickford and King, "Language and Linguistics," 981.
41 June Jordan, "Nobody Mean More To Me Than You and the Future Life of Willie Jordan," *Harvard Educational Review* 58, No. 3 (August 1988): 336–74, 372.
42 Jordan, "Nobody Mean More," 372.
43 Jordan, "Nobody Mean More," 372.

"I choose / anything / anyone / I may lose"
1 June Jordan, "Argument with the Buddha," in *Directed by Desire: The Collected Poems of June Jordan*, ed. Jan Heller Levi and Sara Miles (Copper Canyon Press, 2005), 507.
2 Jordan, "Argument," 509.
3 Jordan, "Argument," 509.
4 Jordan, "Argument," 508.
5 Jordan, "Argument," 508.
6 Jordan, "Argument," 508.

Between the Knuckles of My Own Two Hands
1 June Jordan, "Moving Towards Home," in *Directed by Desire: The Collected Poems of June Jordan*, ed. Jan Heller Levi and Sara Miles (Copper Canyon Press, 2005), 400.
2 Alice Walser, "Can't Hate Anybody and See God's Face," *New York Times*, April 29, 1973, 8.

In Response to "Apologies to All the People in Lebanon"
1 June Jordan, "Apologies to All the People in Lebanon," in *Directed by Desire: The Collected Poems of June Jordan*, ed. Jan Heller Levi and Sara Miles (Copper Canyon Press, 2005), 380.
2 Jordan, "Apologies to All," 382.
3 Jordan, "Apologies to All," 382.

After June Jordan, a Poem About Police Violence
1 Jehan Bseiso, "After June Jordan, a Poem About Police Violence," originally published in *The Funambulist* (2016). Reprinted with permission of the author.

For the Sake of a People's Poetry

1. June Jordan, "For the Sake of a People's Poetry," in *Passion: New Poems, 1977–1980* (Beacon Press, 1980), xix.
2. Jordan, "For the Sake," xxx.
3. June Jordan, "Poem for Nana," in *Directed by Desire: The Collected Poems of June Jordan*, ed. Jan Heller Levi and Sara Miles (Copper Canyon Press, 2005), 249.
4. Jordan, "Poem for Nana," 249.
5. June Jordan, "Poem About Police Violence," in *Directed by Desire: The Collected Poems of June Jordan*, ed. Jan Heller Levi and Sara Miles (Copper Canyon Press, 2005), 272.
6. June Jordan, "Rape Is Not a Poem," in *Directed by Desire: The Collected Poems of June Jordan*, ed. Jan Heller Levi and Sara Miles (Copper Canyon Press, 2005), 304–6.
7. June Jordan, "Case in Point," in *Directed by Desire: The Collected Poems of June Jordan*, ed. Jan Heller Levi and Sara Miles (Copper Canyon Press, 2005), 257–58.
8. Jordan, "Poem for Nana," 251.
9. June Jordon, "Legend of the Holy Night When the Police Finally Held Fire," in *Directed by Desire: The Collected Poems of June Jordan*, ed. Jan Heller Levi and Sara Miles (Copper Canyon Press, 2005), 292–93.
10. Jordan, "Poem About My Rights," in *Directed by Desire: The Collected Poems of June Jordan*, ed. Jan Heller Levi and Sara Miles (Copper Canyon Press, 2005), 309–10.
11. "Poem for South African Women," in *Directed by Desire: The Collected Poems of June Jordan*, ed. Jan Heller Levi and Sara Miles (Copper Canyon Press, 2005), 279.
12. Jordan, "For the Sake," xxii.
13. Walt Whitman, "Democratic Vistas," in *The Portable Walt Whitman*, ed. Mark Van Doren (Penguin, 1977), 325, 369.
14. Whitman, "Democratic Vistas," 380.
15. Jordan, "For the Sake," xxix.
16. June Jordan, "Introduction: Some of Us Did Not Die," in *Some of Us Did Not Die: New and Selected Essays of June Jordan* (Basic/Civitas Books, 2002), 8.
17. June Jordan, "Foreword," *Civil Wars: Observations from the Front Line of America* (Beacon Press, 1981), xi.
18. June Jordan, "Thinking About My Poetry (1977)," in *Civil Wars: Observations from the Front Line of America* (Beacon Press, 1981), 123, 125.
19. Jordan, "Thinking About," 129.

Truth-Telling as an Emancipatory Act: What June Jordan Taught Me About Liberation

1. June Jordan, "Poem About My Rights," in *Directed by Desire: The Collected Poems of June Jordan*, ed. Jan Heller Levi and Sara Miles (Copper Canyon Press, 2005), 311.
2. Jordan, "Poem About My Rights," 310.
3. Jordan, "Poem About My Rights," 311–12.

4   Jordan, "Poem About My Rights," 311.
5   Jordan, "These Poems," in *Directed by Desire: The Collected Poems of June Jordan*, ed. Jan Heller Levi and Sara Miles (Copper Canyon Press, 2005), xxxiii.

Finding "Living Room" with My Drone
1   June Jordan, "Moving Towards Home," in *Directed by Desire: The Collected Poems of June Jordan*, ed. Jan Heller Levi and Sara Miles (Copper Canyon Press, 2005), 399.
2   June Jordan, "Moving Towards Home," 399.
3   June Jordan, "Moving Towards Home," 400.

Love Like a Mango, Obvious
1   June Jordan, "Poem About My Rights," in *Directed by Desire: The Collected Poems of June Jordan*, ed. Jan Heller Levi and Sara Miles (Copper Canyon Press, 2005), 311–12.
2   Jordan, "Poem About My Rights," 310.
3   Jordan, "Poem About My Rights," 309.
4   June Jordan, "Alternative Commencement Address at Dartmouth College, June 14, 1987," in *Technical Difficulties: African-American Notes on the State of the Union* (Pantheon Books, 1992), 44.
5   Jordan, "Alternative Commencement Address," 44.
6   Jordan, "Poem About My Rights," 309–310.
7   Jordan, "Alternative Commencement Address," 45.
8   Jordan, "Poem About My Rights," 311–312.
9   Jordan, "Alternative Commencement Address," 44.

June Jordan: When All Things Are Dear That Disappear
1   June Jordan, "On a New Year's Eve," in *Directed by Desire: The Collected Poems of June Jordan*, ed. Jan Heller Levi and Sara Miles (Copper Canyon Press, 2005), 202.
2   Jordan, "New Year's Eve," 203.
3   Jordan, "New Year's Eve," 203.
4   Jordan, "New Year's Eve," 204.
5   Jordan, "New Year's Eve," 204–5.
6   Jordan, "New Year's Eve," 205–6.
7   Jordan, "New Year's Eve," 206.
8   Jordan, "New Year's Eve," 206.

"Something Like a Sonnet": Reading June Jordan, Finding My Voice, and Becoming an Oral Historian
1   June Jordan, "The Difficult Miracle of Black Poetry in America, or Something Like a Sonnet for Phillis Wheatley," in *On Call: Political Essays* (South End Press, 1985), 87.
2   Jordan, "The Difficult Miracle," 87.

3   James Moseley, "Interview by Kelly E. Navies," Collection of Reginald F. Lewis Maryland Museum of African American History and Culture, March 27, 2002.
4   Jordan, "The Difficult Miracle," 97–98.
5   Jeannie S. Clark, "Interview by Kelly E. Navies," *U Street Oral History Project*, DC Public Library Digital Archive, June 2014, www.dclibrary.org; Alva Marcus, "Interview by Kelly E. Navies," *U Street Oral History Project*, DC Public Library Digital Archive, September 2014, www.dclibrary.org.

Choosing My Mind Between the Mosquitos and the Moon
1   All photos courtesy of the author.
2   Denise Ferreira da Silva, "Radical Praxis or Knowing (at) the Limits of Justice," in *At the Limits of Justice: Women of Colour on Terror*, ed. Suvendrini Perera and Sherene Razack (University of Toronto Press, 2014), 526–37.

Selected Bibliography

Alexander, Elizabeth. *The Light of the World: A Memoir*. Grand Central Publishing, 2015.

Ashbery, John. "John Ashbery Reads 'Self-Portrait in a Convex Mirror' (full poem)." YouTube, uploaded by Zachary Pace, July 28, 2013, www.youtube.com/watch?v=zrvXX9QVAT8&t=363s.

Auden, W. H. "In Memory of W. B. Yeats." *Another Time*. Random House, 1940.

Basso, Keith. "Stalking with Stories." *Wisdom Sits in Places: Landscape and Language Among the Western Apache*. University of New Mexico Press, 1996.

Berry, Chris Aluka, Kelly Elaine Navies, and Maia Surdam. *Affrilachia: Testimonies*. University Press of Kentucky, 2024.

The Bible. 21st century King James version. Deuel Enterprises, 1994.

Boullata, Kamal, ed. *And Not Surrender: American Poets on Lebanon*, Arab American Cultural Foundation, 1982.

Boullata, Kamal, and Kathy Engel, eds. *We Begin Here: Poems for Palestine and Lebanon*. Interlink, 2007. (This book is dedicated to June Jordan—Ed.)

Brien, Shanti B. *Almost Innocent: From Searching to Saved in America's Criminal Justice System*. Amplify, 2021. Brockport Writers Forum, "June Jordan at the Brockport Writers Forum." *YouTube*, October 19, 2017, www.youtube.com/watch?v=Ii4y8MKcrwk&t=441s.

Brown, Ruth Nicole. *Black Girl Celebration: Toward a Hip-Hop Feminist Pedagogy*. Peter Lang, 2008.

Brown University, Watson School of International and Public Affairs. Costs of War Project, 2018.

Bseiso, Jehan. "No Search, No Rescue." In *Making Mirrors: Writing/Righting by and for Refugees*, edited by Jehan Bseiso and Becky Thompson. Interlink, 2019.

Cammarota, Julio, and Michelle Fine, eds. *Revolutionizing Education: Youth Participatory Action Research in Motion*. Routledge, 2008.

Cardenal, Fernando. "The Whole Country Was a Huge School." Interview. *Envío* 289 (2005).

Chen, Nancy. "'Speaking Nearby': A Conversation with Trinh T. Minh-ha." *Visual Anthropology Review* 8, no. 1 (1992): 82–91.

Christian, Barbara. "Being the Subject and the Object." In *New Black Feminist Criticism, 1985—2000*, edited by Gloria Bowles, M. Giulia Fabi, and Arlene R. Keizer. University of Illinois Press, 2007.

Christina, Dominique. "Karma." YouTube, July 20, 2013, https://youtu.be/qPPelxEMRQY?si=-8XfCKVZm3hYTEx6.

Clark, Jeannie S. Interview by Kelly E. Navies. June 2014. "U Street Oral History Project," Washington, DC, Public Library, Digital Archive. www.dclibrary.org.

Cooper, Michael. "Officers in Bronx Fire 41 Shots, And an Unarmed Man Is Killed." *New York Times*, February 5, 1999.

De Veaux, Alexis. "A Conversation with June Jordan." *Essence*, September 2000.

———. "Creating Soul Food June Jordan." *Essence*, April 1981.

———. "Freedom Fighter." In "Remembering June Jordan." *Women's Review of Books* 20, no. 1 (2002): 18.

Dingwaney, Anuradha, and Carol Maier, eds. *Between Language and Cultures: Translation and Cross-Cultural Texts*. University of Pittsburgh Press, 1995.

Ferreira da Silva, Denise. "To Be Announced Radical Praxis or Knowing (at) the Limits of Justice." *Social Text* 31, no. 1 (2013): 43–62.

Forman, Ruth. "What June Taught." In "Remembering June Jordan." *Women's Review of Books* 20, no. 1 (2002): 17.

———. *We Are the Young Magicians*. Beacon Press, 1993.

Freire, Paulo. *Pedagogy of the Oppressed*. Bloomsbury Academic, 1968.

Ganz, Marshall. "What Is Public Narrative: Self, Us & Now." Working paper, 2008.

Ginsberg, Allen. "First Recording of 'Howl' Read by Allen Ginsberg, 1956." YouTube, uploaded by Vincent L. Latham, May 6, 2015, www.youtube.com/watch?v=x-P2fILsLH8.

Gómez, Reid. "The Meaning of Written English: A Place to Dream as One Pleases." *American Indian Culture and Research Journal* 41, no. 4 (2017).

Gumbs, Alexis Pauline, China Martens, and Mai'a Williams, eds. *Revolutionary Mothering: Love on the Front Lines*. PM Press, 2016.

Hammad, Suheir. *Born Palestinian, Born Black*. Harlem River Press, 1996.

Harjo, Joy. "She Had Some Horses." In *She Had Some Horses*. Thunder's Mouth Press, 1983.

Holbrook, Kate. "Even Cacti Grow in Icelandic Winters." In *june jordan's poetry for the people presents: a grip of poems pounding at the door*. Poetry for the People Press, 2002.

———. "Silk Stockings Resistance Poem." Poetry for the People Press, 2004.

hooks, bell. "'this is the oppressor's language / yet I need it to talk to you': Language, a place of struggle." In *Between Language and Cultures: Translation and Cross-Cultural Texts*, edited by Anuradha Dingwaney and Carol Maier. University of Pittsburgh Press, 1995.

Jordan, June. "1977: Poem for Fannie Lou Hamer." In *Directed by Desire: The Collected Poems of June Jordan*, edited by Jan Heller Levi and Sara Miles. Copper Canyon Press, 2005.

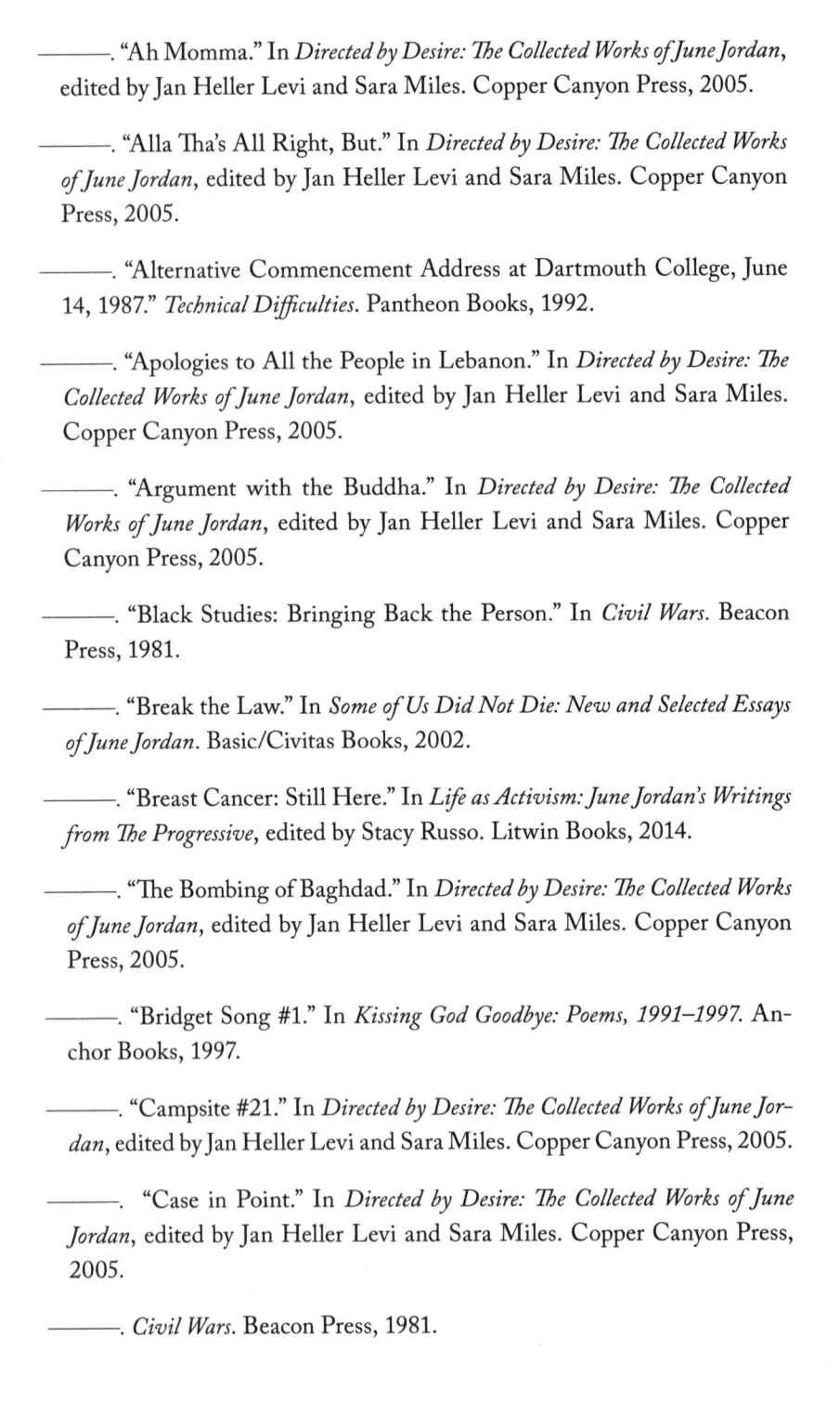

———. "Ah Momma." In *Directed by Desire: The Collected Works of June Jordan*, edited by Jan Heller Levi and Sara Miles. Copper Canyon Press, 2005.

———. "Alla Tha's All Right, But." In *Directed by Desire: The Collected Works of June Jordan*, edited by Jan Heller Levi and Sara Miles. Copper Canyon Press, 2005.

———. "Alternative Commencement Address at Dartmouth College, June 14, 1987." *Technical Difficulties*. Pantheon Books, 1992.

———. "Apologies to All the People in Lebanon." In *Directed by Desire: The Collected Works of June Jordan*, edited by Jan Heller Levi and Sara Miles. Copper Canyon Press, 2005.

———. "Argument with the Buddha." In *Directed by Desire: The Collected Works of June Jordan*, edited by Jan Heller Levi and Sara Miles. Copper Canyon Press, 2005.

———. "Black Studies: Bringing Back the Person." In *Civil Wars*. Beacon Press, 1981.

———. "Break the Law." In *Some of Us Did Not Die: New and Selected Essays of June Jordan*. Basic/Civitas Books, 2002.

———. "Breast Cancer: Still Here." In *Life as Activism: June Jordan's Writings from The Progressive*, edited by Stacy Russo. Litwin Books, 2014.

———. "The Bombing of Baghdad." In *Directed by Desire: The Collected Works of June Jordan*, edited by Jan Heller Levi and Sara Miles. Copper Canyon Press, 2005.

———. "Bridget Song #1." In *Kissing God Goodbye: Poems, 1991–1997*. Anchor Books, 1997.

———. "Campsite #21." In *Directed by Desire: The Collected Works of June Jordan*, edited by Jan Heller Levi and Sara Miles. Copper Canyon Press, 2005.

———. "Case in Point." In *Directed by Desire: The Collected Works of June Jordan*, edited by Jan Heller Levi and Sara Miles. Copper Canyon Press, 2005.

———. *Civil Wars*. Beacon Press, 1981.

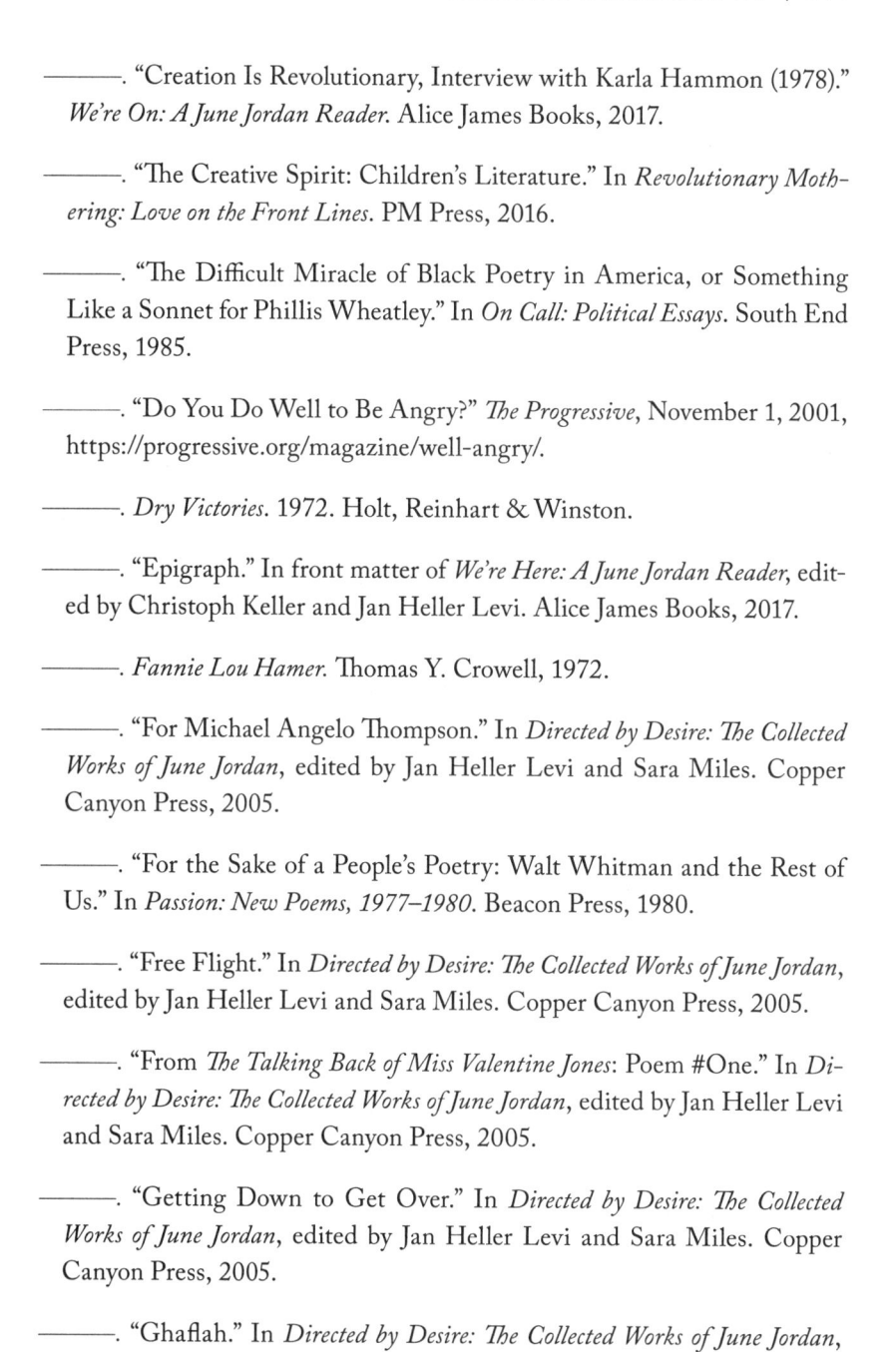

———. "Creation Is Revolutionary, Interview with Karla Hammon (1978)." *We're On: A June Jordan Reader*. Alice James Books, 2017.

———. "The Creative Spirit: Children's Literature." In *Revolutionary Mothering: Love on the Front Lines*. PM Press, 2016.

———. "The Difficult Miracle of Black Poetry in America, or Something Like a Sonnet for Phillis Wheatley." In *On Call: Political Essays*. South End Press, 1985.

———. "Do You Do Well to Be Angry?" *The Progressive*, November 1, 2001, https://progressive.org/magazine/well-angry/.

———. *Dry Victories*. 1972. Holt, Reinhart & Winston.

———. "Epigraph." In front matter of *We're Here: A June Jordan Reader*, edited by Christoph Keller and Jan Heller Levi. Alice James Books, 2017.

———. *Fannie Lou Hamer*. Thomas Y. Crowell, 1972.

———. "For Michael Angelo Thompson." In *Directed by Desire: The Collected Works of June Jordan*, edited by Jan Heller Levi and Sara Miles. Copper Canyon Press, 2005.

———. "For the Sake of a People's Poetry: Walt Whitman and the Rest of Us." In *Passion: New Poems, 1977–1980*. Beacon Press, 1980.

———. "Free Flight." In *Directed by Desire: The Collected Works of June Jordan*, edited by Jan Heller Levi and Sara Miles. Copper Canyon Press, 2005.

———. "From *The Talking Back of Miss Valentine Jones*: Poem #One." In *Directed by Desire: The Collected Works of June Jordan*, edited by Jan Heller Levi and Sara Miles. Copper Canyon Press, 2005.

———. "Getting Down to Get Over." In *Directed by Desire: The Collected Works of June Jordan*, edited by Jan Heller Levi and Sara Miles. Copper Canyon Press, 2005.

———. "Ghaflah." In *Directed by Desire: The Collected Works of June Jordan*, edited by Jan Heller Levi and Sara Miles. Copper Canyon Press, 2005.

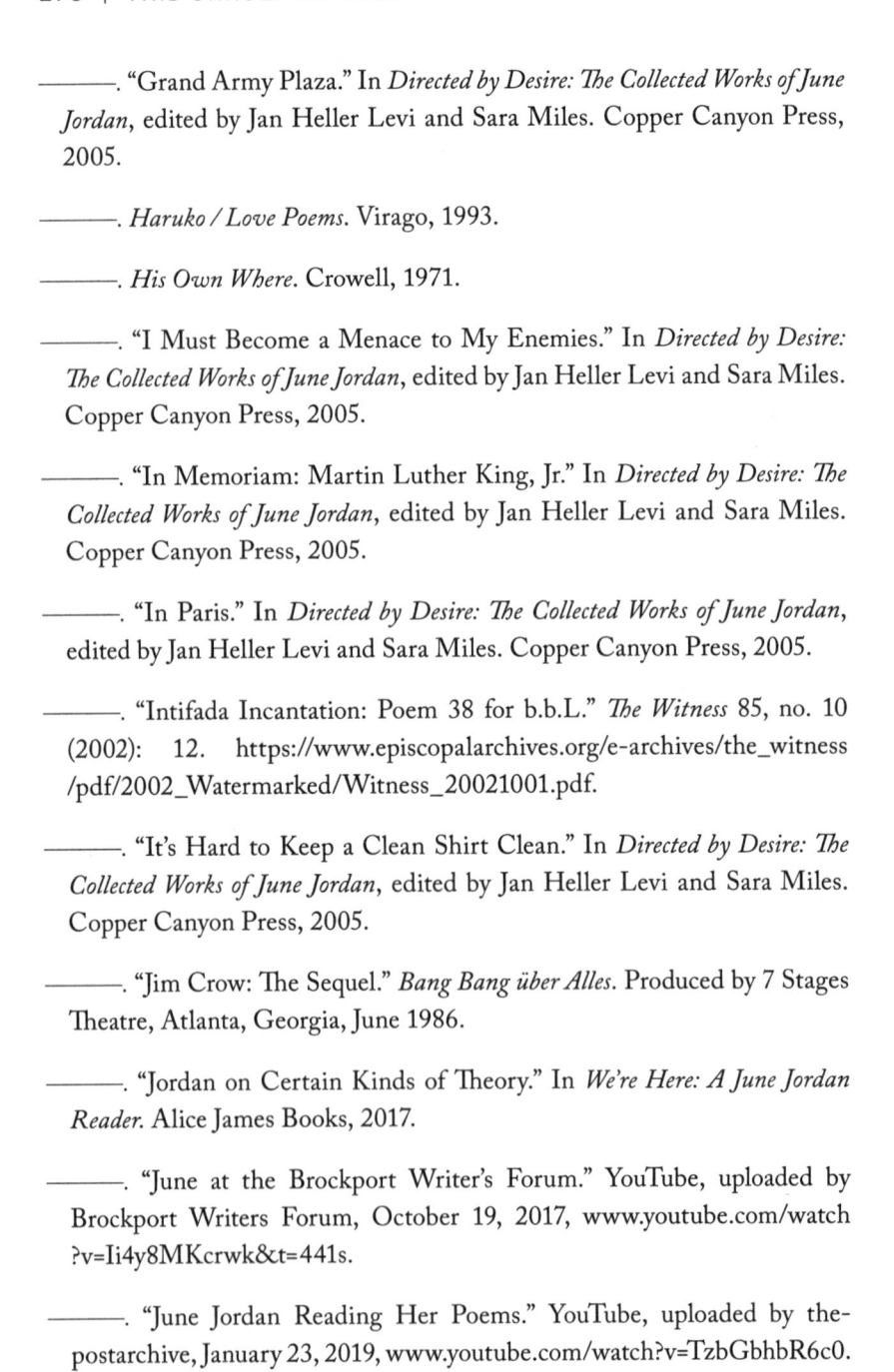

———. "Grand Army Plaza." In *Directed by Desire: The Collected Works of June Jordan*, edited by Jan Heller Levi and Sara Miles. Copper Canyon Press, 2005.

———. *Haruko / Love Poems*. Virago, 1993.

———. *His Own Where*. Crowell, 1971.

———. "I Must Become a Menace to My Enemies." In *Directed by Desire: The Collected Works of June Jordan*, edited by Jan Heller Levi and Sara Miles. Copper Canyon Press, 2005.

———. "In Memoriam: Martin Luther King, Jr." In *Directed by Desire: The Collected Works of June Jordan*, edited by Jan Heller Levi and Sara Miles. Copper Canyon Press, 2005.

———. "In Paris." In *Directed by Desire: The Collected Works of June Jordan*, edited by Jan Heller Levi and Sara Miles. Copper Canyon Press, 2005.

———. "Intifada Incantation: Poem 38 for b.b.L." *The Witness* 85, no. 10 (2002): 12. https://www.episcopalarchives.org/e-archives/the_witness/pdf/2002_Watermarked/Witness_20021001.pdf.

———. "It's Hard to Keep a Clean Shirt Clean." In *Directed by Desire: The Collected Works of June Jordan*, edited by Jan Heller Levi and Sara Miles. Copper Canyon Press, 2005.

———. "Jim Crow: The Sequel." *Bang Bang über Alles*. Produced by 7 Stages Theatre, Atlanta, Georgia, June 1986.

———. "Jordan on Certain Kinds of Theory." In *We're Here: A June Jordan Reader*. Alice James Books, 2017.

———. "June at the Brockport Writer's Forum." YouTube, uploaded by Brockport Writers Forum, October 19, 2017, www.youtube.com/watch?v=Ii4y8MKcrwk&t=441s.

———. "June Jordan Reading Her Poems." YouTube, uploaded by thepostarchive, January 23, 2019, www.youtube.com/watch?v=TzbGbhbR6c0.

———. *June Jordan's Poetry for the People: A Revolutionary Blueprint*, edited by Lauren Muller and the Blueprint Collective. Introduction by June Jordan. Routledge, 1995.

———. "Just Inside the Door." *Progressive*, July 1991.

———. *Kimako's Story*. Houghton Mifflin Harcourt, 1981.

———. "Letter to My Friend." *Some of Us Did Not Die: New and Selected Essays of June Jordan*. Basic/Civitas Books, 2002.

———. "Life After Lebanon." In *On Call: Political Essays*. South End Press, 1985.

———. "Living Room." In *We're On*. South End Press, 1985.

———. "Love's Not the Problem." In *On Call: Political Essays*. South End Press, 1985.

———. "Many Rivers to Cross." In *On Call: Political Essays*. South End Press, 1985.

———. "Moving Towards Home." In *Directed by Desire: The Collected Works of June Jordan*, edited by Jan Heller Levi and Sara Miles. Copper Canyon Press, 2005.

———. *New Life: New Room*. Crowell, 1975.

———. "New Lives." In *Some of Us Did Not Die: New and Selected Essays of June Jordan*. Basic/Civitas Books, 2002.

———. "Nicaragua: Why I Had to Go There." In *Some of Us Did Not Die: New and Selected Essays of June Jordan*. Basic/Civitas Books, 2002.

———. "Nobody Mean More to Me Than You and the Future Life of Willie Jordan." In *On Call: Political Essays*. South End Press, 1985.

———. "Notes Toward a Black Balance Between Hatred and Love." In *Some of Us Did Not Die: New and Selected Essays of June Jordan*. Basic/Civitas Books, 2002.

———. "Of Nightsong and Flight." In *Directed by Desire: The Collected Works of June Jordan*, edited by Jan Heller Levi and Sara Miles. Copper Canyon Press, 2005.

———. "Of Those So Close Beside Me, Which Are You?" In *Technical Difficulties: African American Notes on the State of the Union*. Trafalgar Square, 1993.

———. "On a New Year's Eve." In *Directed by Desire: The Collected Works of June Jordan*, edited by Jan Heller Levi and Sara Miles. Copper Canyon Press, 2005.

———. "On the Occasion of a Clear and Present Danger at Yale (1975)." In *Civil Wars*. Simon & Schuster, 1995.

———. "Out in the Country, of My Country." In *Black Nature: Four Centuries of African American Nature Poetry*. University of Georgia Press, 2009.

———. "Poem About My Rights." In *Directed by Desire: The Collected Works of June Jordan*, edited by Jan Heller Levi and Sara Miles. Copper Canyon Press, 2005.

———. "Poem About Police Violence." In *Directed by Desire: The Collected Works of June Jordan*, edited by Jan Heller Levi and Sara Miles. Copper Canyon Press, 2005.

———. "Poem Against the State (of Things): 1975." In *Directed by Desire: The Collected Works of June Jordan*, edited by Jan Heller Levi and Sara Miles. Copper Canyon Press, 2005.

———. "Poem for a Young Poet." In *Directed by Desire: The Collected Works of June Jordan*, edited by Jan Heller Levi and Sara Miles. Copper Canyon Press, 2005.

———. "Poem for Nana." In *Directed by Desire: The Collected Works of June Jordan*, edited by Jan Heller Levi and Sara Miles. Copper Canyon Press, 2005.

———. "Poem for South African Women." In *Directed by Desire: The Collected Works of June Jordan*, edited by Jan Heller Levi and Sara Miles. Copper Canyon Press, 2005.

———. "Poem in Memory of Alan Schindler, 22 Years Old." In *Directed by Desire: The Collected Works of June Jordan*, edited by Jan Heller Levi and Sara Miles. Copper Canyon Press, 2005.

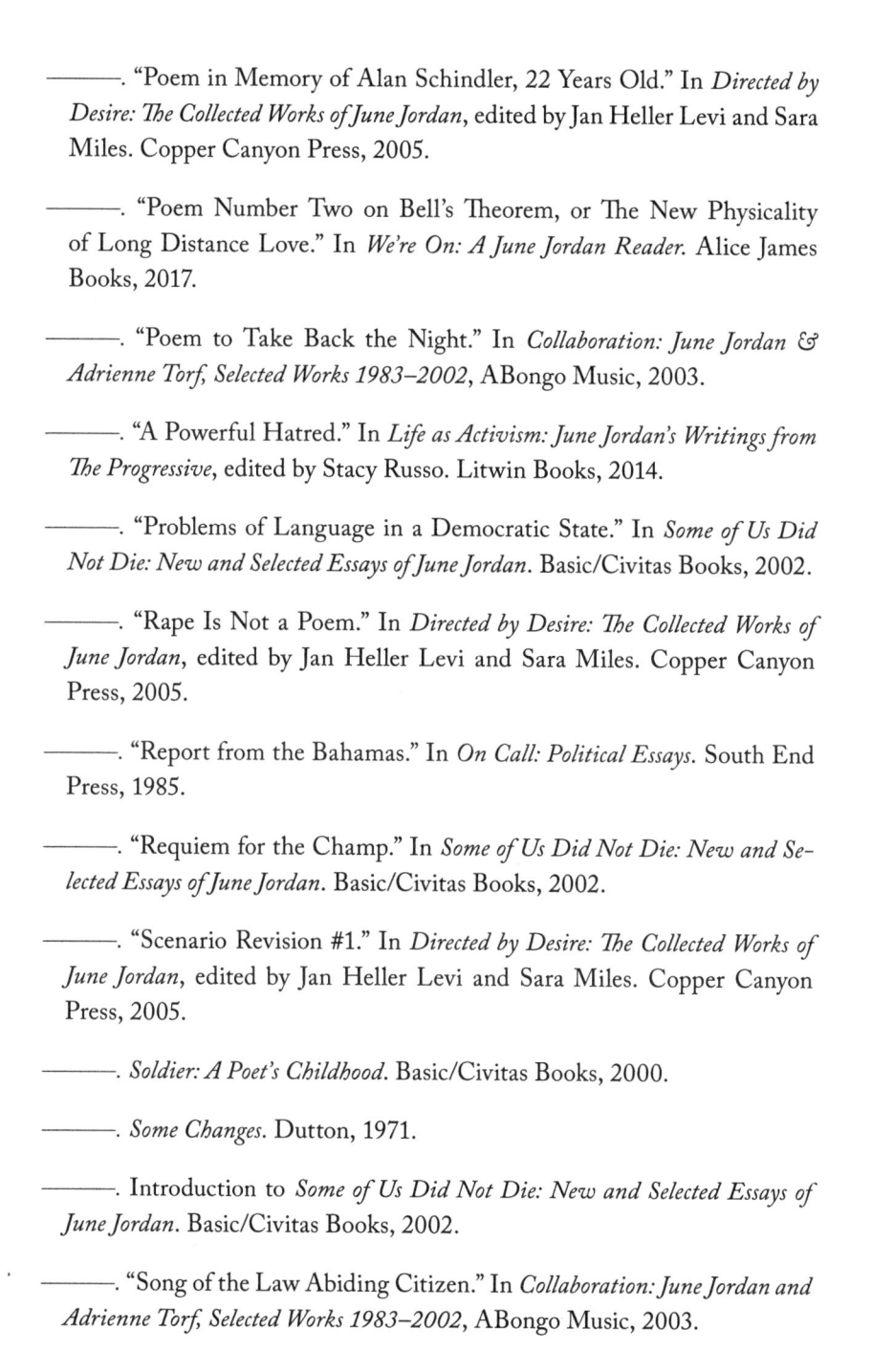

———. "Poem Number Two on Bell's Theorem, or The New Physicality of Long Distance Love." In *We're On: A June Jordan Reader*. Alice James Books, 2017.

———. "Poem to Take Back the Night." In *Collaboration: June Jordan & Adrienne Torf, Selected Works 1983–2002*, ABongo Music, 2003.

———. "A Powerful Hatred." In *Life as Activism: June Jordan's Writings from The Progressive*, edited by Stacy Russo. Litwin Books, 2014.

———. "Problems of Language in a Democratic State." In *Some of Us Did Not Die: New and Selected Essays of June Jordan*. Basic/Civitas Books, 2002.

———. "Rape Is Not a Poem." In *Directed by Desire: The Collected Works of June Jordan*, edited by Jan Heller Levi and Sara Miles. Copper Canyon Press, 2005.

———. "Report from the Bahamas." In *On Call: Political Essays*. South End Press, 1985.

———. "Requiem for the Champ." In *Some of Us Did Not Die: New and Selected Essays of June Jordan*. Basic/Civitas Books, 2002.

———. "Scenario Revision #1." In *Directed by Desire: The Collected Works of June Jordan*, edited by Jan Heller Levi and Sara Miles. Copper Canyon Press, 2005.

———. *Soldier: A Poet's Childhood*. Basic/Civitas Books, 2000.

———. *Some Changes*. Dutton, 1971.

———. Introduction to *Some of Us Did Not Die: New and Selected Essays of June Jordan*. Basic/Civitas Books, 2002.

———. "Song of the Law Abiding Citizen." In *Collaboration: June Jordan and Adrienne Torf, Selected Works 1983–2002*, ABongo Music, 2003.

———. "Study #1." In *Directed by Desire: The Collected Works of June Jordan*, edited by Jan Heller Levi and Sara Miles. Copper Canyon Press, 2005.

———. "Sunflower Sonnet Number Two." In *Directed by Desire: The Collected Works of June Jordan*, edited by Jan Heller Levi and Sara Miles. Copper Canyon Press, 2005.

———. "These Poems." Epigraph to *Directed by Desire: The Collected Works of June Jordan*, edited by Jan Heller Levi and Sara Miles. Copper Canyon Press, 2005.

———. "The Test of Atlanta 1979–." In *Directed by Desire: The Collected Works of June Jordan*, edited by Jan Heller Levi and Sara Miles. Copper Canyon Press, 2005.

———. *Things That I Do in the Dark: Selected Poetry*. Random House, 1977.

———. "Thinking About My Poetry 1977." In *Civil Wars*. Beacon Press, 1981.

———. "Third Poem from Nicaragua Libre: Photograph of Managua." In *Directed by Desire: The Collected Works of June Jordan*, edited by Jan Heller Levi and Sara Miles. Copper Canyon Press, 2005.

———. "To Free Nelson Mandela." In *Collaboration: June Jordan and Adrienne Torf, Selected Works 1983–2002*, ABongo Music, 2003.

———. "Tribute to Paul Robeson." In *Affirmative Acts: Political Essays*, Anchor Book, 1998.

———. "Unemployment Monologue." In *Directed by Desire: The Collected Works of June Jordan*, edited by Jan Heller Levi and Sara Miles. Copper Canyon Press, 2005.

———. "Waking Up in the Middle of Some American Dreams." In *Some of Us Did Not Die: New and Selected Essays of June Jordan*. Basic/Civitas Books, 2002.

———. "Where Is the Love?" In *We're On: A June Jordan Reader*. Alice James Books, 2017.

———. "White English / Black English: The Politics of Translation (1972)." In *Civil Wars: Observations from the Front Line of America*. Simon and Schuster, 1981.

———. *Who Look at Me*, acknowledgments. Thomas Y. Crowell, 1969.

Jordan, June, and Adrienne Torf. *Bang Bang über Alles*. Produced by 7 Stages Theatre, Atlanta, Georgia, June 1986.

———. *Collaboration: June Jordan and Adrienne Torf, Selected Works 1983–2002*, ABongo Music, 2003.

———. "Poem to Take Back the Night." *Collaboration: June Jordan and Adrienne Torf, Selected Works 1983–2002*, ABongo Music, 2003.

———. "Song of the Law Abiding Citizen." *Collaboration: June Jordan and Adrienne Torf, Selected Works 1983–2002*, ABongo Music, 2003.

———. "To Free Nelson Mandela." *Collaboration: June Jordan and Adrienne Torf, Selected Works 1983–2002*, ABongo Music, 2003.

Jordan, June, and Terri Bush, eds. *The Voice of the Children*. Holt, Reinhart & Winston, 1970.

Keane, Paul. "Column: Memories of the Actual 'Animal House.'" *Valley News*, January 13, 2018, https://www.vnews.com/Animal-House-Revisited-14701057.

Kinloch, Valerie. *June Jordan: Her Life and Letters*. Praeger, 2006.

Konigsberg, Eric. "The Fall of Animal House." *Rolling Stone*, September 17, 1992, https://www.rollingstone.com/culture/culture-news/the-fall-of-animal-house-190491/.

Lipsitz, George. *How Racism Takes Place*. Temple University Press, 2011.

Lowell, Robert. "Robert Lowell Reads Skunk Hour." YouTube, uploaded by awetblackbough, August 17, 2010, www.youtube.com/watch?v=hSlcc2b02yc&t=55s.

Marcus, Alva. Interview by Kelly E. Navies. September 2014. "U Street Oral History Project," Washington, DC, Public Library, Digital Archive. www.dclibrary.org.

Marshall, Paule. *Brown Girl, Brownstones*. Feminist Press at CUNY, 1986.

Masini, Donna. *Did You Find Everything You Were Looking For?* Forthcoming.

———. "Some Notes About June." In "Remembering June Jordan." *The Women's Review of Books* 20, no. 1 (2002): 18.

McCarthy, Caitlin. "Demystifying Alpha Delta, the Original 'Animal House.'" *The Dartmouth*, February 12, 2021, https://www.thedartmouth.com/article/2021/02/mccarthy-demystifying-alpha-delta-the-original-animal-house.

Miller, E. Ethelbert. *Fathering Words: The Making of an African American Writer*. St. Martin's Press, 2000.

———. *In Search of Color Everywhere*. Steward, Tabori & Chang, 1994.

———. *Season of Hunger / Cry of Rain*. Lotus Press, 1982.

Morrison, Toni. "Black Studies Center Public Dialogue." Panel discussion. Portland State University, May 30, 1975.

———. "Nobel Lecture." December 7, 1993. https://www.nobelprize.org/prizes/literature/1993/morrison/lecture.

Moseley, James. Interview by Kelly E. Navies. March 27, 2002. Collection of Reginald F. Lewis Maryland Museum of African American History and Culture.

Muller, Lauren. "June Jordan's Poetry for the People Guidelines." In *June Jordan's Poetry for the People: A Revolutionary Blueprint*. Routledge, 1995.

Nehru, Jawaharlal. *Letters from a Father to His Daughter*. Allahabad Law Journal Press, 1929.

Orwell, George. *Such, Such Were the Joys*. Harcourt, Brace, 1953.

Pace, Zachary. "John Ashbery Reads 'Self-Portrait in a Convex Mirror' (full poem)." YouTube, July 28, 2013, www.youtube.com/watch?v=zrvXX9QVAT8&t=363s.

Parmar, Pratibha, dir. *A Place of Rage*. Documentary film. Women Make Movies, 1991.

Rashed, Sara A. "Welcome to America." In *Making Mirrors: Writing/Righting by and for Refugees*, Jehan Bseiso and Becky Thompson, eds. Interlink, 2019.

Rich, Adrienne. Introduction to *Haruko / Love Poems*. High Risk Books / Serpent's Tail, 1994.

Rickford, John R. and Sharese King. "Language and Linguistics on Trial: Hearing Rachel Jeantel (and Other Vernacular Speakers) in the Courtroom and Beyond." *Language* 92, no. 4 (2016): 948–88.

Ross, Diana. "It's My House." YouTube, uploaded by Wayne Blake, June 22, 2016, www.youtube.com/watch?v=PBNbGCCYdyM.

Sharpe, Christina. *In the Wake: On Blackness and Being* (Duke University Press, 2016)

Shange, Ntozake. *for colored girls who have considered suicide / when the rainbow is enuf*. Shameless Hussy Press, 1974.

Shavit, Ari. "How Easily We Killed Them." *New York Times*, May 27, 1996.

Silko, Leslie. *Almanac of the Dead*. Penguin Books, 1991.

———. "Language and Literature from a Pueblo Indian Perspective." In *Yellow Woman and a Beauty of the Spirit: Essays on Native American Life Today*. Simon & Schuster, 1996.

Simpson, Leanne B. *As We Have Always Done: Indigenous Freedom Through Radical Resistance*. University of Minnesota Press, 2017.

Songs from *Bang Bang über Alles*. July 23, 1986. Audio collection of June Jordan, 1970–2000, T-331; Phon-38; CD-13, 101. Schlesinger Library, Radcliffe Institute.

Squires, Catherine R. "Rethinking the Black Public Sphere: An Alternative Vocabulary for Multiple Public Spheres." *Communication Theory* 12, no. 4 (2002): 460.

Sundiata, Sekou. "Space: A Monologue." *The Blue Oneness of Dreams*. Mercury Records, 1997.

Tamura, Keiko. *Forever Foreign: Expatriates Lives in Historic Kobe*. National Library of Australia, 2007.

Tarr, Kathleen. "Linda McCarriston Interview." *TriQuarterly*, February 2012. https://www.triquarterly.org/the-latest-word/interviews/linda-mccarriston-interview.

Torf, Adrienne. Interview. August 21, 2019.

Various. "An Open Letter of Love to Black Students." https://blackspaceblog.com/2014/12/08/an-open-letter-of-love-to-black-students-blacklivesmatter/.

Vlazna, Vacy, ed. *I Remember My Name: Poetry by Samah Sabawi, Ramzy Baroud, Jehan Bseiso*. Novum Pro Verlag, 2016.

Walker, Alice. "Can't Hate Anybody and See God's Face." *New York Times*, April 29, 1973.

———. *In Search of Our Mother's Gardens*. Harcourt Brace Jovanovich, 1983.

Whitman, Walt. "Democratic Vistas." In *The Portable Walt Whitman*, edited by Mark Van Doren. Penguin, 1977.

Williams, Jesse. "BET Awards Speech." YouTube, uploaded by Contrecia Tanyae, June 26, 2016, www.youtube.com/watch?v=TbJUzqw1E-g.

X, Malcolm. "Who Taught You to Hate Yourself?" Speech, May 22, 1962, Los Angeles, CA.

"Yaser Murtaja, and His Dreams of Travelling." *Al Jazeera*, April 7, 2018.

Yazzie, Evangeline P., and Margaret Speas. *Diné Bizaad Bínáhoo'aah: Rediscovering the Navajo Language*. Salina Bookshelf, 2009.

Index

A

Advocates for Indigenous California Language Survival (AICLS), 153, 154
"After All Is Said and Done" (Miller), 98
Alexander, Elizabeth, 9, 12, 13–14
Almanac of the Dead (Silko), 163
ancestors
　Black daughters learning from, 235–36, 240–41, 242–43
　in grammar of colonialism class, 155–56, 160–63
　our connection with, 78–79, 211
　as portals to answers, 165–66, 240–41, 252
anger, 117–18, 190–91
anti-Blackness
　Black English and, 161–62, 165
　documented in June's poetry, 18–19, 89–91, 95, 209–10, 224
　as foundational to the US, 24, 66–69, 114, 190–91
　KKK and, 17–18
　of police violence, 95, 159–61, 192, 198
　trauma of, 24–25, 66–69, 207
　See also colonialism; racism
anti-intellectualism, 60–63
"Apologies to All the People of Lebanon" (Jordan), 172, 196–97
"Argument with the Buddha" (Jordan), 141–142, 167–69
Attica uprising, 91–92
Azzam, Zeina, 220

B

Bang Bang über Alles (Jordan and Torf), 17
Barkley, Elliott James "LD," 91–92

Bhansali, Rajasvini, 104–6, 107, 109
bisexuality, 12, 86, 89, 201
Black daughters
　birthing, 68
　June as, 25–26, 71, 86–87, 91, 210
　learning from ancestors, 235–36, 240–41, 242–43
Black English
　June's class on art of, 119–20, 157–60, 165
　in June's poetry, 22, 119
　marvelous language of, 25
　See also grammar of colonialism (class); language
Black feminism, 192, 193–94
Black girlhood studies, 244–45, 246–50, 253–55
Black Lives Matter movement, 161, 187, 191, 198
Black masculinity, 66–69, 185
Black Power movement, 187–88, 190, 193–94
Black women
　Black girlhood and, 253–56
　Black masculinity and, 66–69
　friendships between, 173–74, 180, 181–83
　June's claim of the identity, 48, 53, 88
　June's class in search of, 158–59
　June's tributes to, 33, 201
　language of, 159, 162–163
　oral histories of, 235–36, 239, 241–43
　social movement labor of, 54, 180–81, 184–85, 187–88, 193–94
　writers, 158–59, 181, 237–38, 240–41
the blues, 22–26, 95
"The Bombing of Baghdad" (Jordan), 110–11, 112, 113, 114–15

Born Palestinian, Born Black (Hammad), 88–89
Boullata, Kamal, 55, 56, 88
breath, 19, 29–31, 111, 142, 169
Brien, Shanti Bright, 111–15
Brooks, Gwendolyn, 29–30, 240
brown, adrienne maree, 196–97
Brown, Ruth Nicole, 244–45, 246–50, 251, 253
Brown, Wesley, 231–34
Browne, Mahogany L., 66–70
bruise
  abuse as, 22–23
  within friendships, 52
  racism as, 24, 67
  writing as antidote to, 23, 25–26, 134, 168
Bseiso, Jehan, 78, 198–99

C

cancer, 11, 132, 133–34, 152, 172
Candelaria, Xochiquetzal, 117–18, 121
Cardenal, Fernando, 62
Causa Justa / Just Cause, 64–65
Citizenship Amendment Act (India), 107–108
civil rights movement, 173, 187, 193–94
Civil Wars (Jordan), 12, 54, 180, 204
class (socioeconomic)
  anti-intellectualism and, 60–63, 64–65
  citizenship and, 107–8, 258
  colonization and, 113, 157–58, 161–62, 237
  education and, 61–62, 145, 147–48
  impact of language on, 157–58, 161–62
  in June's poetry, 90, 209–10
  in Margo Okazawa-Rey's family, 39, 41
  stratification, 61–62, 104–6, 107–8, 113
  See also anti-Blackness; racism
colonialism
  as breaking of imagination, 128
  entanglement of racism and, 113–14, 127–30, 156, 163–64
  as foundational to the US, 42, 111–12, 113, 127–30
  grammar of, 154, 155–56, 160, 200–201
  grief of, 66–69, 127–30, 155–56, 161–62, 163
  impact of home on, 38–41, 99, 217–18, 219–20
  oral history as rebellion against, 238–39
  shame as tool of settler-, 68, 155–56, 162–63, 249
  as upheld by universities, 12–13, 224–25
  See also anti-Blackness; grammar of colonialism (class)
The Color Purple (Walker), 159
creative spirit, 1, 147–48, 150
critical consciousness, 61–64, 151
Critical Conversations Series (UC Berkeley), 179–80

D

darkness
  of the 1980s and 1990s, 188–89, 190, 191–92
  importance of doing things in, 1–2, 73–74, 97, 98, 215
  in June's poetry, 18–20, 72, 215, 229
Dartmouth Community for Divestment (DCD), 221–25
Darwish, Mahmoud, 49, 55, 108
Davis, Angela Y., 181–82, 183–86, 191–94
desire
  for connection, 13, 19–20, 141–42, 167–69, 229
  as personal, 87–88
  as sacred, 167–69
  as sensual, 30–31, 72–73, 87–88
  wonderment and, 116–17, 231–34
De Veaux, Alexis, 22, 25, 26, 56
Diné Bizaad, 153–54
displacement
  caused by settler-colonialism, 38–39, 99, 127–30, 217–18, 219
  many rivers to cross created by, 75–76
  of nature, 250
  as obscured by passive language, 74–75
  as strategy of elites, 104–6, 107

See also colonialism; prison
Dunbar, Paul Laurence, 29–30, 237

E

Ellison, Ralph, 174
Engel, Kathy, 51–54, 55–57, 58–59

F

Fathering Words: The Making of an African American Writer (Miller), 85–86, 96–97
for colored girls who have considered suicide / when the rainbow is enuf (Shange), 32
forgetting, sin of, 78, 104–6, 107
   See also remembering
Forman, Ruth, 122–24, 154, 166
Free Angela Campaign, 186
"Free Flight" (Jordan), 73, 120
Freire, Paulo, 62–63
friendship
   between Black women, 173–74, 180, 181–83
   bruises within, 52
   love as June's legacy in, 12, 52–54, 96–97, 173–74, 227–28
fuchsias, 116, 117, 120

G

Gabriel, Dani, 168–69, 170
ghaflah, 78, 104–6, 107
ghosts, 127–30, 207, 211
Ginsberg, Allen, 29
Gómez, Reid, 153–54, 165–66
   See also grammar of colonialism (class)
grammar of colonialism (class)
   ancestors addressed in, 155–56, 160–63
   assignments in, 161
   Black Red English as centered in, 158
   as built on love, 164–65
   "Nobody Mean More to Me Than You and the Future Life of Willie Jordan" in, 158–60
   students in, 163–64
   syllabus of, 154, 156–58, 164
   theory of the safety zone in, 163–64
   "White English / Black English: The Politics of Translation (1972)" in, 156–58
"Grand Army Plaza" (Jordan), 93–94
Great March of Return (2018), 217–18, 219
grief
   in the body, 214–15
   of colonization, 66–69, 127–30, 155–56, 161–62, 163
   holding space and language for, 137
   in June's poetry, 88, 140–43, 167–68, 218
   of language loss, 153–54
"Guidelines for Critiquing a Poem" (Jordan), 122–23, 125, 131–35, 139–40
Gumbs, Alexis Pauline, 1–3, 56, 78, 146

H

Hacker, Marilyn, 46–50
Hamer, Fannie Lou, 173–74
Hammad, Suheir, 88–89
Hardwick, Gwendolen, 80–82
Harjo, Joy, 94, 112–13
Harlem, 22, 29, 47, 49, 173
HEAL Initiative, 174–75
heart
   colonization's devastation of, 128, 196
   connected at the, 38, 58, 122
   June as, 73
   of June's poetry, 23, 27
   knowledge of, 118, 133
   poetry as, 101
heartbeat, 120, 208, 235–36
Hilal, Dima, 99, 100, 101–3
Hill, Dominique C., 253–56
His Own Where (Jordan), 157, 158, 160, 164
historical trauma, 127–30, 207
Holbrook, Kate, 137–41, 143
home
   as belonging, 43–44
   colonization's impact on, 38–41, 68, 99, 217–18, 219–20
   language as, 153–54, 164–65
   question of, 39–41, 127–30
Horter, Will, 221–25, 226–30
Huang, Jessica Wei, 144–46, 149–50, 152
Hughes, Langston, 29–30

I

identity politics
  collective connections and, 37, 43–45, 194
  June on, 37, 53, 77
  locating oneself in relation to, 37, 38–39, 107, 125–26, 206–7
  question of home and, 39–41, 127–30
  within and across US social movements, 42–43
If They Come in the Morning (Davis), 193
imagination
  Black English as accessible to, 157
  as central to June's writing, 23, 58, 256
  colonization as breaking of, 128
  importance of, 64, 260
  as therapeutic, 214
imperialism. *See* US imperialism
In Mad Love and War (Harjo), 94
interdependence, 133
intergenerational trauma, 125–26, 207
Islamophobia, 100, 102–3, 104–6, 107–8
Israel, 38–39, 58, 172, 196, 218–19

J

jazz, 29–31, 192, 259
Jeantel, Rachel, 161–62
Jordan, Granville Ivanhoe, 11, 22–23, 25
Jordan, June
  bisexuality of, 89
  childhood of, 22–23, 25
  as a daughter, 25–26, 71, 86–87, 91, 210
  death of, 12, 47–49
  energy and presence of, 85–86, 118, 125, 259
  fight against breast cancer, 11, 131–32, 133–34, 172
  as a fighter, 11, 25, 48–50, 122, 209
  laughter of, 53, 60, 116, 122, 239
  as a mother, 23, 87
  as a musician, 29, 120
  as New World poet, 202–5
  as outside Black nationalism, 24
  as passionate tennis player, 187
  poetic existence of, 184
  romance of, 15–16, 17–20
  as self-sustaining, 185–86
  synthesizing abilities of, 120
  teachers of, 173–74
  as underrecognized, 26, 51
  as well versed in world religions, 100, 167
  as willing witness for change, 72, 119–20, 258–59
Jordan, June, as a teacher
  on appreciation for Black English, 119–20, 157–60, 165
  "Guidelines for Critiquing a Poem" by, 125, 131–35, 139–40
  on how to name abuse, 206–7, 208–9, 210–11
  listening as important to, 74–75, 168, 211
  nurturing students as important to, 51–52, 57, 100–101, 121, 239–40
  on passive voice, 75, 139–40
  of Poetry for the People, 63–64, 99–100, 125
  shared leadership as important to, 11, 76, 100–101, 125, 151
  solidarity as important to, 43, 77, 172–75, 187, 192–93
  See also legacy, teaching as June's
Jordan, June, books by
  Civil Wars, 12, 54, 180, 204
  Haruko, 13, 87–88
  His Own Where, 157, 158
  June Jordan's Poetry for the People: A Revolutionary Blueprint, 10, 122, 131–35, 138
  On Call: Political Essays, 236
  Passion, 93
  Soldier: A Poet's Childhood, 11, 22, 25–26
  Some of Us Did Not Die, 131, 143, 203
  Things That I Do in the Dark & Other Poems, 30–31, 91–92
  Who Look at Me, 11, 18, 20
Jordan, June, essays by
  "Alternative Commencement Address at Dartmouth College, June 14, 1987," 223, 224–25, 225–26
  "The Creative Spirit," 1, 2, 147
  "The Difficult Miracle of Black Poetry in America, or Something Like a Sonnet for Phillis Wheatley," 235, 236–37, 238

"Eyewitness in Lebanon," 99
"For the Sake of People's Poetry: Walt Whitman and the Rest of Us," 95–96, 200–201, 202, 203
"Letter to My Friend," 51
"Many Rivers to Cross," 71–72, 74, 252
"A New Politics of Sexuality," 89
"Nicaragua: Why I Had to Go There," 94, 108–9
"Nobody Mean More to Me Than You and the Future Life of Willie Jordan," 76, 119, 158–60, 165–66, 259
"Of Those So Close Beside Me, Which Are You?," 174
"Problems of Language in a Democratic State," 75, 139, 140
"A Report from the Bahamas," 37, 45, 258
"White English / Black English: The Politics of Translation (1972)," 156–58
Jordan, June, journalism of
 in the Bahamas, 45, 258
 in Lebanon, 99
 in Nicaragua, 61–62, 108–9
 in poetry, 90, 94–95, 110–11, 140–41, 172, 201
 about police violence, 165
 See also journalists
Jordan, June, legacy of. *See* legacy, advocacy as June's; legacy, love as June's; legacy, praxis as June's; legacy, teaching as June's; legacy in poetry, June's
Jordan, June, poetry of
 anti-Blackness documented in, 18–19, 89–91, 209–10, 224
 Black English in, 22, 119
 breath in, 19, 111, 142, 169
 as comforting and nourishing, 22, 148, 196–97
 as crafted for liberation, 209
 darkness in, 18–20, 72, 215, 229
 democratic impulse of, 27, 185, 201
 depictions of global interconnectedness in, 91–92, 110–11, 196–97, 201
 epigraphs for, 78
 as grappling with shame, 111, 113–14, 196–97
 grief in, 88, 140–43, 167–68, 218
 influences on, 29–30, 95
 love as central to, 86, 87–88, 93–94, 204, 227–28
 musical collaboration and, 16–20
 pain as part of, 140–143, 155, 191–92
 as particular and immense, 110–11, 116–17, 140–42, 189, 231–34
 personal as political in, 87, 90, 119, 209–10, 215
 police violence documented in, 95
 rape in, 90, 201, 222
 reading style of, 27–31, 33–34
 socioeconomic class in, 90, 209–10
 syntax of, 16, 30–32, 95, 140–41, 201
 water in, 72–73
 "we" as site of, 13, 111, 114–15, 155, 203
 See also Jordan, June, writing of; poetry
Jordan, June, poetry of (list)
 "Ah, Momma," 87
 "Alla Tha's All Right, but," 72–73
 "Apologies to the People of Lebanon," 172, 196–97
 "Argument with the Buddha," 141–42, 167–69
 "The Bombing of Baghdad," 110–11, 112, 113, 114–15
 "Bridget Song #1," 117
 "Campsite #21," 116–17
 "For Michael Angelo Thompson," 141
 "Free Flight," 73, 120
 "From The Talking Back of Miss Valentine Jones: Poem # One," 30–31, 31–32
 "Grand Army Plaza," 93–94
 "It's Hard to Keep a Clean Shirt Clean," 173
 "Lullabye for Ella," 53, 54
 "Moving Towards Home," 77, 88, 172, 218
 "Of Nightsong and Flight," 72
 "On a New Year's Eve," 137, 231–34
 "Poem About My Rights," 89–91, 154–55, 201, 209–10, 221–22, 224–25

"Poem About Police Violence," 95
"Poem Against the State (of Things)," 91–93
"Poem for Nana," 201
"Poem for South African Women," 133, 201
"Poem for Will Horter and Claudia Campbell on the Occasion of Their Joining Together—August 21, 1993," 227–28, 230
"Poem in Memory of Alan Schindler, 22 Years Old," 140–41
"Scenario Revision #1," 133–34
"Solidarity," 182–83, 184
"Study #1," 139–40
"The Test of Atlanta 1979–," 94–95
"These Poems," 72, 88, 215
"Third Poem from Nicaragua Libre: Photograph of Managua," 61–62, 119
Jordan, June, writing of
  as a balm, 23, 25–26, 196–97
  Black feminism as shaped by, 192
  the blues as reflected in, 22–26, 95
  as collective, 185, 204
  different world envisioned through, 192
  as embodied work, 72, 233, 252
  imagination as central to, 23, 58, 256
  nine categories of, 86
  power examined in, 155, 157–60, 209–10
  as prolific, 11, 26, 179
  as resistance, 133–34, 155
  water in, 71–73, 74, 252
  as witness, 92, 94–95, 99, 108–9
  See also Jordan, June, poetry of
Jordan, Mildred, 71, 87, 91
Jordan, Reggie, 119–20, 159–60
Jordan, Willie, 119–20, 159–60, 165
journalists, 56, 217–18, 219–20
  See also Jordan, June, journalism of
June Jordan: Her Life and Letters (Kinloch), 86
June Jordan School for Equity
  community of, 145–46
  history of, 145, 147–48
  mission of, 145, 147
  Poetry for the People class at, 144, 146–47, 148, 150–52
  shooting in parking lot of, 144–45, 146, 152
June Jordan's Poetry for the People: A Revolutionary Blueprint (Jordan), 10, 122, 131–35, 138

K

King, Martin Luther, Jr., 13, 96, 207
Ku Klux Klan (KKK), 17, 223

L

language
  as home, 153–54, 164–65
  as political, 75, 139–40, 157–60, 161–63, 165–66
  power of one's own, 119, 153–54, 159
  as symptomatic, 254
  as a tool, 259
  See also Black English; grammar of colonialism (class)
"Language and Linguistics on Trial: Hearing Rachel Jeantel (and Other Vernacular Speakers) in the Courtroom and Beyond" (Rickford and King), 161–62, 164
legacy, advocacy as June's
  for literacy, 24, 63–64
  for Palestine, 49, 55, 171–73, 187–89, 218–19
  reflected among change agents, 71, 77–79, 132–35, 168–69
  reflected in poetry of others, 7, 48–50, 80–81, 198
  at Yale, 12–13
legacy, love as June's
  expansive, 1–2, 13, 76, 88, 147
  in friendships, 12, 52–54, 96–97, 173–74, 227–28
  and guidance for us, 1–3, 20, 45, 51, 165–66
  in her writing, 1, 2, 13, 20, 204
  reflected in poetry of others, 7, 73–74, 98
  See also love
legacy, praxis as June's, 252–56
legacy, teaching as June's, 52, 56, 122–23, 156–61, 258–59
  See also Jordan, June, as a teacher; Poery for the People (class)

legacy in poetry, June's
  reading style as, 27–31, 33–34
  reflected by poetry of others, 35, 53–54, 73–74, 104–6, 198
  reflected in performance poetry of others, 32–34
  witnessing as, 92, 94–95, 108–9
liberation
  Black women's organizing in movements for, 54, 180–81, 184–85, 187–88, 193–94
  critical consciousness as tool for, 63–64
  love as part of struggle for, 227
  necessity of intersectional movements for, 180, 188–89, 193–94, 198
  shared dreams of, 45
  spiritual practice of, 138
  truth-telling as acts of, 207–8, 211–14
lifeforce, 1–3, 147–48, 151–52
literacy brigades, 61–63
love
  bravery required for self-, 109
  carrying us away from suicide, 10, 76
  as central to June's poetry, 86, 87–88, 93–94, 204, 227–28
  grammar of colonialism class as built on, 164–65
  is lifeforce, 1–3, 152
  as organizing principle, 120
  as part of the struggle for liberation, 227
  as a politic, 213
  power of, 10, 18–20, 147, 152
  as ultimate connection, 13, 43, 77
  See also legacy, love as June's
Lowell, Robert, 28, 31
Luckey, Ariel, 125–26, 127–30
lynching, 235
  See also police violence

M
MADRE, 51, 52–53
Malcolm X, 13, 173
"Many Rivers to Cross" (Jordan), 71–72, 74, 252
Martin, Trayvon, 161
Masini, Donna, 202, 205

mass incarceration, 81, 188–89, 192
  See also prison
McCarty, Teresa, 163–64
Menezes, Sheila, 131–35, 135–36
Meyer, Christopher David, 23, 87
Meyer, Elizabeth Riva, 206–10, 211–15, 215–16
Miller, E. Ethelbert, 85–86, 89, 91, 93–94, 96–98
Mitchell, Blackhorse, 156
Morris, Monica, 158–59
Morrison, Toni, 56, 85, 161–62, 181
"Moving Towards Home" (Jordan), 77, 88, 172, 218
Muller, Lauren, 144, 146, 151–52
Murdered and Missing Indigenous Women, 163
Murtaja, Yaser, 217–18, 219, 220

N
National Register of Citizens (India), 107–8
Navajo language, 153–54
Navies, Kelly Elaine, 235–36, 237–40, 241, 242–43
New World poet, 202–5
"Nicaragua: Why I Had to Go There" (Jordan), 94, 108–9
"Nobody Mean More to Me Than You and the Future Life of Willie Jordan" (Jordan), 76, 119, 158–60, 165–66, 259
Nye, Naomi Shihab, 7–8

O
Okazawa-Rey, Margo, 37–39, 39–42, 43–45
"On a New Year's Eve" (Jordan), 137, 231–34
oppression, genealogies of, 42, 181, 188
  See also colonialism; police violence
oral history, 235–39, 241–43

P
Palestine
  Israeli occupation of, 38–39, 58, 196, 203–4, 218–19
  June's unwavering commitment to, 49, 55, 171–73, 187–89, 218–19

liberation movement for, 187, 198, 217–18, 219
Margo Okazawa-Rey's experiences in, 37–39, 43–44
Parmar, Pratibha, 180–81, 183, 186, 190–91, 195
passive voice, 74–75, 139–40
PEN, 55
Perez, Ranya, 162–63
Perry, Imani, 258–59
A Place of Rage (film), 180, 185–86, 187, 190–91
Poblet, María, 60–61, 64–65
"Poem About My Rights" (Jordan), 89–91, 149, 154–55, 201, 209–10, 221–22, 224–25
"Poem for Nana" (Jordan), 201
"Poem for South African Women" (Jordan), 133, 201
poetry
　as belonging with the people, 75–76, 126, 134
　as embodiment, 203, 214
　influenced by June's reading style, 32–34
　inspired by June, 149–50, 246–50, 254–55, 257
　for June, 35, 73–74, 80–81, 98, 131
　as linked to history, 237, 238–39, 242–43
　as praxis, 138–40
　reading styles of, 28–31
　as remembering, 35, 46–50, 98, 104–7, 109
　as resistance, 133–34, 138, 155
　as truth-telling, 125, 127–30, 148–50, 208, 244–50
　as a way through oppression, 167–69
　work of, 9–10, 133–34, 208–9, 211
　See also Jordan, June, poetry of
Poetry for the People (class)
　critical consciousness development in, 63–64, 151
　at June Jordan School for Equity, 144, 146–47, 148, 150–52
　student-teacher poet experiences of, 99–100, 125, 137–41, 171, 208–9

truth-telling as core tenet of, 208–9, 210–11
police violence
　anti-Blackness of, 95, 159–60, 161, 192, 198
　documented in June's poetry, 95
　as foundational to US, 190–91
　in India, 107–8
　responses to, 159–60, 165, 191, 192, 198
　victims of, 119–20, 159–61, 190–91, 192, 198
　See also colonialism
praxis, 138–40, 252–56
prison
　anti-Blackness of, 68
　Gaza as open-air, 77
　industrial complex, 188–89
　teaching poetry in, 63–64, 134–45
　uprising at Attica, 91–92
　See also anti-Blackness; colonialism; displacement
"Problems of Language in a Democratic State" (Jordan), 75, 139, 140

R

racism
　as bruise, 24, 67
　campaign against Brazil's, 193
　entanglement of colonialism and, 113–14, 127–30, 156, 163–64
　as foundational to US, 24, 42, 191
　in France, 183
　as upheld by universities, 12–13, 224–25
　See also anti-Blackness; colonialism; Islamophobia
Raiford, Leigh, 195
rape, 11, 90–91, 201, 222
refugees
　many rivers crossed by, 75–76
　poetry by, 75–76, 217–18
　settler-colonialism and, 127–30, 219
　violence against, 99, 105–6, 172, 193, 218–20
remembering
　as disallowed by whiteness, 206–7
　importance of, 55–56, 96–97, 231–34
　June's presence, 52, 118, 125, 234, 259

oral histories as, 237–39, 241
poetry as, 35, 46–50, 98, 104–7, 109
as weapon against coercive revisionist history, 55–56, 66–69, 109, 196–97
"A Report from the Bahamas" (Jordan), 37, 45, 258
Revolutionary Mothering: Love on the Front Lines (Gumbs), 78, 146
Rich, Adrienne, 87–88
Rogow, Zack, 27, 34, 35–36

S

Saadawi, Nawal El, 58
Sabra and Shatila massacre (1982), 172, 218, 219
Sandinista Front for National Liberation, 61–63, 65, 108–9
Saving Our Lives Hear Our Truths (SOLHOT), 253, 254
self-determination, 155, 209–11, 221–22, 225
Shamasunder, Sriram, 172, 173–75
shame
  as grappled with by June, 111, 113–14, 196–97, 203
  as tool of settler-colonialism, 68, 155–56, 162–63, 249
Shange, Ntozake, 32, 236
Sharpe, Christina, 160
Silko, Leslie Marmon, 163
Simpson, Leanne Betasamosake, 155
slavery, 23, 160, 236, 238–39
Sogorea Te' Land Trust, 126
Soldier: A Poet's Childhood (Jordan), 11, 22, 25–26
solidarity, 43, 77, 172–75, 187, 192–93
"Solidarity" (Jordan), 182–83, 184
Some of Us Did Not Die (Jordan), 131, 143, 203
South African apartheid, 221, 225–26
"Study #1" (Jordan), 139–40
Sundiata, Sekou, 32–33
syllabus, confronting power through, 156–58, 158–60, 164

T

theory of the safety zone, 163–64

therapy as political, 211–15
"These Poems" (Jordan), 72, 88, 215
Things That I Do in the Dark & Other Poems (Jordan), 30–31, 91–92
Thompson, Becky, 73–74, 74–77, 78–79
Torf, Adrienne B., 15–17, 18–20, 20–21, 29
trauma. *See* bruise; historical trauma; intergenerational trauma
truth-telling
  as acts of liberation, 207–8, 211–14
  as core tenet of Poetry for the People, 208–9, 210–11
  oral history as, 237–38
  poetry as, 125, 127–30, 148–50, 208, 244–50
Tuckey, Melissa, 53–54

U

US imperialism
  and assassinations, 210
  Islamophobia of, 102–3, 138
  in support of Israel, 38, 111–12, 196–97
  See also colonialism

W

wake work, 160
Walker, Alice, 159
water
  as connection with ancestors, 78–79
  in June's writing, 71–73, 74, 96–97, 252
  as keeping us alive, 74
Weaver, Afaa M. 尉雅風, 257
We Begin Here: Poems for Palestine and Lebanon (Boullata and Engel), 55
Wheatley, Phillis, 236–37
"White English / Black English: The Politics of Translation (1972)" (Jordan), 156–58
Whitman, Walt, 202–3, 204
Who Look at Me (Jordan), 11, 18, 22–24, 28, 256
women, violence against, 11, 90–91, 110, 112, 114, 201, 222

Y

Yale Attica Defense, 12–13

About the Editors

Lauren Muller (1959–2023): How to write a biographical sketch for someone who has traveled from this realm to another? Do you start at the beginning or the end? Shall we use her words or those who carry her with them now? Lauren was an early spring magnolia tree in bloom, a vulnerable, giving spirit who listened to the first panel of papers that became the nucleus of this book from her phone as she was getting a chemo treatment in San Francisco. Originally raised in Sewanee, Tennessee (Appalachia), with her three sisters, Lauren was a transplant to Berkeley (home of the Muwekma Ohlone and other descendants of the Verona Band) where she was a graduate student, taught Poetry for the People, and eventually became the beloved chair of interdisciplinary studies at City College of San Francisco for over two decades. A sea at the turning of the tides, Lauren drew on energy around her to nurture new courses and programs—Critical Middle East Studies, Critical Pacific Island and Oceania Studies, and Trauma Prevention and Recovery. Lauren coedited (with Hertha D. Sweet Wong and Jana Sequoya Magdaleno) *Reckonings: Contemporary Short Fiction by Native American Women* (Oxford University Press, 2008) and shepherded many people's poems into the wide world. From her broom-closet office she fashioned a workstation where her door and heart were always open. From her work as June Jordan's hand-chosen editor of the collectively inspired *Poetry for the People: A Revolutionary Blueprint*, to her accompanying June to chemo treatments and spreading June's ashes, to her vision for this collection, June and Lauren were family to each other. In her last letter Lauren wrote, "June is with us in this project. I send you love and gratitude." On the day before she traveled, Lauren was still talking about the book, telling one of us (Becky): "Contact Joy [Harjo]. She wants to be part of it. Check in with Cornelius [Eady]." When an elder had asked Lauren which ancestor she wanted to guide her to the next realm, she said, "June is real close now." In the last hours of her life, Lauren's family read two Jordan poems to her: "Poem About My Rights" and "Free Flight." Your flight is free, Lauren. The book is flying now.

Becky Thompson, poet, scholar, activist, and yogi, is the author of several books, including *To Speak in Salt* (Ex Ophidia Press, 2022), *Teaching with Tenderness: Toward an Embodied Practice* (University of Illinois Press, 2017), and *Making Mirrors: Righting/Writing by and for Refugees* (coedited with Jehan Bseiso; Interlink, 2019), all of which were guided by Jordan's pedagogy and activism. Her teaching in Thailand, Greece, the US, and China has also been touched by *June Jordan's Poetry for the People: A Revolutionary Blueprint*.

Dominique C. Hill is a creative and vulnerability guide whose scholarship interrogates embodiment with foci in Black girlhood, education, and performance. Hill's art and scholarship illuminate tensions between race and gender, identity and structures, and reality and possibility. Hill is the coauthor of *Who Look at Me?!: Shifting the Gaze of Education Through Blackness, Queerness, and the Body* (with Durrell M. Callier; Brill, 2019), which interrogates the gaze afforded Blackness and queerness in education. Hill's pedagogy and praxis of Black feminism is informed by Jordan's cultural work, audacious living, and approach to education beyond the confines of schools. Hill is an assistant professor of women's studies at Colgate University.

Durell M. Callier is an artist-scholar who employs Black feminist and queer methodologies to explore the interconnectivity of race, gender, sexuality, and culture. His research documents, analyzes, and interrogates the lived experiences of Black youth and their communities. Analyzing these dynamics, Callier's scholarship illuminates how Black art and creative practices subvert, respond to, and reimagine Black life amidst anti-Black and antiqueer violence.

About Haymarket Books

Haymarket Books is a radical, independent, nonprofit book publisher based in Chicago. Our mission is to publish books that contribute to struggles for social and economic justice. We strive to make our books a vibrant and organic part of social movements and the education and development of a critical, engaged, and internationalist Left.

We take inspiration and courage from our namesakes, the Haymarket Martyrs, who gave their lives fighting for a better world. Their 1886 struggle for the eight-hour day—which gave us May Day, the international workers' holiday—reminds workers around the world that ordinary people can organize and struggle for their own liberation. These struggles—against oppression, exploitation, environmental devastation, and war—continue today across the globe.

Since our founding in 2001, Haymarket has published more than nine hundred titles. Radically independent, we seek to drive a wedge into the risk-averse world of corporate book publishing. Our authors include Angela Y. Davis, Arundhati Roy, Keeanga-Yamahtta Taylor, Eve Ewing, Aja Monet, Mariame Kaba, Naomi Klein, Rebecca Solnit, Olúfẹ́mi O. Táíwò, Mohammed El-Kurd, José Olivarez, Noam Chomsky, Winona LaDuke, Robyn Maynard, Leanne Betasamosake Simpson, Howard Zinn, Mike Davis, Marc Lamont Hill, Dave Zirin, Astra Taylor, and Amy Goodman, among many other leading writers of our time. We are also the trade publishers of the acclaimed Historical Materialism Book Series.

Haymarket also manages a vibrant community organizing and event space in Chicago, Haymarket House, the popular Haymarket Books Live event series and podcast, and the annual Socialism Conference.